D1520203

The Mathematics
of Life Insurance

Second Edition

The Mathematics of Life Insurance

A Practical Guide to the Application of Insurance Principles

WALTER O. MENGE
Fellow of the Society of Actuaries

CARL H. FISCHER
Fellow of the Society of Actuaries
Professor Emeritus
The University of Michigan
Ann Arbor, Michigan

ULRICH'S BOOKS, INC.
549 E. University, Ann Arbor, Michigan

© 1965

Walter O. Menge and Carl H. Fischer

ISBN: 0-914004-00-X

SEVENTH PRINTING 1985

Earlier edition, entitled *An Introduction to the Mathematics of Life Insurance,* copyright 1935 by The Macmillan Company; copyright renewed 1963 by Walter O Menge.

LIBRARY OF CONGRESS CATALOG CARD NUMBER: 65-12855

Ulrich's Books Inc.
Ann Arbor, Michigan 48104

Printed in the United States of America

Preface

This edition is a revision of a textbook published originally under the authorship of Walter O. Menge and James W. Glover. Much of the material has been rewritten and new exercises for the student have been added. It is intended primarily as a text for beginning courses in the mathematics of life insurance in colleges and universities. It also should prove of interest to readers, other than college students, who wish to understand the fundamentals of life insurance. For the study of this text no mathematical preparation, other than that usually included in the high school course, is necessary; but elementary courses in college mathematics and the theory of interest will be found very useful, especially if only a short time is to be devoted to its study.

The material included in this work has been obtained from many sources, including practical actuarial work in the application of the principles as well as many years of teaching the subject. The scope of the book is limited to single life contingencies, together with the application of these probabilities in combination with the theory of interest. The notation used, that of standard actuarial publications, allows the student to continue without interruption with the study of more advanced topics after completing the material contained herein.

The general scheme of the book is to provide some elasticity in the time required to cover the material. This is accomplished by the inclusion of many applied problems that should be solved by the student when a complete course is desired. For a shorter survey course many problems may be omitted. Several hundred odd exercises are included with answers. The majority of these require little or no numerical work in their solution. The tables, which are appended, while not entirely complete, are more extensive than those usually included in books of this character and afford greater accuracy than most published books of tables.

The authors are indebted to many friends for valuable suggestions and criticisms which have resulted in conspicuous improvements in the original text.

Walter O. Menge
Carl H. Fischer

Contents

The Mathematics
of Life Insurance

CHAPTER 1

The Life Table

1.1 INTRODUCTION

No prediction can be made with confidence in regard to the time of death of an individual. Although it may be true, as Benjamin Franklin once said, that nothing is certain except death and taxes, it is equally true for the individual life that nothing is so uncertain as the time of death.

It may be known with relative certainty that, out of a large group of persons chosen at random, some will die within a given period of time, but it is not known which particular ones will die. It is this uncertainty, inherent in human life, which gives rise to the necessity for some form of protection against the losses resulting from death. The relative number of deaths from a large group of persons can be predicted with sufficient accuracy to warrant life insurance companies furnishing insurance protection to persons who satisfy certain requirements in regard to health. Changes in vitality and longevity of the general population progress slowly, and it is possible, by a careful observation of past experience, to estimate quite closely the number of persons out of a given large group that will die in a year.

The structure of life insurance depends fundamentally upon three elements: (a) the probability of the death of a given individual in a given period of time, (b) the interest rate which can be earned on invested funds, and (c) the rate of expense incurred in the sale and maintenance of a life insurance policy. Inasmuch as the subject of probability plays an important role in the study of the mathematical theory of life insurance, consideration will be given in this chapter to some of the basic principles of this subject.

[1]

1.2 PROBABILITY, *A PRIORI* DEFINITION

If an event can happen in h ways and fail in f ways, all of which are equally likely, the probability p of the occurrence of the event is

$$p = \frac{h}{h+f} \qquad (1.1)$$

and the probability q of the failure of the event is

$$q = \frac{f}{h+f}. \qquad (1.2)$$

This mathematical definition gives a precise meaning to the words *chance* or *probability* as used in regard to the occurrence of an event. Thus, if a bag is known to contain ten balls, seven of which are white, and the other three black, the probability that a ball drawn at random will be white is 7/10. In this problem the number h of the equally likely ways of drawing a white ball is seven, while the number f of equally likely ways in which one can fail to obtain a white ball is three. It should be noted that the denominators of expressions (1.1) and (1.2) are the total number of equally likely ways in which the event can either happen or fail.

From definitions (1.1) and (1.2), it is obvious that p and q are both less than or equal to unity, while their sum is

$$p + q = \frac{h+f}{h+f} = 1.$$

Thus, the probability of the occurrence of an event plus the probability of the failure of the event is equal to unity. Furthermore, when $f = 0$, $p = 1$, and hence, if an event is certain to occur, the probability of its occurrence is unity.

1.3 EMPIRICAL PROBABILITY

There are many important classes of events in which it is impossible to enumerate all of the ways in which an event can happen or fail, and, indeed, impossible to ascertain whether such ways as can be enumerated are "equally likely." In fact, this is normally the case in real life situations. Thus, in life insurance, as in many other fields, the *a priori* definition is impractical as a means of determining the basic underlying probabilities. Recourse must be made to the method of determining an approximation to the true underlying probability by means of observations. In such cases it is necessary that the probability be determined empirically by an observation of the proportion of cases in which the event happens on a large number of occasions. Thus, if it be observed that an event has happened *m* times in *n* possible cases (*n,* a large number) then, in the absence of further information, it may be assumed that *m/n* is a satisfactory estimate of the probability of the event, and that confidence in the reliability of this estimate increases as *n* increases.

For example, if it be determined that out of 100,000 men alive at exact age 20, the number who died in the following year was 162, an approximation to the probability that such a man aged 20 will die in the following year is 0.00162.

A precise formulation of the definition of probability from this empirical point of view would require the limit of the ratio *m/n* as the number *n* is increased without bound. It is necessary to assume the existence of such a limit in making precise statements in the theory of probability. Assuming that the limit does exist, it is possible to define the probability of the occurrence of an event as

$$p = \lim_{n \to \infty} \frac{m}{n}. \tag{1.3}$$

In statistical applications the limit *m/n* cannot, in general, be determined, but it is possible to find approximations to the limit which are satisfactory for many practical purposes.

It should be noted that the value of the probability from the empirical point of view is determined by past experience and its use for prediction of future events involves the assumption that the experience of the future will duplicate that of the past. This expectation, of course, will not always be fulfilled, but where large numbers are involved, slight variations will have little significance, and, in any case, the assumption is the best and most convenient one available.

It is important to recognize that the statement "the probability of an event is 2/3" means (a) if a large number of trials are taken it is expected that approximately 2/3 of them will be successful, and (b) that as the number of trials is increased, the ratio of successes to trials will approach the limit 2/3. This statement does not mean that in a given number of trials, say 60, exactly 2/3 of them, or 40, will be successful, but rather that the number 40 represents the best prediction of the number of successful trials. It may happen in an actual case that more or less than this expected number will occur.

1.4   THEOREMS ON PROBABILITY

Two or more events are said to be *mutually exclusive* if the occurrence of any one of them excludes the occurrence of any of the others. Two events are said to be *dependent* or *independent* according as the occurrence of either one of them does or does not affect the probability of the occurrence of the other.

THEOREM I. *The probability of the occurrence of any one of a number of mutually exclusive events is the sum of the respective probabilities of the individual events.*

Let the probabilities $p_1, p_2, \ldots, p_r$ of r mutually exclusive events be (after reducing to a common denominator)

$$\frac{h_1}{n}, \frac{h_2}{n}, \ldots, \frac{h_r}{n},$$

respectively. Then any one of these events can happen in

$$h_1 + h_2 + \cdots + h_r$$

equally likely ways, and the probability of the occurrence of any one of the events is

$$\frac{h_1 + h_2 + \cdots + h_r}{n} = p_1 + p_2 + \cdots + p_r.$$

THEOREM II. *The probability of the occurrence of all of a set of independent events is the product of the respective probabilities of the individual events.*

Let the probabilities of two independent events be $p_1 = h_1/n_1$ and $p_2 = h_2/n_2$, respectively, where h_1 and h_2 represent respectively the number of equally likely ways in which the events can happen. For each way in which the first event can happen there are h_2 ways in which the second can also happen, so that both events can succeed in $h_1 \cdot h_2$ equally likely ways. In a similar way, the total number of ways in which the two events can happen or fail is $n_1 \cdot n_2$, and hence from the definition the probability of the occurrence of both events is

$$\frac{h_1 \cdot h_2}{n_1 \cdot n_2} = p_1 \cdot p_2.$$

The extension of this proof to more than two events is left to the student.

THEOREM III. *If the probability of a first event is p_1, and if, after this has happened, the probability of a second event is p_2, the probability that both events will happen in the specified order is $p_1 \cdot p_2$.*

The proof of this theorem is entirely analogous to that of the previous theorem. The extension of Theorem III to any number of events is obvious.

Exercises

1. If the probabilities that A and B survive a certain period are 0.7 and 0.8 respectively, what is the probability
   (a) that both A and B survive,
   (b) that at least one dies?

Solution. (a) Assuming that the deaths of A and B are independent events, the desired probability is, by Theorem II,

$$0.7 \times 0.8 = 0.56.$$

(b) Events (a) and (b) are mutually exclusive events, one of which is certain to happen. Hence, the probability of the occurrence of one or the other of these events is unity. Employing Theorem I, we find for the probability of event (b)

$$1 - 0.56 = 0.44.$$

2. A bag contains five white, three red, and four black balls. If a ball is drawn at random, what is the probability that it is a red ball? A white ball? A white or red ball?
3. If three balls are drawn successively from the bag in Exercise 2 without being replaced, what is the probability that they are all black?
4. If two dice are thrown, what is the probability of two threes? Two fours? A three paired with a four?
5. The probability of an individual aged 30 living ten years is 0.9 and the probability of an individual aged 40 living ten years is 0.8. What is the probability that an individual aged 30
   (a) lives to reach age 50,
   (b) dies between ages 40 and 50,
   (c) dies before reaching age 40?
6. Two cards are drawn at random without replacement from a deck of 52. What is the probability that both the cards drawn are aces? Both kings? An ace followed by a king? A king followed by an ace? An ace and a king drawn in either order?
7. Three cards are drawn without replacement from a deck of 52. What is the probability that all the cards are aces? Two aces followed by a king? An ace, king, and queen drawn in any order?
8. Answer questions (6) and (7) under the assumption that the cards are replaced after each drawing.
9. A traveler has four connections to make in order that he may reach his destination on time. If the probability of making each connection is 3/4, what is the probability of his making all of the connections?

10. The probability of team A winning a game from team B is 3/5. What is the probability that A will win two or more out of a series of three?

11. What is the probability of a particular baseball team winning all three of a series of games, assuming the teams are evenly matched? Winning two and losing one in any order?

12. If the probabilities of A, B, C, and D surviving a certain period are 3/4, 4/5, 5/6, and 6/7, respectively, what is the probability that
   (a) all four will survive the period,
   (b) all four will die in the period,
   (c) at least one dies in the period,
   (d) at least one survives the period?

13. Two dice are thrown and the sum of the upper faces computed. What is the probability of throwing a seven? A two? An eleven? Any number greater than eight?

14. If a bag contains four red and three white balls, and a second bag contains two red and five white balls, what is the probability of drawing one red and one white ball in two drawings, one from each bag?

15. If a ball is drawn from the first bag in Exercise 14 and, without its color being observed, is placed in the second bag, what is the probability that if a ball is now drawn from the second bag it will be red?

16. What is the probability of throwing n heads in n throws of a coin? One tail and the rest heads?

17. If the probability that the age of a man, selected at random from a group of men, is between 20 and 35 years is 2/3, and the probability that it is between 20 and 25 is 1/4, what is the probability that his age is between 25 and 35?

18. If the probabilities of surviving ten years are 0.8, 0.7, and 0.6 for persons of ages 30, 40, and 50, respectively, what is the probability that an individual now age 30 will die between ages 50 and 60?

19. A has three coins and B has two. The coins are all to be tossed and it is agreed that the player showing the greatest number of heads shall be the winner. In the case of an equal number of heads, B wins. What is A's probability of winning?

20. The probability that a man aged 25 and another aged 45 will both survive a period of twenty years is 0.7. The probability that a man aged 25 will survive ten years is 0.9. Find the probability that a man aged 35 will live to age 65.

1.5 MORTALITY TABLES

The basis of the theory of life insurance is the mortality or life table. A mortality table has been defined as "the instrument by means of which are measured the probabilities of life and death." A mortality table is primarily a record of past experience and naturally its use in predicting future events implies the expectation that the experience of the past will be duplicated in the future. In the construction of a mortality table, the investigations which are undertaken are designed to yield at each age the *rate of mortality,* that is, the probability that a life of a given age will die within a year. The two principal sources of life tables are general population statistics obtained from the census and the mortality records of life insurance companies.

Many important mortality tables have been based upon the experience of the general population. The number of deaths is obtained at each age from the official records of deaths, and the rate of mortality at each age is obtained by dividing the number of deaths by an adjusted figure representing the number exposed to the risk of death at that age. Such a table is unsuitable for use by a life insurance company. Insured lives form a "select" group, from which those lives subject to high rates of mortality have been eliminated by medical examination or otherwise. The population table, however, includes many in poor health, and others engaged in hazardous or unhealthy occupations. It is to be expected, therefore, that the rates of mortality in a table constructed from population records will be higher than the rates of mortality in a table based on the experience of life insurance companies.

The rates of mortality among the general population in the United States have been calculated and published after each decennial census since 1890. However, the earlier tables did not represent national mortality since they were based only upon data from states which required statewide registration of births and deaths. By 1940, all of the states were in this category, so that the mortality rates of the tables published thereafter do reflect nationwide experience.

The United States Life Tables contain separate tabulations by states, and each is further subdivided to show the rates of mortality in respect to white and nonwhite persons, male and female lives, native-born and foreign-born and among those residing in urban and rural districts. Generally speaking, the rate of mortality is lower among white persons than among those of other races, is lower for females than for males, and is lower for rural districts than for urban. Geography also makes a difference. In general, the north central section covering the plains states has shown the lowest rates of mortality while those of the southeastern section have been the highest.

There are in existence many life tables formed from the experience of one or more life insurance companies. In the construction of such a table the number of deaths at each age is recorded and compared with the number of lives exposed to the risk of death at that age. The quotient of these two figures gives the rate of mortality. Experience has shown that, regardless of the source from which the statistics are obtained, the empirical data will not yield a smooth sequence of rates from age to age. The irregularities are generally attributed to chance fluctuations. Since it appears reasonable to assume that the rates of death do proceed smoothly from age to age, the actuary makes use of a process of "graduation" to smooth out the irregularities. Hence it may be said that the published table represents an idealized version of the mortality which actually occurred among the lives studied.

Among the best known tables used for life insurance purposes in the United States have been the American Experience Table, first published in 1868 and used for many years, the American Men Mortality Table, based on the combined records of many insurance companies for the period 1900–1915, and the Commissioners' 1941 Standard Ordinary Mortality Table, generally designated as the 1941 CSO Table. This latter table became the generally recognized legal standard for reserve and nonforfeiture purposes in most of the states but is now being superseded by the 1958 CSO Mortality Table for these purposes. This most recent table was based upon the experience of several life insurance companies from 1950 to 1954 for policies that had been in force more than five years.

Past experience has shown that mortality rates are lower for annuitants than for holders of life insurance policies so that it would be unsound to issue annuities at rates calculated upon life insurance tables. Accordingly, mortality studies have been made on the lives of annuitants and corresponding annuity mortality tables constructed. The table presently in use as a minimum reserve standard is the 1937 Standard Annuity Table, but its mortality rates seem now to be too high. Several more recent tables with lower rates of mortality have been constructed and are in extensive use for premium calculations and also for reserve purposes, since they produce reserves greater than the legal minimum reserves.

It should be noted that if the actuary wishes to build an element of conservatism into his table, he can arrange to increase slightly the rates of mortality if the table is to be used for life insurance, and similarly he can decrease the rates of mortality if the table is to be used for annuity purposes. It is not uncommon to find such a "margin" in insurance and annuity tables.

1.6 CONSTRUCTION OF A MORTALITY TABLE

With the rates of mortality by age available, it is a simple matter to construct a mortality table. An initial age is chosen and a convenient number of lives is assumed to exist at that precise age. This number, called the *radix*, is usually a round number such as 100,000 1,000,000, or 10,000,000. Thus, the 1958 CSO Table for males (see Table II of the Appendix) begins with a radix of 10,000,000 at age 0. The mortality rate of 0.00708 at this age applied to an exposure of 10,000,000 lives would produce 70,800 deaths between the ages of 0 and 1. Hence, at age 1 there would remain 9,929,200 survivors. The rate of 0.00176 at age 1 applied to an exposure of 9,929,200 produces 17,475 deaths which, subtracted from the exposure, leaves 9,911,725 survivors at age 2. This same process is repeated, age by age, up to the limiting age of the table which is defined as the first age at which no survivors exist. This limiting age is designated by the symbol ω. In the case of the 1958 CSO Table for males, $\omega = 100$.

One should not assume that the compiler of the mortality table believes that any such limiting age is the maximum length of life; rather, this age is merely a convention, of relatively minor importance in the financial computations based upon the table, but necessary because a table must end somewhere.

The completed mortality table, then, consists of a column showing the number of survivors at each age and the number of deaths that occur at each age—that is, between the attainment of the indicated age and the attainment of the next succeeding age. In standard actuarial notation, a tabular age is usually represented by the symbol x, and the function corresponding to that age by some other letter with x appearing as a subscript. Thus, the number of survivors of the original group who began at the initial tabular age and have now attained precise age x is designated by l_x. The number of persons in the group who die after attaining precise age x but before reaching age $x + 1$ is represented by d_x.

At once, it is evident that

$$l_{x+1} = l_x - d_x, \tag{1.4}$$

that is, the number of survivors at age $x + 1$ must equal the number at age x less the number who die before reaching age $x + 1$.

One important use of the mortality table is to determine various probabilities related to survival from any age to any other age. In such a case, we may be said to employ the *a priori* definition of probability. To illustrate, suppose we wish to determine the probability, according to the 1958 CSO Table, that a person now aged exactly 25 will survive to age 26. We note that according to the table of the 9,575,637 persons aged 25, 9,557,155 survive to age 26. This is analogous to a situation in which we have an urn containing 9,575,637 balls of which 9,557,155 are white and 18,481 are black.

Then, if the drawing of each of these balls is equally likely, the probability of survival is equal to that of drawing a white ball which, by our *a priori* definition of probability, is 9,557,155/9,575,637.

In the general case, we define the probability that a person now of precise age x years, designated in standard actuarial practice by the symbol (x), will survive to age $x + 1$ as

$$p_x = \frac{l_{x+1}}{l_x},\tag{1.5}$$

and the probability that (x) will die before the attainment of age $x + 1$ as

$$q_x = \frac{d_x}{l_x}.\tag{1.6}$$

Since $l_{x+1} + d_x = l_x$, it is evident that

$$p_x + q_x = 1,\tag{1.7}$$

a relationship which satisfies our intuition as well as the laws of probability.

Exercises

1. Prove by means of equations (1.4) and (1.5) the following identities:
    (a) $l_x = d_x + d_{x+1} + \cdots + d_{\omega-1}$.
    (b) $l_x - l_{x+n} = d_x + d_{x+1} + \cdots + d_{x+n-1}$.
    (c) $l_{x+n} = l_x \cdot p_x \cdot p_{x+1} \cdots p_{x+n-1}$.
2. Given that $l_{15} = 100,000$, and the rates of mortality at ages 15, 16, 17, 18, and 19 are 0.0020, 0.0021, 0.0023, 0.0026, and 0.0030, respectively, compute columns of l_x, d_x, and p_x for these ages.
3. Verify equations (1.4) and (1.6) for the 1958 CSO Table for ages 40 to 45, inclusive.
4. Check numerically the identities given in Exercise 1 for the 1958 CSO Table, using $x = 94$ and $n = 3$.
5. Given the following items from a certain table of mortality, deduce the corresponding values for d_x, q_x, p_x.

x	92	93	94	95	96	97	98
l_x	1000	500	230	92	29	6	0

6. Verify in the 1958 CSO Table that

$$l_{20} - l_{25} = d_{20} + d_{21} + d_{22} + d_{23} + d_{24}.$$

7. Using the result in Exercise 6, find the probability that a person aged 20 will die before reaching age 25.
8. What are the probabilities that a man aged 40 and subject to the mortality of the 1958 CSO Table will die in each of the decades 40–49 inclusive, 50–59, 60–69, respectively.
9. From the data of Exercise 5, find the probability that a person aged 92 will die between the ages of 94 and 96.

1.7 NOTATION

The symbol $_np_x$ means the probability that (x) will live to reach age $x + n$. Out of the l_x persons alive at age x there are l_{x+n} survivors at age $x + n$; consequently

$$_np_x = \frac{l_{x+n}}{l_x}. \tag{1.8}$$

The probability that (x) will die before reaching age $x + n$ is denoted by $_nq_x$. Hence

$$_nq_x = \frac{d_x + d_{x+1} + \cdots + d_{x+n-1}}{l_x} = \frac{l_x - l_{x+n}}{l_x}. \tag{1.9}$$

The symbol $_m|q_x$ is used to denote the probability that a person now aged x will die in the year following the attainment of age $x + m$, or between ages $x + m$ and $x + m + 1$. Since, according to the mortality table, d_{x+m} individuals will die in this age interval out of l_x alive at age x, it follows that

$$_m|q_x = \frac{d_{x+m}}{l_x}.$$

The probability that (x) will die in the n-year period following the attainment of age $x + m$, or in the period of time between age $x + m$ and age $x + m + n$, is denoted by the symbol $_m|_nq_x$. It follows immediately that

$$_m|_nq_x = \frac{d_{x+m} + d_{x+m+1} + \cdots + d_{x+m+n-1}}{l_x},$$

or

$$_m|_nq_x = \frac{l_{x+m} - l_{x+m+n}}{l_x} = _mp_x - _{m+n}p_x. \tag{1.10}$$

In considering the foregoing notation it should be noted that the letter "p" with proper subscripts is used to denote the probability of an individual living a given period; whereas, the letter "q" is used to denote the probability of an individual dying during a given period. The notation $_{m|n}q_x$ is entirely general and may be specialized to yield the following results:

$$q_x = {}_{0|1}q_x, \qquad _nq_x = {}_{0|n}q_x, \qquad _{m|}q_x = {}_{m|1}q_x .$$

Exercises

1. From the 1958 CSO Table find the numerical values of the following probabilities (give the proper symbol in each case):
   (a) that a man aged 20 will live at least 25 years more.
   (b) that a man aged 30 will die in the year following the attainment of age 45,
   (c) that a man aged 35 will die between ages 60 and 70,
   (d) that a man aged 40 will live to age 55 but not to age 60,
   (e) that a man aged 45 will die within five years,
   (f) that a man aged 20 will die between ages 45 and 50.
   (g) Explain why the answer to (f) is the product of the answers to parts (a) and (e).

2. State in words the probabilities represented by the following symbols:

$$_{10}p_{21}; \quad p_{21}; \quad _{10|}q_{30}; \quad _{10|2}q_{30}; \quad q_{40}; \quad _{15|5}q_{50}.$$

3. The probability $_np_x$ may be considered as the probability of the compound event consisting of (x) living one year, $(x + 1)$ living one year, $(x + 2)$ living one year . . ., and $(x + n - 1)$ living one year. From Theorem II the probability of this compound event is

$$p_x \cdot p_{x+1} \cdot p_{x+2} \cdots p_{x+n-1}.$$

   Show algebraically that this expression is equal to $_np_x$.

4. Prove the following identities:
   (a) $_{m+1}p_x + {}_{m|}q_x = {}_mp_x,$
   (b) $_{m+n}p_x + {}_{m|n}q_x = {}_mp_x,$
   (c) $_{m+n}p_x = {}_mp_x \cdot {}_np_{x+m} = {}_np_x \cdot {}_mp_{x+n}.$

5. The probability that a man aged 30 and another man aged 50 will both survive a period of twenty years is 0.4. Out of 48,000 men alive at age 30, 3000 will die before they attain age 40. Calculate the probability that a man now aged 40 will die within the next thirty years.

6. Prove the following identities:
   (a) $_{m|}q_x = {}_mp_x \cdot q_{x+m},$
   (b) $_{m|n}q_x = {}_mp_x \cdot {}_nq_{x+m}.$

7. At what age, according to the 1958 CSO Table, is a man now aged 85 most likely to die? What is the probability that he will die at that age?

8. Prove the identity:

$$_np_x = \frac{_np_x - {}_{n+1}p_x}{q_{x+n}}.$$

9. Using the 1958 CSO Table, compare the probability that a man 25 years old will die between the ages of 65 and 70 with the probability that a man aged 50 will die between those same ages.

10. Prove the identity:

$$q_x + p_x \cdot q_{x+1} + {}_2p_x \cdot q_{x+2} + {}_3p_x \cdot q_{x+3} + \cdots = 1.$$

11. Given that $q_x = .02x - 1.5$ for values of x between 85 and 95, inclusive, and that $l_{85} = 1000$, form the l_x and d_x columns from 85 to 95. Find the probability that (85) lives to age 92; that (85) dies between 90 and 92. Without using the values of l_x and d_x, find the probability that (88) dies within the year; that he survives to 91.

1.8 EXPECTATION OF LIFE

By the expression *expectation of life at age x* is meant the average number of years to be lived in the future by persons now aged x. If we assume that all the deaths that occur in any year take place at the very beginning of that year, out of an original group of l_x persons at age x there will be l_{x+1} persons who survive to the end of the first year, and there will be a total of l_{x+1} years lived by the whole group during the first year following age x. Similarly, the group will live a total of l_{x+2} additional years during the second year following age x, l_{x+3} additional years during the third year, and so on. Adding these whole years together and dividing by the number of persons, l_x, in the original group, we find the average number of years to be lived in the future by individuals now aged x,

$$e_x = \frac{l_{x+1} + l_{x+2} + l_{x+3} + \cdots + l_{\omega-1}}{l_x}. \qquad (1.11)$$

This fraction is called the *curtate expectation* since it neglects the fractional parts of years lived by those who die in any year.

Under the assumption that the deaths during any year of age are distributed uniformly throughout the year, so that on the average each person will live half a year in the year of his death, the *complete expectation* of life at age x is found by adding $1/2$ to the curtate expectation. Hence,

$$\mathring{e}_x = e_x + \frac{1}{2} = \frac{1}{2} + \frac{l_{x+1} + l_{x+2} + \cdots + l_{\omega-1}}{l_x}, \qquad (1.12)$$

approximately.

The expectation of life is often useful in making rough analyses of problems which would otherwise have to be solved by more elaborate means to be considered later. It is often supposed, however, by those unacquainted with actuarial methods that the expectation of life is fundamental in actuarial calculations. That this is not the case will be seen from the developments of the succeeding chapters.

Exercises

1. Check the values of the expectation of life given in the 1958 CSO Table for ages 75, 85, and 90.
2. Assuming that deaths are uniformly distributed throughout the year, show that

$$\mathring{e}_x = \tfrac{1}{2}(q_x + 3 \cdot {}_1|q_x + 5 \cdot {}_2|q_x + 7 \cdot {}_3|q_x + \cdots).$$

3. Prove

$$e_x = p_x + {}_2p_x + {}_3p_x + \cdots.$$

4. (a) Show that

$$e_x = p_x(1 + e_{x+1}).$$

(b) Prove

$$\frac{e_x \cdot e_{x+1} \cdot e_{x+2} \cdots e_{x+n-1}}{(1 + e_{x+1})(1 + e_{x+2})(1 + e_{x+3}) \cdots (1 + e_{x+n})} = {}_np_x.$$

5. Show that

$$1 + e_x = q_x + p_x(1 + q_{x+1}) + {}_2p_x(1 + q_{x+2}) + \cdots.$$

6. From the data of Exercise 5, page 10, find e_{92} and $\mathring{e}_{93}$.
7. Assuming a uniform distribution of deaths throughout each year, prove that

$$({}_{1/2}p_x - p_x) + ({}_{3/2}p_x - {}_2p_x) + ({}_{5/2}p_x - {}_3p_x) + \cdots = \tfrac{1}{2}.$$

1.9 SELECTION

A *select* group is one which has not been chosen at random. The *selection* of such a group may be deliberate, as in the case of a life insurance company requiring a satisfactory medical examination prior to insurance. A group chosen in this manner may be expected to live longer on the average than a group chosen at random. The selection of a group may be automatic as in the case of emigration from one country to another, where it may be expected that only persons in reasonably good health will migrate. Individuals purchasing life annuities, payable only during the life of the individual, from insurance companies form a select group, inasmuch as an individual in poor health usually will not buy such an annuity.

It has been observed that the effect of these types of selection upon the mortality rate of the select group diminishes with the lapse of time from the date of selection and usually has decreased sufficiently in a period of five or ten years so that it may, for practical purposes, be assumed to have disappeared. Thus, two groups of persons, one formed from the survivors of those who insured fifteen years ago at age 30, and the other from the survivors of those insured ten years ago at age 35 (all the members of the two groups being, therefore, now of the same age), would probably show about the same mortality rate.

An example of a modern table of *select* and *ultimate* mortality rates may be found in Anderson's* Select Modification of Mortality Table X_{18}. This table shows not only the *ultimate* rate of mortality for the period after the effect of medical selection has disappeared (assumed to be five years), but also shows the adjusted rates of mortality, called *select* rates, for each of the years of the five-year period during which the medical examination and other selection methods are effective. The following extract from this table shows the mortality rates for a selected range of ages.

MORTALITY TABLE X_{18}
(with Anderson's Select Modification)
RATE OF MORTALITY PER 1000

Age at Issue	Policy Year						Attained Age
	1	2	3	4	5	6 and Over	
30	.78	.88	.99	1.10	1.25	1.41	35
31	.80	.91	1.02	1.17	1.33	1.53	36
32	.82	.94	1.08	1.24	1.44	1.68	37
33	.84	.98	1.14	1.33	1.57	1.87	38
34	.88	1.03	1.22	1.45	1.74	2.10	39
35	.92	1.10	1.33	1.61	1.95	2.36	40
36	.97	1.19	1.46	1.79	2.19	2.64	41
37	1.04	1.30	1.62	2.00	2.44	2.95	42
38	1.13	1.44	1.80	2.22	2.72	3.28	43
39	1.24	1.59	1.99	2.47	3.01	3.63	44
40	1.36	1.74	2.20	2.72	3.32	4.02	45
41	1.48	1.91	2.41	2.99	3.67	4.45	46
42	1.61	2.09	2.64	3.29	4.05	4.92	47
43	1.74	2.27	2.89	3.61	4.46	5.46	48
44	1.87	2.46	3.16	3.97	4.93	6.06	49

*James C. H. Anderson, "Gross Premium Calculations and Profit Measurement for Nonparticipating Insurance," *Transactions of the Society of Actuaries,* **XI**, pp. 393–4.

In the preceding table the figure 1.62 given for the third year of insurance at age 37 indicates that 0.00162 is the probability that an individual now aged 39, who was accepted for life insurance two years ago at age 37, will die before attaining age 40.

Not only the rates of mortality, but the numbers of survivors and of deaths at each age and duration of insurance appear in a complete select mortality table. From these may be calculated other actuarial functions on a select basis. Although one might expect that select tables would be employed extensively in life insurance calculations, in actual practice they receive only limited use. In many instances the actual monetary difference in results based upon select tables rather than ultimate tables is relatively small, not large enough to justify the additional labor and expense which would be involved in their use. In this book we will make no further use of select tables until Chapter VI, Gross Premiums, is reached.

Exercises

Fill in the numerical values from the Select Mortality Table X_{18} for each of the following problems but do not multiply.

1. What is the probability that a man now aged 36, who was accepted for insurance a year ago, will live to reach 38?

Solution.   The probability of such an individual, age 36, dying within one year is 0.00110 according to the table. Hence the probability of living one year is $1 - 0.00110 = 0.99890$. The probability of an individual age 37, accepted for life insurance two years ago, living one year is $1 - 0.00133 = 0.99867$. Hence, by Theorem II, the desired probability is (0.99890) multiplied by (0.99867).

2. What is the probability that a man now being accepted for life insurance at age 41 will live to reach age 45?

3. What is the probability that an individual now aged 35, who was accepted for insurance two years ago, will die between ages 36 and 37?

4. What is the probability that an individual now aged 32, who was accepted for insurance at age 30, will live to reach age 40?

5. What is the probability that a man now being accepted for insurance at age 35 will die before reaching 40?

6. What is the probability that a man now aged 40, who was accepted for insurance at age 32, will die in the next year? Will die before reaching age 45?

7. Consider two policyholders, both aged 35, one of whom has just been accepted for insurance while the other has had his policy for ten years. Find the probability that both will live to age 37; that at least one will die before age 38; that both will die before age 36.

8. Consider two groups of insured persons all aged 40. The first group con-

sists of 1000 newly insured persons while the second group consists of 1000 who were insured initially at age 35. How many fewer deaths will be expected among the newly insured group during the next five years than among the members of the other group?

Review Exercises

1. Given the following table of mortality, deduce columns for d_x, q_x, p_x, e_x, and $\mathring{e}_x$.

x	90	91	92	93	94	95	96
l_x	850	450	210	75	20	4	0

2. If $l_x = k(86 - x)$, where k is a constant, show that

$$d_x = k; \quad p_x = \frac{85 - x}{86 - x}; \quad q_x = \frac{1}{86 - x}.$$

3. From the Select Mortality Table X_{18}, Section 1.9, find the probability that an individual now being accepted for life insurance at age 32 will
   (a) survive to age 35,
   (b) die between ages 33 and 34,
   (c) survive to age 34.

4. The probability that at least one of the two lives A and B will die in the next ten years is 0.44. The probability that at least one of the two lives will survive the period is 0.94. Find the probability that A will be living at the end of the ten years.

5. A husband is aged 22 and a wife 24 at the date of their marriage; what is the probability that they will live to celebrate their silver wedding? Their golden wedding? Use the 1958 CSO Table to answer this problem.

6. Using the 1958 CSO Table find numerical answers to the following probabilities:
   (a) that (30) will die between ages 65 and 70,
   (b) that (50) will survive to age 70,
   (c) that (20) will die between ages 80 and 85.

7. Plot a graph showing, at age intervals of five years, the values of q_x as given by the 1958 CSO Table.

8. Between what two consecutive ages, according to the 1958 CSO Table, is a man now aged 35 most likely to die? What is the probability that he will die in that year?

9. The probability that (22) will live ten years is 0.96 and that he will live 30 years is 0.72. Find the probability that a person aged 32 will live to age 52.

10. If $l_x = k(100 - x)$, find p_{85}; $_3p_{65}$; $_{10|5}q_{50}$.

11. (a) Complete the following table:

x	l_x	d_x	p_x	q_x
98	160			
99		40		
100	24			0.667
101			0.250	
102				1.000

(b) Find e_{98} and $\overset{\circ}{e}_{98}$ from the above table.

CHAPTER 2

Annuities

2.1 COMPOUND INTEREST

The mathematical theory of life insurance involves the assumption that money is constantly productive. Life insurance probably constitutes the best example of long-time finance, or investment extended over a considerable period of time, and thus it is necessary that some consideration be given to the most important principles of interest. Methods of computing interest may be classified generally into two classes: (a) *simple interest,* in which the principal is considered as remaining constant throughout the transaction, and (b) *compound interest,* in which the interest previously earned is periodically "compounded," or added to the principal, thus producing a new principal to be used in the ensuing period. Life insurance companies invariably use compound interest with a period of one year as the time between the successive "compoundings"; our discussion here will be limited to interest calculated upon this basis.

If we denote the annual rate of interest by i, then the interest earned on a principal of A in one year will be $A \cdot i$, and the total accumulated amount, including both principal and interest, will be $A(1 + i)$ by the end of one year. This new principal, $A(1 + i)$, when invested for the second year earns interest of $A(1 + i)i$, and the total accumulated amount at the end of that year will be

$$A(1 + i) + A(1 + i)i = A(1 + i)^2.$$

Similarly, during the third year the principal invested will be $A(1 + i)^2$, the interest earned $A(1 + i)^2 i$, and the total accumulated amount is

$$A(1 + i)^2 + A(1 + i)^2 i = A(1 + i)^3.$$

[19]

In general, after n years have elapsed, the total accumulated amount S, including the original principal of A and the interest earned in the meantime, is

$$S = A (1 + i)^n, \tag{2.1}$$

Dividing this equation by $(1 + i)^n$, we obtain

$$A = S(1 + i)^{-n} = S \cdot v^n, \tag{2.2}$$

where $v = (1 + i)^{-1}$.

The principal A is called the *present value* or *discounted value* of S. It may be considered as the sum which placed at compound interest at the rate i will amount or accumulate to S by the end of the n years.

Tables of the functions $(1 + i)^n$ and v^n at 3% interest are given in Table I in the Appendix.

2.2   ANNUITY CERTAIN

An *annuity certain* is a sequence of periodic payments, usually of equal size, payable over a fixed term of years, it being assumed that each payment is sure to be made at the time when it is due. The time between successive payments is called the *payment interval*. We will restrict the present discussion to annuities with a payment interval of one year. It is convenient to consider that each annuity payment pertains to some payment interval, either immediately preceding or immediately following the payment. The time from the beginning of the first payment interval to the end of the last payment interval is called the *term* of the annuity. The *annual rent* of an annuity is the sum of the payments which occur in any one year, and since only annuities with annual payments are under consideration, the annual rent will be the annuity payment. An annuity whose payments are made at the beginning of each payment interval is called an annuity *due,* whereas the term annuity *immediate* is applied whenever the payments are made at the end of each payment interval. The *present value* or *single premium* for an annuity is the sum of the present values of the payments taken at the beginning of its term, whereas the *amount* of an annuity is the sum of the accumulated amounts of the payments taken at the end of its term, each payment being accumulated from the date when it was due. Obviously, the present value and the amount of an annuity will depend for their values upon the interest rate to be used. Since the present value and the amount of an annuity represent the values of the same payments taken at different times, the present value is equal to the amount discounted over the term of the annuity.

Consider an annuity with a payment of $1 paid at the end of the first year, $1 paid at the end of the second year, and so on until finally $1 is paid at the end of the nth year. Such a sequence of payments forms, according to the definition, an annuity immediate with annual rent $1. Let $s_{\overline{n}|}$ denote the sum of the accumulated values of the payments taken at the end of the nth year at the interest rate i, compounded annually. The payment made at the end of the first year will accumulate for $n - 1$ years, the payment made at the end of the second year will accumulate for $n - 2$ years, and so on, the final payment of $1 earning no interest. Upon successively applying equation (2.1), one has

$$s_{\overline{n}|} = (1 + i)^{n-1} + (1 + i)^{n-2} + \cdots + (1 + i) + 1.$$

The multiplication of both sides of this equation by $(1 + i)$ yields

$$(1 + i)s_{\overline{n}|} = (1 + i)^n + (1 + i)^{n-1} + \cdots + (1 + i)^2 + (1 + i).$$

Subtracting the first equation from the second, we obtain

$$i \cdot s_{\overline{n}|} = (1 + i)^n - 1,$$

whence it follows that

$$s_{\overline{n}|} = \frac{(1 + i)^n - 1}{i}. \tag{2.3}$$

Let $a_{\overline{n}|}$ denote the present value of the same annuity, that is, the discounted value of these payments at the beginning of the first year. To obtain an expression for $a_{\overline{n}|}$, discount the amount $s_{\overline{n}|}$ for n years (the term of the annuity) and obtain

$$a_{\overline{n}|} = (1 + i)^{-n} s_{\overline{n}|} = \frac{(1 + i)^{-n}(1 + i)^n - (1 + i)^{-n}}{i};$$

hence

$$a_{\overline{n}|} = \frac{1 - v^n}{i}. \tag{2.4}$$

Tables of the values of $s_{\overline{n}|}$ and $a_{\overline{n}|}$ at 3% interest are found in Table I in the Appendix.

Let us suppose that the payments described above were made at the beginning of each year instead of at the end of each year. Such an annuity would be called an annuity *due* and each of its payments would be equivalent to $(1 + i)$ paid at the end of the same year. Hence, if $\ddot{s}_{\overline{n}|}$ and $\ddot{a}_{\overline{n}|}$ denote, respectively, the amount and present value of the annuity due, it follows that

$$\ddot{s}_{\overline{n}|} = (1 + i)s_{\overline{n}|}$$

$$\ddot{a}_{\overline{n}|} = (1 + i)a_{\overline{n}|}.$$

Inserting the value of $s_{\overline{n}|}$ given by equation (2.3), we obtain

$$\ddot{s}_{\overline{n}|} = (1 + i)\left[\frac{(1 + i)^n - 1}{i}\right] = \frac{(1 + i)^{n+1} - (1 + i)}{i}$$

$$= \frac{(1 + i)^{n+1} - 1}{i} - 1.$$

Hence it follows that

$$\ddot{s}_{\overline{n}|} = s_{\overline{n+1}|} - 1. \qquad (2.5)$$

Similarly

$$\ddot{a}_{\overline{n}|} = (1 + i)\frac{1 - v^n}{i} = \frac{(1 + i) - v^{n-1}}{i} = 1 + \frac{1 - v^{n-1}}{i},$$

and hence

$$\ddot{a}_{\overline{n}|} = 1 + a_{\overline{n-1}|}. \qquad (2.6)$$

Equations (2.5) and (2.6) are useful in obtaining the numerical values of $\ddot{s}_{\overline{n}|}$ and $\ddot{a}_{\overline{n}|}$ from the values of $s_{\overline{n+1}|}$ and $a_{\overline{n-1}|}$, respectively, given in Table I.

It should be noted that $a_{\overline{n}|}$ represents the value of a sequence of payments one interval before the first payment is to be made; $\ddot{a}_{\overline{n}|}$ represents the value at the time of the first payment; $s_{\overline{n}|}$ the value at the time of the last payment; and $\ddot{s}_{\overline{n}|}$ the value one payment interval after the last payment is made.

Exercises

Assume an interest rate of 3%, compounded annually, in the following problems.

1. A beneficiary under a life insurance policy is offered the option of $10,000 cash or a sequence of equal payments at the end of each year for ten years. Find the annual payment.

Solution.   Let R be the amount of each annual payment. Then the present value of the annuity immediate of R per year may be represented by the product

$$R \cdot a_{\overline{10}|}.$$

Since this option is to be equivalent to $10,000 in cash, one immediately
writes the equation

$$R \cdot a_{\overline{10|}} = 10,000,$$

whence, using Table I, we find

$$R = \frac{10,000}{a_{\overline{10|}}} = \frac{10,000}{8.5302028}$$

$$= \$1,172.30$$

2. Solve Exercise 1 when the payments are to be made at the beginning of
each year for ten years. For fifteen years.

3. (a) Find the accumulated amount of $2000 invested for twenty years.
Seventy years.
(b) What is the present value of $1000 due at the end of ten years? A
hundred years?

4. An individual aged 30 pays $5000 to a life insurance company in ex-
change for a contract in which the company agrees to pay a fixed sum
when the individual reaches age 60. If the individual dies before age 60
the company agrees to return immediately to his heirs the $5000 and
accumulated interest to the date of his death. What amount should the
individual receive when he attains age 60?

5. If d (called the *rate of discount*) satisfies the equation $d = iv$, show that

(a) $d = 1 - v$,

(b) $\ddot{s}_{\overline{n|}} = \dfrac{(1 + i)^n - 1}{d}$,

(c) $\ddot{a}_{\overline{n|}} = \dfrac{1 - v^n}{d}$.

(d) $\dfrac{1}{s_{\overline{n|}}} = \dfrac{1}{\ddot{a}_{\overline{n|}}} - d.$

6. Prove the identities:

(a) $a_{\overline{n+1|}} = a_{\overline{n|}} + v^{n+1}$,

(b) $s_{\overline{n+1|}} = s_{\overline{n|}} + (1 + i)^n$,

(c) $v^n = v \cdot \ddot{a}_{\overline{n|}} - a_{\overline{n-1|}}$,

(d) $v^n = 1 - i \cdot a_{\overline{n|}}.$

(e) $\dfrac{1}{a_{\overline{n|}}} - \dfrac{1}{s_{\overline{n|}}} = i.$

7. Approximately how long will it take an investment to double itself? To
triple itself?

8. A man borrows $1000, agreeing to pay his creditor $500 at the end of
two years and to make a final payment at the end of five years. What
will be the size of this final payment?

9. A man deposits $250 in a savings bank at the end of each year for ten
years. How much will be in the account just after the tenth deposit?

10. A debtor agrees to repay his debt of $10,000 by means of annual payments, beginning at the end of the first year, of $1000 each as long as necessary, followed by a final smaller payment. How many payments of $1000 will be made? What will be the size of the final payment?

11. A man wishes to accumulate a fund of $1500 at the end of twelve years. How much must he deposit at the beginning of each year in order to achieve this goal?

12. What is the present value of an annuity certain of $800 paid at the beginning of each year for eight years?

13. If one deposits $100 at the beginning of each year for ten years, how much can be taken out each year in equal amounts for five years, first withdrawal at the end of the tenth year?

14. If one deposits $100 at the end of each year for ten years, how much can be taken out each year in equal amounts for five years, first withdrawal at the end of the eleventh year? Relate the answer here to that in Exercise 13.

15. If in Exercise 13 the first withdrawal had been made at the end of the fourteenth year, how large would each of the five withdrawals have been?

2.3 NET SINGLE PREMIUMS

In many of the following sections we will be interested in finding the *present value* of future sums, the payment of each of which is contingent upon either the death or survival of a designated life or group of lives. This present value, particularly in the case of life insurance, is often termed the *net single premium* for the contingent benefit. The net single premium may be defined as a sum paid at the inception of the contract which, under certain basic assumptions, would be necessary and sufficient to provide the scheduled benefit payments. The basic assumptions are the following:

1. the mortality table employed will represent precisely the mortality to be experienced by the group of lives concerned;

2. all net single premiums received will be immediately invested and will earn precisely the assumed rate of interest until withdrawn to pay benefits;

3. all net single premiums paid on behalf of the group of lives involved, plus all interest earned, will ultimately be paid to members of the group in the form of contractual benefits payments. In other words, any expenses, taxes, profits, losses, and the like, will be taken care of outside of the net premium structure.

As a direct consequence of these assumptions, we have the fol-

lowing fundamental equation underlying the definition of the term
net single premium:

$$
\left\{
\begin{array}{l}
\text{Present value at the incep-}\\
\text{tion of the contract of all net}\\
\text{single premiums to be paid}\\
\text{by a life or group of lives for}\\
\text{contractual benefits}
\end{array}
\right\}
=
\left\{
\begin{array}{l}
\text{Present value at the incep-}\\
\text{tion of the contract of all}\\
\text{contractual benefits to be}\\
\text{received by this life or group}\\
\text{of lives}
\end{array}
\right\}
$$

2.4   PURE ENDOWMENT

Let us suppose that l_x persons, all of age x, desire by equal contributions at the present time to provide a payment of $1 to each one that
survives the succeeding n years. As l_{x+n} survivors will be living at the
end of the n-year period, a fund of l_{x+n} dollars must be on hand at
that time. The present value of this fund is $v^n l_{x+n}$. Since this amount
is to be raised at the present time from the l_x persons, each of whom
makes an individual contribution which we will denote by $_nE_x$, we
can equate the total present value of the net single premiums paid at
the inception of the contract by the l_x lives entering into the contract
to the total present value of the benefits to be paid to the group and
obtain $l_x \cdot {_nE_x} = v^n \cdot l_{x+n}$. Solving for $_nE_x$, we have

$$
{_nE_x} = \frac{v^n l_{x+n}}{l_x} = v^n \cdot {_np_x}. \tag{2.7}
$$

The preceding method of derivation is commonly referred to as
the *mutual fund method.* It will be employed from time to time in this
text. The benefit described above constitutes for each individual
what is known as a *pure endowment*—that is, a payment to be made
at the end of a specified number of years only in event that a designated individual (x) survives to receive it. The individual's contribution or *net single premium,* $_nE_x$, depends for its value upon the rate of
interest and the probability that the final payment of $1 will be
received, and may be considered as the present value of the pure endowment.

The present value A of an n-year pure endowment of R payable to
a man now aged x if he survives the n years is

$$
A = R \cdot {_nE_x} = R \cdot v^n \cdot {_np_x}.
$$

If both the numerator and denominator of the second member of equation (2.7) are multiplied by v^x, we obtain

$$_nE_x = \frac{v^{x+n}l_{x+n}}{v^x l_x}.$$

Designate by D_x the product $v^x \cdot l_x$ and by D_{x+n} the product $v^{x+n}l_{x+n}$. Thus we write $D_{25} = v^{25}\,l_{25}$, $D_{50} = v^{50}\,l_{50}$, and so on. Inserting these symbols in the previous equation, we have

$$_nE_x = \frac{D_{x+n}}{D_x}. \tag{2.8}$$

The notation D_x is one of several auxiliary symbols, known as *commutation symbols,* which play an important role in practical calculations. It will be noticed as the theory develops that direct use of the values given in a mortality table is rarely made, except to compute the values of the commutation symbols.

Tables of the values of D_x and other commutation symbols upon the basis of the 1958 CSO Table with various rates of interest have been computed and are in common use. Unless otherwise specified, all computations in the numerical problems are to be based upon this table with interest at 3% per annum. Commutation columns at this rate of interest are given in Table III, whereas values of $_nE_x$ and its reciprocal, for selected values of n, are given in Tables VII and VIII, respectively.

Exercises

1. Two payments of $1,000 each are to be received at the end of five and ten years, respectively. Find their present value
   (a) if they are certain to be received;
   (b) if they are to be received only if (45) is alive to receive them.

   Solution. (a) Since the payments are assumed to be paid in any event, discount due to the interest factor only need be considered, and we have immediately

   present value $= 1000\,(1.03)^{-5} + 1000\,(1.03)^{-10} = \$1,606.70.$ (Table I)

   (b) In this case the payments constitute two pure endowments payable at ages 50 and 55, respectively. Hence, the total present value is

   $$1000\,_5E_{45} + 1000\,_{10}E_{45}$$

   Employing Table VII to find numerical values for the pure endowment symbols, we have

$$1000\,(0.835279) + 1000\,(0.685079) = \$1{,}520.36.$$

2. A man now aged 20 is promised a gift of $5000 when he reaches age 35. Find the present value of the promise.

3. Show that
   (a) $_mE_x \cdot {_nE_{x+m}} = {_{m+n}E_x};$
   (b) $_nE_x = {_1E_x} \cdot {_1E_{x+1}} \cdot {_1E_{x+2}} \cdots {_1E_{x+n-1}};$
   (c) Use the first identity to compute the numerical value of $_9E_{30}$ from the available tables.

4. (a) To what would the formula for $_nE_x$ reduce if (x) were sure to survive the n years?
   (b) To what would it reduce if money were unproductive?
   (c) To what would it reduce if money were unproductive and (x) were sure to survive the n years?

5. A man now aged 25 has $1000 cash. If he deposits this with an insurance company what sum should he receive at age 45 if he agrees to forfeit all rights in event of death before age 45?

6. Check by computation the values of D_{20}, D_{55}, $_{15}E_{25}$, and $1/_5E_{50}$ given in the tables.

7. Prove that $D_{x+1} = v \cdot p_x \cdot D_x.$

8. What pure endowment payable at age 65 could a man aged 30 purchase with $2000 cash?

9. Find the present value of a pure endowment
   (a) of $1000, due in thirty years and purchased at age 25;
   (b) of $500, due in ten years and purchased at age 60.

10. Compute the values of $_{10}E_{70}$ and $1/_{20}E_{65}.$

2.5   LIFE ANNUITIES

A *life annuity* is a set of periodic payments, usually of equal size, payable over a period of years, each payment contingent upon the survival of a designated individual, called the *annuitant,* to the time of payment. The terms, *payment interval, annual rent, term, immediate,* and *due,* are applicable to life annuities in the same manner as to annuities certain. If the annuity is to continue through the entire life of the annuitant, the annuity is called a *whole life* annuity, whereas if the payments cease at the end of a specified time, even though the annuitant be then still living, the annuity is called a *temporary* life annuity. Unless otherwise specified, the words *life annuity* usually imply a whole life annuity, rather than a temporary life annuity. It is obvious that a pure endowment is a special case of a temporary life annuity, that is, a temporary life annuity having only one payment.

Annuities are classified according to the time at which the term begins with respect to the present age of the annuitant. If the term begins at the present age of the annuitant, the annuity is called *ordinary;* if the term begins sometime in the future, the annuity is *deferred;* whereas if the term of the annuity began sometime in the past, the annuity is called a *forborne* annuity.

2.6 WHOLE LIFE ANNUITY

Suppose that l_x persons, all of age x, desire to provide a fund from which amounts are to be withdrawn each year sufficient to pay \$1 to each survivor, the payments to continue as long as there are any survivors. At the end of the first year there will be l_{x+1} survivors according to the mortality table and l_{x+1} dollars will be needed then, or $v \cdot l_{x+1}$ dollars now. Similarly, at the end of the second year there will be l_{x+2} survivors and $v^2 \cdot l_{x+2}$ dollars now will be needed to take care of the payments to be made at that time. Likewise $v^3 \cdot l_{x+3}$ dollars now will be necessary to take care of the payments to be made to the survivors at the end of the third year, and so on to the end of the mortality table. If we denote by a_x the contribution to be made by each individual into the fund at age x, equating the total contributions to the total present value of the payments, we obtain

$$l_x \cdot a_x = vl_{x+1} + v^2 l_{x+2} + v^3 l_{x+3} + \cdots + v^{\omega - x - 1} l_{\omega - 1},$$

and, upon dividing by l_x,

$$a_x = \frac{vl_{x+1} + v^2 l_{x+2} + v^3 l_{x+3} + \cdots + v^{\omega - x - 1} l_{\omega - 1}}{l_x}. \tag{2.9}$$

It is to be noted that each individual of the above group receives from the fund \$1 payable at the end of each year as long as he survives, and that a_x represents the present value or *net single premium* which he pays for this benefit, which in this case constitutes a *whole life annuity immediate.*

Multiplying equation (2.9) in numerator and denominator by v^x, we obtain

$$a_x = \frac{v^{x+1} l_{x+1} + v^{x+2} l_{x+2} + v^{x+3} l_{x+3} + \cdots + v^{\omega - 1} l_{\omega - 1}}{v^x l_x},$$

or

$$a_x = \frac{D_{x+1} + D_{x+2} + D_{x+3} + \cdots + D_{\omega - 1}}{D_x}, \tag{2.10}$$

since $D_x = v^x l_x$; $D_{x+1} = v^{x+1} l_{x+1}$, and so on.*

Represent by the commutation symbol N_x the following sum

$$N_x = D_x + D_{x+1} + D_{x+2} + \cdots + D_{\omega-1},$$

the sum being taken to the limiting age of the table. For example,

$$N_{25} = D_{25} + D_{26} + D_{27} + \cdots + D_{\omega-1},$$
$$N_{30} = D_{30} + D_{31} + D_{32} + \cdots + D_{\omega-1}.$$

Replacing the numerator of the right member of equation (2.10) by N_{x+1}, we find

$$a_x = \frac{N_{x+1}}{D_x}. \qquad (2.11)$$

The net single premium for a whole life annuity immediate, a_x, can be obtained also by considering it as the sum of a series of pure endowments due at the end of one year, two years, three years, and so on. Using this method, we find the formula

$$a_x = {}_1E_x + {}_2E_x + {}_3E_x + \cdots + {}_{\omega-x-1}E_x,$$

or

$$a_x = \frac{D_{x+1} + D_{x+2} + D_{x+3} + \cdots + D_{\omega-1}}{D_x} = \frac{N_{x+1}}{D_x}.$$

---

*The reason for the introduction of commutation symbols will be clarified by the following comparison. Let us suppose that the numerical values of life annuities immediate are required at ages 30 and 31. Applying formula (2.9), we have, using the 1958 CSO Table,

$$a_{30} = \frac{v l_{31} + v^2 l_{32} + v^3 l_{33} + \cdots + v^{69} l_{99}}{l_{30}},$$

$$a_{31} = \frac{v l_{32} + v^2 l_{33} + v^3 l_{30} + \cdots + v^{68} l_{99}}{l_{31}}.$$

A total of 137 multiplications are required to find these numerical values, 69 in the first numerator and 68 in the second numerator, since there are no duplicates. Assuming that the values of the commutation symbols D_x and N_x are not available, and using formula (2.10), we obtain

$$a_{30} = \frac{D_{31} + D_{32} + \cdots + D_{99}}{D_{30}}, \qquad a_{31} = \frac{D_{32} + D_{33} + \cdots + D_{99}}{D_{31}},$$

which would require a total of only 69 multiplications, since all of the terms in the second numerator are duplicates of terms in the first. The difference between the two formulas would be further emphasized if a larger number of annuities were to be calculated. Hence, commutation symbols not only give a convenient means of expressing the rather cumbersome formula (2.9), but they also shorten to a large extent the number of numerical calculations to be made.

When referring to whole life annuities, the student should note that the only difference between an annuity immediate and an annuity due is the payment made at the beginning of the first year under the latter annuity. All of the other payments under the two types will coincide; hence, if the present value or single premium for a whole life annuity due be represented by $\ddot{a}_x$, it follows that

$$\ddot{a}_x = 1 + a_x = 1 + \frac{N_{x+1}}{D_x} = \frac{D_x + N_{x+1}}{D_x},$$

or

$$\ddot{a}_x = \frac{N_x}{D_x}. \tag{2.12}$$

Table IV gives the values of the whole life annuity due $\ddot{a}_x$.

Exercises

1. Compute the net single premiums for a whole life annuity immediate and a whole life annuity due, of $600 per year, purchased at age 30. At age 50.
2. A man now aged 60 has $10,000 cash. What annuity payment per year, first payment at age 61, can he purchase?
3. A man aged 65 is promised a pension of $500 at the end of each year for as long as he lives. What is the present value of the pension?
4. A man aged 30 agrees to pay a life insurance company $50 at the beginning of each year as long as he lives. What single payment at age 30 is equivalent to this annuity?
5. Derive by means of mutual fund method the formula for the single premium for a whole life annuity due for an individual now aged 30.
6. Show that

   (a) $\ddot{a}_x = 1 + v \cdot p_x \cdot \ddot{a}_{x+1};$ (b) $\ddot{a}_{x+1} = \dfrac{(1 + i)a_x}{p_x}.$

7. Assuming that the rate of interest is zero, show that $a_x = e_x$.
8. Prove that $a_x < 1/i$.
   HINT. $l_x > l_{x+1} > l_{x+2} > \cdots.$
9. Prove algebraically, and by verbal interpretation, the formula

   $$\ddot{a}_x = \ddot{a}_{\overline{1}|} \cdot q_x + \ddot{a}_{\overline{2}|} \cdot {}_1|q_x + \ddot{a}_{\overline{3}|} \cdot {}_2|q_x \cdots.$$

10. Use the identity of problem 6(a) to find l_{20} and l_{21}, if, at 4%,

    $$a_{20} = 18.662, \qquad a_{21} = 18.517, \qquad a_{22} = 18.379, \qquad l_{22} = 94,932.$$

11. A whole life annuity immediate to (x) provides payments as follows: 1.03, $(1.03)^2$, $(1.03)^3$, and so on. If the annuity value is computed at 3%

compound interest, show that the present value of this annuity is e_x.

12. A man aged 35 deposits $100 at the beginning of each year with an insurance company under an agreement that the money will accumulate at 3% interest until he reaches age 65 at which time he will start to receive a life annuity. The accumulated deposits are to be returned to his heirs in the event of his death before age 65. Thereafter, no death benefit is payable. Find the size of the annual payments he will receive, first payment at age 65.

13. It is estimated that $1200, payable at the end of the year, is the cost of maintaining an inmate in a penitentiary. Assuming mortality according to the 1958 CSO Table and interest at 3%, estimate the discounted value of the cost of keeping a man, now aged 23, in the penitentiary for the remainder of his life.

14. Show that

$$a_x = v p_x + v^2 \cdot {}_2 p_x \cdot \ddot{a}_{x+2}$$

2.7 TEMPORARY AND DEFERRED LIFE ANNUITIES

Let $\ddot{a}_{x:\overline{n}|}$ denote* the present value or net single premium for a temporary life annuity due with annual rent $1, that is, a sequence of n one dollar payments to be made at the beginning of each year, each payment being contingent upon the survival of (x) to receive it. The annuity ceases at the end of n years, even though (x) be still alive. Such a net single premium may be considered as the sum of the present values of a series of pure endowments of $1, payable at the beginning of each year for the next n years; hence

$$\ddot{a}_{x:\overline{n}|} = {}_0 E_x + {}_1 E_x + {}_2 E_x + \cdots + {}_{n-1} E_x,$$

or

$$\ddot{a}_{x:\overline{n}|} = \frac{D_x + D_{x+1} + D_{x+2} + \cdots + D_{x+n-1}}{D_x}.$$

Since

$$N_x = D_x + D_{x+1} + \cdots + D_{x+n-1} + D_{x+n} + \cdots + D_{\omega-1},$$
$$N_{x+n} = \qquad\qquad\qquad\qquad\qquad\quad D_{x+n} + \cdots + D_{\omega-1},$$

we have, upon subtraction,

$$N_x - N_{x+n} = D_x + D_{x+1} + \cdots + D_{x+n-1},$$

---

*The internationally accepted actuarial notation provides the alternative symbols ${}_n\ddot{a}_x$ and ${}_{n|m}\ddot{a}_x$, respectively, in addition to the symbols used here, $\ddot{a}_{x:\overline{n}|}$ and ${}_{n|}\ddot{a}_{x:\overline{m}|}$. This latter notation has the advantage of producing symmetrical-appearing relationships in succeeding chapters.

and hence

$$\ddot{a}_{x:\overline{n}|} = \frac{N_x - N_{x+n}}{D_x}. \tag{2.13}$$

Numerical values of $\ddot{a}_{x:\overline{n}|}$ are given in Table IX for selected values of n.

Let $_n|\ddot{a}_x$ denote the present value or net single premium for a deferred whole life annuity due with annual rent \$1, that is, a sequence of one-dollar payments to be made at the end of n years, $n + 1$ years, and so on, each payment contingent upon the survival of (x) to receive it. There are no payments made during the deferred period of n years but they continue thereafter at the beginning of each succeeding year as long as (x) is alive.

It is evident that

$$_n|\ddot{a}_x = {_nE_x} + {_{n+1}E_x} + {_{n+2}E_x} + \cdots + {_{\omega-x-1}E_x},$$

or

$$_n|\ddot{a}_x = \frac{D_{x+n} + D_{x+n+1} + D_{x+n+2} + \cdots + D_{\omega-1}}{D_x},$$

and hence

$$_n|\ddot{a}_x = \frac{N_{x+n}}{D_x}. \tag{2.14}$$

Let $_n|\ddot{a}_{x:\overline{m}|}$ denote the present value or net single premium for a deferred temporary life annuity due of annual rent \$1, that is, a sequence of one-dollar payments payable at the end of n years, $n + 1$ years, $\cdots$, $n + m - 1$ years, each payment contingent upon the survival of (x) to receive it. This is the most general type of life annuity, since any sequence of payments in the future could be reproduced by giving the quantities m and n suitable values. Considering this single premium as the sum of a sequence of pure endowments, one has

$$_n|\ddot{a}_{x:\overline{m}|} = {_nE_x} + {_{n+1}E_x} + {_{n+2}E_x} + \cdots + {_{n+m-1}E_x},$$

or

$$_n|\ddot{a}_{x:\overline{m}|} = \frac{D_{x+n} + D_{x+n+1} + D_{x+n+2} + \cdots + D_{x+n+m-1}}{D_x},$$

and hence

$$_n|\ddot{a}_{x:\overline{m}|} = \frac{N_{x+n} - N_{x+n+m}}{D_x}. \tag{2.15}$$

Let $a_{x:\overline{n}|}$, ${}_n|a_x$ and ${}_n|a_{x:\overline{m}|}$ represent the present values of the corresponding annuities immediate. Comparing the dates upon which the payments are to be made, we observe that

$$a_{x:\overline{n}|} = {}_1|\ddot{a}_{x:\overline{n}|} = \frac{N_{x+1} - N_{x+n+1}}{D_x},$$

$${}_n|a_x = {}_{n+1}|\ddot{a}_x = \frac{N_{x+n+1}}{D_x},$$

$${}_n|a_{x:\overline{m}|} = {}_{n+1}|\ddot{a}_{x:\overline{m}|} = \frac{N_{x+n+1} - N_{x+n+m+1}}{D_x}.$$

DIAGRAM ILLUSTRATING ANNUITY PAYMENTS
(ON THE ASSUMPTION THAT (x) WILL DIE AFTER n + m YEARS)

	x	x+1	x+2	⋯	x+n-1	x+n	x+n+1	⋯	x+n+m	⋯	y
Attained Age	←──── *n* years ────→					←──── *m* years ──→					
a_x =		1	1	⋯	1	1	1	⋯	1	⋯	1
$\ddot{a}_x$ = 1		1	1	⋯	1	1	1	⋯	1	⋯	1
$a_{x:\overline{n}|}$ =		1	1	⋯	1	1					
$\ddot{a}_{x:\overline{n}|}$ = 1		1	1	⋯	1						
${}_n|a_x$ =							1	⋯	1	⋯	1
${}_n|\ddot{a}_x$ =						1	1	⋯	1	⋯	1
${}_n|a_{x:\overline{m}|}$ =							1	⋯	1		
${}_n|\ddot{a}_{x:\overline{m}|}$ =						1	1	⋯			
${}_nE_x$ =						1					

Exercises

1. (a) Prove algebraically the following identities:
   (1) ${}_n|\ddot{a}_x = {}_nE_x \cdot \ddot{a}_{x+n}$;
   (2) $\ddot{a}_{x:\overline{m+n}|} = \ddot{a}_{x:\overline{n}|} + {}_mE_x \cdot \ddot{a}_{x+m:\overline{n}|}$;
   (3) ${}_n|\ddot{a}_{x:\overline{m}|} = {}_nE_x \cdot \ddot{a}_{x+n:\overline{m}|}$.
   (b) Use the identities in (a) to compute from the available tables of $\ddot{a}_x$, $\ddot{a}_{x:\overline{n}|}$, and ${}_nE_x$ the numerical values of

   (1) ${}_{10}|\ddot{a}_{30}$;   (2) $\ddot{a}_{25:\overline{14}|}$;   (3) ${}_4|\ddot{a}_{35:\overline{20}|}$.

2. Derive the formulas for each of the following by the mutual fund method:

   (a) ${}_n|\ddot{a}_x$;   (b) $a_{x:\overline{n}|}$.

3. Prove the identities:

   (a) $\ddot{a}_{x:\overline{n}|} = 1 + a_{x:\overline{n-1}|}$;   (b) ${}_n|\ddot{a}_x = \ddot{a}_x - \ddot{a}_{x:\overline{n}|}$;

   (c) $\ddot{a}_{x:\overline{n}|} = \ddot{a}_x - {}_nE_x \cdot \ddot{a}_{x+n}$.

4. Show that

$$\text{(a)} \quad \ddot{a}_{x:\overline{n}|} < \ddot{a}_{\overline{n}|}; \qquad\qquad \text{(b)} \quad {}_n|\ddot{a}_{x:\overline{m}|} < v^n \ddot{a}_{\overline{m}|}$$

5. An individual aged 35 pays $5000 to an insurance company in return for a contract to pay him a fixed annual income for life, starting with a payment on his fifty-fifth birthday. No payment is to be made by the company if he dies before age 55.

(a) Find the annual income if the company makes no charge for expense.

(b) What will the annual income be if the company deducts 5% of the premium for expenses?

6. A certain life insurance policy calls for the payment of premiums of $100 at the beginning of each year for twenty years by an individual now aged 34. Find the present value of the premiums.

7. A man aged 20 agrees to pay $50 at the beginning of each year for as long as he lives. What is the present value of the payments? If the last payment is to be made when the man reaches age 84, what is the present value of the payments?

8. A certain life insurance policy matures when the policyholder is of age 50 and gives him $10,000 in cash or at his option a sequence of equal payments at the beginning of each year for ten years and as long thereafter as he may live. If he dies during the first ten years the payments are to be continued to his heirs until a total of ten have been made. Find the annual payment under the optional plan.

HINT. The optional plan gives an annuity certain and a life annuity deferred ten years. Hence, if R denotes the annual payment, it follows that

$$R(\ddot{a}_{\overline{10}|} + {}_{10}|\ddot{a}_{50}) = 10,000.$$

9. Fill in the missing quantities in the following table, assuming that $v = 0.9$ (carry computations to three decimal places).

Age x	l_x	d_x	q_x	p_x	a_x	e_x	$\mathring{e}_x$
90	600	100					
91							
92	400			0.75			
93							
94	200		0.50				
95							
96	0						

10. To provide for his son's future college expenses, a father pays $6000 to an insurance company for a four-year temporary life annuity, first payment to be made at age 18. If the boy is now 10 years old, what will be the size of the annual payments?

11. How much would (33) have to pay at the beginning of each year for twenty years for a life income of $2400 per year, first payment at age 65? No payment would be made if his death occurred prior to age 65.

12. In Exercise 11, if the payments were considered as deposits, refundable with interest in the event of death prior to age 65, what would be the size of the payments to provide the $2400 whole life annuity beginning at age 65?

13. Given $q_{40} = 0.0040$, $q_{41} = 0.0041$, and $q_{42} = 0.0042$, find the numerical value of $\ddot{a}_{40:\overline{4}|}$ if interest is at 3%.

14. A man aged 45 has a contract for a deferred whole life annuity of $1000 per year, first payment at age 65. He wishes to replace this by a twenty-year temporary life annuity due (first payment to be made at once). What will be the size of these new payments?

2.8 FORBORNE ANNUITY

Consider a group of l_x individuals forming a fund into which each individual contributes a fixed amount at the beginning of each year for a stated number of years. These contributions are to be invested at compound interest at rate i and at the end of the given period of years the total accumulated fund is to be divided among the survivors. No return is made from the fund when a member dies, but his contributions assist in increasing the amount which each survivor receives. This type of fund is called a *tontine fund*. Each survivor receives what is known as a *forborne annuity*. We will consider the problem of determining the amount which each survivor will receive at the end of the stated period, say n years.

Let the share of each survivor at the end of the n-year period be denoted by $\ddot{s}_{x:\overline{n}|}$, or* by $_nu_x$, and assume that each individual contributes one dollar at the beginning of each year. The fund receives l_x dollars at the beginning of the first year, which accumulate to $l_x(1 + i)^n$ at the end of the n years. At the beginning of the second year there will be l_{x+1} lives remaining, each of whom pays a second dollar, and the total accumulation of which at the end of n years will be $l_{x+1}(1 + i)^{n-1}$, and so on until at the beginning of the last year there will be l_{x+n-1} survivors who will contribute a dollar each producing an accumulation of $l_{x+n-1}(1 + i)$ at the end of the n-year period. After dividing the total of these accumulated values by the number of survivors at the end of the n-year period, we have

---

*Before the international symbol $\ddot{s}_{x:\overline{n}|}$ was adopted in 1947, the symbol $_nu_x$ had been used by American actuaries for many years. It is still in fairly common use. Accordingly, we will use $_nu_x$ as an alternate notation from time to time, particularly in Chapters 4 and 5 and in Table XII.

$$\ddot{s}_{x:\overline{n}|} = \frac{l_x(1 + i)^n + l_{x+1}(1 + i)^{n-1} + \cdots + l_{x+n-1}(1 + i)}{l_{x+n}}.$$

Multiplying numerator and denominator by v^{x+n} and reducing to commutation symbols, we obtain

$$\ddot{s}_{x:\overline{n}|} = \frac{D_x + D_{x+1} + D_{x+2} + \cdots + D_{x+n-1}}{D_{x+n}},$$

and hence

$$\ddot{s}_{x:\overline{n}|} = \frac{N_x - N_{x+n}}{D_{x+n}}. \qquad (2.16)$$

The symbol $\ddot{s}_{x:\overline{n}|}$ is frequently referred to as the *accumulated value of the individual survivor's payments with the benefit of interest and survivorship*. Formula (2.16) may also be obtained by setting $\ddot{a}_{x:\overline{n}|}$ (the present value of the payments) equal to the present value of a pure endowment of amount $\ddot{s}_{x:\overline{n}|}$ due at the end of n years. Thus

$$\ddot{a}_{x:\overline{n}|} = \ddot{s}_{x:\overline{n}|} \cdot {}_nE_x,$$

or

$$\ddot{s}_{x:\overline{n}|} = \ddot{a}_{x:\overline{n}|}\left(\frac{1}{{}_nE_x}\right) = \frac{N_x - N_{x+n}}{D_{x+n}}.$$

The reciprocal $1/{}_nE_x$ as used in the above equation appears as an accumulation factor with benefit of interest and survivorship and will be used in this sense in succeeding sections.

When $n = 1$, the notation u_x is often used instead of $\ddot{s}_{x:\overline{1}|}$ or the older symbol ${}_1u_x$, hence

$$u_x = \frac{N_x - N_{x+1}}{D_{x+1}} = \frac{D_x}{D_{x+1}}. \qquad (2.17)$$

Numerical values of $\ddot{s}_{x:\overline{n}|}$ (or ${}_nu_x$) and u_x are shown in Tables XII and VI, respectively.

2.9 GENERAL ANNUITY FORMULA

It is now possible to set up a general expression for the value at any time of a sequence of payments of the same size, where each payment is contingent upon the survival of a designated life. Thus

$$R \cdot \frac{N_a - N_b}{D_c} \qquad (2.18)$$

gives the value at age c of a series of annual payments of R dollars each, the first payment payable at age a and the last payment payable at age $b - 1$. Whenever the age b is beyond the limiting age of the table the second term in the numerator disappears. The difference $b - a$ indicates the number of annual payments or, alternatively, the length of the term of the annuity. By properly choosing the ages a, b, and c, expression (2.18) may be adapted to produce the formulas for $\ddot{a}_x$, a_x, $\ddot{a}_{x:\overline{n}|}$, $a_{x:\overline{n}|}$, $_n|\ddot{a}_{x:\overline{m}|}$, $_nE_x$, $\ddot{s}_{x:\overline{n}|}$, and u_x.

Exercises

1. A man aged 30 wishes to provide a life annuity of $1000 per year, first payment to be made when he reaches age 60. What annual payment should he deposit with an insurance company at the beginning of each year for the next thirty years
   (a) if his contract specifies that no return of payments will be made in event of his death,
   (b) if his contract specifies that, in event of his death prior to age 60, the company will return immediately all of his deposits with interest?
   Solution. (a) Under this condition his accumulation at age 60 is the accumulated value of a forborne annuity. Hence it follows that

$$R \cdot \ddot{s}_{30:\overline{30}|} = 1000\ddot{a}_{60},$$

and, by Tables IV and XII.

$$R = \frac{1000\ddot{a}_{60}}{\ddot{s}_{30:\overline{30}|}} = \frac{1000(12.6347)}{57.5396} = \$219.58.$$

(b) Under this latter condition he receives only the benefit of interest on his deposits prior to age 60 and, since the annual payments constitute an annuity due, it follows that

$$R \cdot \ddot{s}_{\overline{30}|} = 1000\ddot{a}_{60} \qquad \text{or} \qquad R(s_{\overline{31}|} - 1) = 1000\ddot{a}_{60},$$

and, by Tables IV and I,

$$R = \frac{1000\ddot{a}_{60}}{s_{\overline{31}|} - 1} = \frac{1000\,(12.6347)}{49.00268} = \$257.84.$$

2. (a) Prove that

$$_{m+n}u_x = {_m}u_x \cdot \frac{1}{_nE_{x+m}} + {_n}u_{x+m}.$$

(b) Use the identity in (a) to find the numerical value of $\ddot{s}_{20:\overline{17}|}$ from the available tables.

3. Prove that

   (a) $\ddot{a}_{x+1} = (\ddot{a}_x - 1)u_x;$

(b) $\ddot{s}_{x:\overline{n}|} = \dfrac{\ddot{a}_x}{{}_nE_x} - \ddot{a}_{x+n};$

(c) $\ddot{a}_x = vp_x(u_x + \ddot{a}_{x+1}).$

4. A man now aged 20 has an annuity of $5000 a year due him at ages 25, 26, 27, 28, and 29, each payment contingent upon his survival to that age. He desires to trade these payments for a life annuity beginning at the present time. What will be the annual rent of the new annuity?

5. An individual now aged 40 desires to purchase a deferred life annuity of $1000 a year, first payment to occur at the end of twenty years. He wishes to buy this annuity by means of equal annual premiums at the beginning of each year for the next ten years. If no return of premiums is to be made in event of his death at any time, calculate the net premium he is to pay.

6. A boy aged 17 is to receive a legacy of $10,000 if living on his twenty-fifth birthday. He wishes to change this to an income payable at the end of each of the next four years, if living, first payment at age 18. Express the annual rent of the new annuity in terms of commutation symbols.

7. A man aged 35 has an income of $10,000 payable annually at the end of each year to his estate for the next ten years whether he lives or dies. He desires to exchange this for a deferred life annuity, first payment at age 65. What will be the annual rent of this annuity?

8. Express in terms of commutation symbols the present value of a life annuity due on the life of an individual now aged 30 providing for a sequence of payments of $50 each for the first ten years, then increasing to $100 each year thereafter.

9. A man aged 30 wishes to provide for a life annuity of $1000 per year, first payment at age 50. If he desires no return of payments in event of his death, what annual payment at the beginning of each year for the next twenty years should he deposit with an insurance company?

10. Compute the present value of a temporary life annuity due on the life of an individual now aged 30 providing for a sequence of payments of $500 a year for fifteen years followed by a sequence of ten payments of $1000 each year.

11. Show that $\ddot{s}_{x:\overline{n}|} > \ddot{s}_{\overline{n}|}$ and explain verbally why this inequality must be true.

12. Each of a group of men aged 26 agrees to deposit $100 at the beginning of each year for fifteen years, then to allow the fund to accumulate at 3% interest until it is divided among the survivors reaching age 60. How much will each survivor receive?

13. A group of men aged 30 agree to pay $250 at the end of each year into a fund earning interest at 3%, the last payment to occur at age 65. Thereafter, the survivors are to receive life annuities, first payment at age 66. Find the size of the annuity payments.

14. How much must each member of a group of men aged 30 deposit at the beginning of each year for the next twenty-five years if each of the

surviving members is to receive $10,000 at age 60? What would be the size of the deposits if the estates of those who died before reaching age 60 were also to share in the division? What would be the size of the deposits if these estates were also required to continue making deposits just as if the individual were still alive?

2.10   INCREASING LIFE ANNUITIES

Consider a regularly increasing temporary life annuity due consisting of a payment of $1 at the beginning of the first year, $2 at the beginning of the second year, $3 at the beginning of the third year, and so on, the payments increasing by $1 a year until a final payment of $n is paid at the beginning of the nth year, all payments contingent upon the survival of (x) to receive them. The present value or net single premium, denoted by $(I\ddot{a})_{x:\overline{n}|}$, of such an annuity consists of the sum of the present values of a series of increasing pure endowments; hence

$$(I\ddot{a})_{x:\overline{n}|} = 1 \cdot {}_0E_x + 2 \cdot {}_1E_x + 3 \cdot {}_2E_x + \cdots + n \cdot {}_{n-1}E_x,$$

$$= \frac{D_x + 2D_{x+1} + 3D_{x+2} + \cdots + n \cdot D_{x+n-1}}{D_x}.$$

Since

$$D_x + D_{x+1} + D_{x+2} + \cdots + D_{x+n-1} = N_x - N_{x+n}$$
$$D_{x+1} + D_{x+2} + \cdots + D_{x+n-1} = N_{x+1} - N_{x+n}$$
$$D_{x+2} + \cdots + D_{x+n-1} = N_{x+2} - N_{x+n}$$
$$\cdots \qquad\qquad \cdots$$
$$D_{x+n-1} = N_{x+n-1} - N_{x+n},$$

the sum of these equations yields

$$D_x + 2D_{x+1} + 3D_{x+2} + \cdots + n \cdot D_{x+n-1}$$
$$= N_x + N_{x+1} + N_{x+2} + \cdots + N_{x+n-1} - n \cdot N_{x+n}.$$

If we define the commutation symbol

$$S_x = N_x + N_{x+1} + N_{x+2} + \cdots + N_{\omega-1}$$

and hence

$$S_{x+n} = N_{x+n} + N_{x+n+1} + \cdots + N_{\omega-1},$$

subtracting, we find

$$S_x - S_{x+n} = N_x + N_{x+1} + N_{x+2} + \cdots + N_{x+n-1}$$

and hence

$$D_x + 2D_{x+1} + 3D_{x+2} + \cdots + n \cdot D_{x+n-1} = S_x - S_{x+n} - n \cdot N_{x+n}$$

and

$$(I\ddot{a})_{x:\overline{n}|} = \frac{S_x - S_{x+n} - n \cdot N_{x+n}}{D_x}. \tag{2.19}$$

If we chose for n a value such that $x + n$ is beyond the limit of the mortality table, we have

$$(I\ddot{a})_x = \frac{S_x}{D_x} \tag{2.20}$$

to represent the net single premium for a regularly increasing whole life annuity with no terminating age.

It should be noted that the increasing whole life annuity, the present value of which is given by (2.20), has its first payment equal to the increase, or "step," between successive payments. If it is desired to find the present value of an annuity whose first payment is different from the regular difference between the successive payments, this can be done readily by analyzing the annuity into its component parts. Thus, if we have an annuity with payments of $50, $55, $60, $65, and so forth for life, it can be considered as the sum of a level life annuity of $45 per year plus a standard increasing life annuity with a first payment and step equal to $5.

Combinations of formulas (2.19) and (2.20) may be used to evaluate other types of regularly increasing annuities, and also annuities which decrease regularly. For example, an annuity which increases for a time and then remains level for life thereafter may be evaluated by adding an increasing temporary life annuity and a level deferred life annuity with appropriate annual rents. Also, a deferred increasing annuity may be evaluated by subtracting an increasing temporary life annuity and a deferred level life annuity from an increasing whole life annuity. A decreasing life annuity may be considered as a level whole life annuity decreased by an increasing life annuity. Most students will find it helpful to draw diagrams of the scheduled payments in analyzing problems involving increasing or decreasing annuities.

Exercises

1. A man now aged 30 has a temporary life annuity with successive payments of $500, $450, $400, $350, $300, and $250, the first payment to be made immediately. Compute the present value.

Solution 1. The successive payments constitute a series of six pure endowments due at the beginning of each of the next six years. Hence, if K represents their present value, we have

$$K = 500_0E_{30} + 450_1E_{30} + 400_2E_{30} + 350_3E_{30} + 300_4E_{30} + 250_5E_{30},$$

$$= 50\frac{10D_{30} + 9D_{31} + 8D_{32} + 7D_{33} + 6D_{34} + 5D_{35}}{D_{30}}$$

Upon adding the six equations

$$\begin{aligned}
5(D_{30} + D_{31} + D_{32} + D_{33} + D_{34} + D_{35}) &= 5(N_{30} - N_{36}) \\
D_{30} + D_{31} + D_{32} + D_{33} + D_{34} &= (N_{30} - N_{35}) \\
D_{30} + D_{31} + D_{32} + D_{33} &= (N_{30} - N_{34}) \\
D_{30} + D_{31} + D_{32} &= (N_{30} - N_{33}) \\
D_{30} + D_{31} &= (N_{30} - N_{32}) \\
D_{30} &= (N_{30} - N_{31}),
\end{aligned}$$

we obtain

$$\begin{aligned}
10D_{30} + 9D_{31} + 8D_{32} &+ 7D_{33} + 6D_{34} + 5D_{35} \\
&= 10N_{30} - (N_{31} + N_{32} + N_{33} + N_{34} + N_{35} + 5N_{36}) \\
&= 10N_{30} - (S_{31} - S_{36}) - 5N_{36}.
\end{aligned}$$

Hence, using Table III, we have,

$$K = 50\frac{10N_{30} - (S_{31} - S_{36}) - 5N_{36}}{D_{30}}$$

$$= 50\frac{10(91698462) - (1532429399 - 1130140150) - 5(70021353)}{3905782.0}$$

$$= \quad \$2,106.99.$$

Solution 2.   From a six-year temporary annuity due with payments of $550, we subtract a six-year temporary increasing annuity due with a first payment and a step of $50, using formula (2.19). Thus, we have

$$550\frac{N_{30} - N_{36}}{D_{30}} - 50\frac{S_{30} - S_{36} - 6N_{36}}{D_{30}} = 50\frac{11N_{30} - S_{30} + S_{36} - 5N_{36}}{D_{30}}$$

$$= 50\frac{10N_{30} - S_{31} + S_{36} - 5N_{36}}{D_{30}} = \$2,106.99, \text{ as before.}$$

2. Show that the present value of an increasing life annuity due payable on the life of (x) is

$$\frac{hN_x + kS_{x+1}}{D_x},$$

if the first payment of h is made immediately, and the succeeding annual payments increase by k per year.

3. Show that the net single premium for a temporary decreasing life annuity due with successive payments of $n, n - 1, n - 2, \ldots, 2, 1$ is

$$\frac{n \cdot N_x - (S_{x+1} - S_{x+n+1})}{D_x}.$$

4. A man now aged 35 has a temporary life annuity with successive annual payments of $10, 8, 6, 4, 2, 4, 6, 8, and 10, the first payment to be made immediately. Compute the present value.

5. Express in terms of commutation symbols the present value of each of the following:

   (a) Life annuity to a man aged 24 beginning at once with a payment of $10 and increasing by $1 a year until a payment of $25 has been reached after which the annuity payment remains constant.

   (b) Life annuity to a man now aged 30 beginning with an initial payment of $100 at once decreasing by $5 a year until the payment becomes zero.

6. Describe the annuity whose present value is represented by each of the following:

   (a) $\dfrac{S_{x+1}}{D_x}$; (b) $\dfrac{S_{x+1} - S_{x+n+1}}{D_x}$; (c) $\dfrac{S_{x+1} - S_{x+n+1} - n \cdot N_{x+n+1}}{D_x}$.

7. Find the present value of a life annuity issued to (50) which provides for annual payments beginning at once with a payment of $100 and increasing by $100 each year until $1000 is paid at age 59, followed by level annual payments of $500 for the rest of life.

8. Express in commutation symbols the net single premium for an annuity immediate to (x) providing for annual payments of $100 the first year, $400 the second year, $700 the third year, increasing by $300 until $1600 is reached, after which the payments decrease by $400 annually until a level of $400 is reached and maintained thereafter for the remainder of life.

9. Find the net single premium for a deferred life annuity issued at age 40 under which the first payment of $2000 is due at age 70, the next payment of $1950 at age 71, the third of $1900 at age 72, and so on to the end of the 1958 CSO Table.

10. Find the present value of an eleven-year temporary life annuity due issued at age 50 under which payments start at $1000, decrease annually by $100 until $500 is reached, followed by annual payments of $700, $900, $1100, $1300, and $1500.

2.11 ANNUITIES PAYABLE MORE THAN ONCE A YEAR

Life insurance and life annuity contracts often provide that the periodical payments shall be made more frequently than once a year. Life insurance premiums are often payable semiannually, quarterly, or monthly, industrial insurance premiums are payable weekly, and pensions in many cases are payable monthly.

It is necessary therefore to consider the present values of annuities payable m times per year, where m is any given integer. The symbol $\ddot{a}_x^{(m)}$ is used to denote the present value of a life annuity due with annual rent of $1 payable in m installments of $1/m$ each, the first installment of $1/m$ to be made immediately, and the succeeding installments to be made at the beginning of each succeeding period of $1/m$ year for as long as (x) is alive. Upon considering this annuity as a sequence of pure endowments, one has

$$\ddot{a}_x^{(m)} = \frac{1}{m}(1 + {}_{\frac{1}{m}}E_x + {}_{\frac{2}{m}}E_x + {}_{\frac{3}{m}}E_x + \cdots),$$

or

$$\ddot{a}_x^{(m)} = \frac{1}{m}(1 + v^{\frac{1}{m}} \cdot {}_{\frac{1}{m}}p_x + v^{\frac{2}{m}} \cdot {}_{\frac{2}{m}}p_x + v^{\frac{3}{m}} \cdot {}_{\frac{3}{m}}p_x + \cdots).$$

An evaluation of this expression presents peculiar difficulties. Since the mortality table gives no information as to the probability of an individual living a fractional part of a year, an exact evaluation is ordinarily impossible. However, an approximation satisfactory for most purposes can be obtained by means of the following simple device.

Consider the two identities:

$$_{0}|\ddot{a}_x = \ddot{a}_x - 0, \qquad _{1}|\ddot{a}_x = \ddot{a}_x - 1.$$

Linear interpolation between these values for the deferred life annuity $_{\frac{1}{m}}|\ddot{a}_x$ yields

$$_{\frac{1}{m}}|\ddot{a}_x \doteqdot \ddot{a}_x - \frac{1}{m},$$

where the symbol $\doteqdot$ means "approximately equal." Similarly, by interpolation,

$$_{\frac{2}{m}}|\ddot{a}_x \doteqdot \ddot{a}_x - \frac{2}{m},$$

and, in general,

$$_{\frac{k}{m}}|\ddot{a}_x \doteqdot \ddot{a}_x - \frac{k}{m},$$

where $k \leqq m$. Suppose that we have m annuities, each of annual rent $1, and each payable once per year, the first payments of which fall due at the ends of 0, $1/m$, $2/m$, ..., $(m - 1)/m$ years, respectively. Together these annuities form an annuity due with annual rent of m dollars, payable m times per year. Hence, the sum of the present values of these anuities will be $m \cdot \ddot{a}_x^{(m)}$; it follows that

$$m \cdot \ddot{a}_x^{(m)} \doteqdot \left[\ddot{a}_x + \left(\ddot{a}_x - \frac{1}{m} \right) + \left(\ddot{a}_x - \frac{2}{m} \right) + \cdots + \left(\ddot{a}_x - \frac{m-1}{m} \right) \right].$$

The right member of this equation is the sum of an arithmetical progression with a common difference of $-1/m$. Summing the series, we have

$$m \cdot \ddot{a}_x^{(m)} \doteqdot m \cdot \ddot{a}_x - \frac{m(m-1)}{2m},$$

and hence, dividing by m, we have,

$$\ddot{a}_x^{(m)} \doteqdot \ddot{a}_x - \frac{m-1}{2m}. \tag{2.21}$$

If $a_x^{(m)}$ denotes the present value of a life annuity immediate with annual rent $1, payable m times per year, then it follows that

$$a_x^{(m)} \doteqdot \ddot{a}_x^{(m)} - \frac{1}{m} \doteqdot \ddot{a}_x - \frac{m+1}{2m},$$

or

$$a_x^{(m)} \doteqdot a_x + \frac{m-1}{2m}. \tag{2.22}$$

As special cases of formulas (2.21) and (2.22), we have the following approximations:

$$\begin{array}{ll} \ddot{a}_x^{(2)} \doteqdot \ddot{a}_x - \frac{1}{4}, & a_x^{(2)} \doteqdot a_x + \frac{1}{4}, \\ \ddot{a}_x^{(4)} \doteqdot \ddot{a}_x - \frac{3}{8}, & a_x^{(4)} \doteqdot a_x + \frac{3}{8}, \\ \ddot{a}_x^{(12)} \doteqdot \ddot{a}_x - \frac{11}{24}, & a_x^{(12)} \doteqdot a_x + \frac{11}{24}. \end{array}$$

Similarly, for the temporary life annuity due, we may write

$$\ddot{a}_{x:\overline{n}|}^{(m)} = \ddot{a}_x^{(m)} - {}_n|\ddot{a}_x^{(m)} = \ddot{a}_x^{(m)} - {}_nE_x\,\ddot{a}_{x+n}^{(m)}$$

$$\doteqdot \ddot{a}_x - \frac{m-1}{2m} - {}_nE_x\left(\ddot{a}_{x+n} - \frac{m-1}{2m} \right)$$

$$\doteqdot [\ddot{a}_x - {}_nE_x\,\ddot{a}_{x+n}] - \frac{m-1}{2m}(1 - {}_nE_x);$$

hence we have

$$\ddot{a}_{x:\overline{n}|}^{(m)} \doteq \ddot{a}_{x:\overline{n}|} - \frac{m-1}{2m}(1 - {}_nE_x). \qquad (2.23)$$

Exercises

1. Compute the present value of an annuity of $500 semiannually for the life of an individual now age 25:
    (a) when the payments are made at the beginning of each six months,
    (b) when the payments are made at the end of each six months.
2. The value of a life annuity of $100 a year to be paid at the end of each year for the lifetime of a certain individual is $1798.54. What is the present value of an annuity of the same annual rent, if the payments are made at the end of each month?
3. A life annuity contract provides for the payment of $100 per annum for the life of the annuitant, first payment at age 60. If, upon attaining age 60, the annuitant desires payments at the beginning of each month, what would be the equitable amount of each monthly payment? If the payments are to be made at the beginning of each quarter, what would be the equitable quarterly payment?
4. (a) The symbol $\ddot{a}_{\overline{n}|}^{(m)}$ is used to denote the present value of an annuity certain due with annual rent $1, payable m times per year in install-ments of $1/m$. By considering an individual who is *certain* to live n years, show that formula (2.23) can be written in the form

$$\ddot{a}_{\overline{n}|}^{(m)} \doteq \ddot{a}_{\overline{n}|} - \frac{m-1}{2m}(1 - v^n).$$

   (b) Using the result of part (a), solve the following problem: What quarterly payment at the beginning of each three months for ten years is equivalent to an annual payment of $100 at the beginning of each year for the same period, assuming the payments are certain to be made?
5. Show that

$$_n|\ddot{a}_x^{(m)} \doteq {}_nE_x\left(\ddot{a}_{x+n} - \frac{m-1}{2m}\right).$$

6. Show that

    (a) $a_{x:\overline{n}|}^{(2)} \doteq \frac{1}{4}(3a_{x:\overline{n}|} + \ddot{a}_{x:\overline{n}|}),$

    (b) $a_{x:\overline{n}|}^{(4)} \doteq \frac{1}{8}(5a_{x:\overline{n}|} + 3\ddot{a}_{x:\overline{n}|}).$

7. If $s_{x:\overline{n}|}^{(m)}$ represents the accumulated value of a forborne annuity of annual rent $1, payable m times per year, show that

$$s_{x:\overline{n}|}^{(m)} \doteq s_{x:\overline{n}|} - \frac{m-1}{2m}\left(\frac{1}{{}_nE_x} - 1\right).$$

8. If $(I\ddot{a})_x^{(m)}$ denotes the present value of an increasing life annuity due, payable m times per year, with annual rent of $1 in the first year, $2 in the second year, $3 in the third year, and so on for the life of an individual now aged (x), show that

$$(I\ddot{a})_x^{(m)} \doteq (I\ddot{a})_x - \frac{m-1}{2m}\ddot{a}_x.$$

9. What payment at the end of each month can an annuitant aged 63 receive in place of the $600 annually which is now due him, first payment at the end of the first year?

10. Find the present value of a deferred whole life annuity of $100 per month, first payment at age 65, issued to (40).

11. What size monthly payments, beginning at age 55 and continuing for fifteen years, can be purchased by a man aged 45 for $6000?

12. A group of men aged 35 agree to deposit $300 at the start of each year for twenty-five years. At the end of thirty years, when they are aged 65, the survivors will start drawing equal monthly annuities for life. Find the size of these life annuity payments.

Review Exercises

1. A whole life annuity immediate on the life of (x) provides for a sequence of payments of (1.035) at the end of one year, $(1.035)^2$ at the end of the second year, $(1.035)^3$ at the end of the third year, and so on. Show that the present value of this annuity at $3\frac{1}{2}\%$ is e_x.

2. Show that the present value of a perpetuity of $1 per annum, first payment to be made at the end of the year in which (x) dies, is $1/i - a_x$.

3. A is aged 30 and B is aged 40. They wish to contribute equally to a charity. A promises to pay $500 a year on each of his birthdays from the thirtieth to fourty-fourth, inclusive. B agrees to pay R dollars if and when he attains age 45. Find the value of R.

4. Find in commutation symbols an expression for $\ddot{a}_{30}$ where the interest rate is to be 4% for the first ten years and 5% thereafter.

5. Compute the present value at age 30 of a whole life annuity immediate having an annual rent of $120 payable in equal installments (a) annually, (b) semiannually, (c) quarterly, and (d) monthly.

6. Show that

(a) $\ddot{s}_{x:\overline{n}|} = (\ddot{s}_{x:\overline{n-1}|} + 1)u_{x+n-1}.$

(b) $\ddot{a}_{x+1} = (\ddot{a}_x - 1)u_x.$

7. A man aged x offers a single premium of

$$\frac{\ddot{a}_{x-n} - \ddot{a}_{x-n:\overline{2n}|}}{{}_nE_{x-n}}$$

for a deferred life annuity, first payment at age $x + n$. Find the annual rent of the annuity.

8. Prove

$$_r|\ddot{a}_{x:\overline{n}|}^{(m)} \doteq {_r|\ddot{a}_{x:\overline{n}|}} - \frac{m-1}{2m}(_rE_x - {_{n+r}E_x}).$$

9. If $(I\ddot{a})_{x:\overline{n}|}^{(m)}$ denotes the present value of an increasing temporary life annuity due, payable m times per year, with annual rent of $1 in the first year, $2 in the second year, $3 in the third year, and so on until finally n dollars is paid in the nth year, show that

$$(I\ddot{a})_{x:\overline{n}|}^{(m)} \doteq (I\ddot{a})_{x:\overline{n}|} - \frac{m-1}{2m}[\ddot{a}_{x:\overline{n}|} - n \cdot {_nE_x}].$$

10. A beneficiary now aged 50 is offered one of the following options:
  (a) $10,000 in cash, or
  (b) Equal payments at the beginning of each month for as long as she lives, or
  (c) Equal payments at the beginning of each month for as long as she lives, the payments in any event to be made for at least 120 months.
  Compute the monthly payment under options (b) and (c).
  HINT. See Exercise 8, Section 2.7 and Exercises 4(a) and 5, Section 2.11.

11. A young man of 20 is to receive $5000 if he is alive at age 35. He decides to exchange this benefit for a life annuity payable monthly, first payment at age 60. Find the size of the monthly payments.

12. (a) Find the present value of a whole life annuity due to (35) of $1000 per year for thirty years followed by $2000 per year for the remainder of life.
  (b) Find the present value of a temporary life annuity due to (35) of $2000 per year for twenty-five years followed by $1000 per year for an additional ten years.

13. Find the present value of a twenty-year temporary life annuity immediate with payments of $500 at the end of one-half year, one and one-half years, two and one-half years, and so on, plus payments of $1000 at the end of one year, two years, three years, and so on until a total of forty payments in all have been made. The annuity is issued to (33).

14. A group of men aged 23 agree to deposit $10 at the start of each month for fifteen years. At that time—that is, at age 38—the survivors divide the fund equally. How much will each receive?

CHAPTER 3

Net Premiums

3.1 INTRODUCTION

Life insurance is on a sound basis only when a large number of individuals are insured by one organization or company, so that individual losses may be distributed over the whole group according to some scientific principle of mutuality. When an individual is insured by a company, he and the company agree to a written contract, called a *policy*. In the policy the *insured*, or *policyholder*, agrees to make certain payments to the company. These payments are usually referred to as *gross premiums*. In consideration of the premiums paid to the company by the insured, the company in turn agrees to pay a stipulated sum of money, called the *face* amount of insurance, if certain events occur. The person to whom the face amount of insurance is to be paid is called the *beneficiary*. The *policy date* or *date of issue* is the date upon which the insurance contract is made, and the successive years after this date are called *policy years*. Most life insurance companies charge gross premiums which are determined by the age the *insured* attained or will attain on his birthday nearest to the date of issue.* This *age nearest birthday* is referred to as the *age at issue*.

The *net* premiums for a policy are those whose total present value is equal to the present value of the policy benefits under the following assumptions: (a) the benefits under the policy will be paid at the ends of the policy years in which they fall due; (b) the company's invested funds will earn interest at exactly the assumed rate; and (c) the deaths among the policyholders will occur at

---

*Recently, a few life insurance companies began to base their gross premiums, and other factors, upon the *age at last birthday*. In such cases a variation of the standard mortality table, adjusted for this difference in recording ages, is employed.

exactly the rates given by the adopted mortality table. Under these assumptions, if a company were run without profit or expense, it could afford to issue policies in return for these net premiums. Whenever the net premiums are assumed to be the same for all policy years in which the premium is paid, the premiums are called *net level premiums*. When a policy provides for the payment of all of the insured's premium obligations in one installment, this install-ment is payable immediately on the policy date and is called the *single premium* for the policy. The present value of all benefits under the assumptions (a), (b), and (c) is called the *net single premium*.

The actual gross premium charged by the company is the net premium plus a certain amount, called *loading,* which provides for the expenses of the company and for the added disbursements due to the violation of the conditions (a), (b), and (c). Attention will be given later to the problem of computing gross premiums, while the present chapter will be devoted entirely to the discussion of net premiums and related questions. It should be noted that a policy-holder invariably agrees to pay, in addition to the loading, a series of net premiums whose present value is equal to the present value of all of the policy benefits. Thus, a policyholder always agrees to pay for what he receives under the policy, and if the net premium for one policy is less than that for another policy, computed on the same mortality table and interest rate, but payable for the same period of time, it follows that the benefits under the first policy have a smaller present value. The question of which policy is best for a given individual is largely a question of fitting the type of benefits and the size of the premium to the individual's needs and resources.

3.2   WHOLE LIFE INSURANCE

A *whole life insurance* may be defined as a benefit consisting of a fixed sum to be paid to the beneficiary at the time of the death of the insured regardless of when it occurs. A policy containing this provision is called a *whole life* policy. The net single premium for a whole life insurance is the present value, under a definite assump-tion regarding mortality and interest, of the face amount of the policy payable at the end of the year in which the death of the insured occurs.

Let A_x denote the net single premium for a whole life insurance of $1 on the life of (x), that is, the present value of $1 to be paid at the end of the year in which (x) dies. If a company insured l_x individuals, each of age x, on the same policy date, the total single premium col-lections would be $l_x \cdot A_x$. During the first policy year d_x deaths would occur among this group and d_x dollars would be payable at the end of the first year to beneficiaries. In order to meet this obligation vd_x dollars would be needed now. During the second policy year d_{x+1} deaths would occur and v^2d_{x+1} dollars would be needed now to care for the payments to beneficiaries; during the third year d_{x+2} deaths would occur and v^3d_{x+2} dollars would be needed now, and so on until all of the l_x individuals, originally insured, had died. Equating the total net premiums collected by the company to the total present value of the benefits, we have

$$l_x A_x = vd_x + v^2d_{x+1} + v^3d_{x+2} + v^4d_{x+3} + \cdots + v^{\omega-x}d_{\omega-1},$$

or

$$A_x = \frac{vd_x + v^2d_{x+1} + v^3d_{x+2} + v^4d_{x+3} + \cdots + v^{\omega-x}d_{\omega-1}}{l_x}.$$

Multiplying numerator and denominator of the right member of this equation by v^x, we find

$$A_x = \frac{v^{x+1}d_x + v^{x+2}d_{x+1} + v^{x+3}d_{x+2} + v^{x+4}d_{x+3} + \cdots + v^{\omega}d_{\omega-1}}{v^x l_x}.$$

Let the product $v^{x+1}d_x$ be represented by the commutation symbol C_x. For example:

$$C_{25} = v^{26}d_{25}; \qquad C_{30} = v^{31}d_{30}; \text{ and so forth.}$$

Introducing the commutation* symbols C_x, C_{x+1}, C_{x+2}, $\cdots$ into the expression for A_x, we have

$$A_x = \frac{C_x + C_{x+1} + C_{x+2} + C_{x+3} + \cdots + C_{\omega-1}}{D_x}.$$

Denote by the commutation symbol M_x the sum

$$M_x = C_x + C_{x+1} + C_{x+2} + C_{x+3} + \cdots + C_{\omega-1}.$$

Thus

$$M_{25} = C_{25} + C_{26} + C_{27} + \cdots + C_{\omega-1},$$
$$M_{30} = C_{30} + C_{31} + C_{32} + \cdots + C_{\omega-1}.$$

It follows immediately that

---

*The student should note that these new commutation symbols are introduced not only for simplicity in representation, but also because they materially reduce the number of necessary numerical calculations.

$$A_x = \frac{M_x}{D_x}. \qquad (3.1)$$

Similarly, the net single premium for a whole life insurance of R on the life of (x) is

$$R \cdot A_x = R \cdot \frac{M_x}{D_x}.$$

Values of the single premium A_x and its reciprocal are given in Table IV, whereas values of the commutation symbols C_x and M_x are to be found in Table III.

Exercises

1. Verify the entries in the tables of C_x and M_x at ages 99, 98, and 97. Verify the entries in the table of A_x at ages 20, 35, 50.
2. Find the net single premium for a whole life insurance of $4000 on the life of a man (a) aged 20; (b) aged 40; (c) aged 85.
3. How much whole life insurance can a man aged 40 purchase with $2000 cash, assuming that the gross and net premiums are the same?
4. Derive by the mutual fund method an expression in terms of commutation symbols for the present value of a whole life insurance of amount R issued at age 30.
5. Prove that $A_x = v(q_x + p_x A_{x+1})$.
6. Show that $A_x u_x = A_{x+1} + q_x/p_x$.
7. Show that

   (a) $p_x = \dfrac{1 - (1 + i)A_x}{1 - A_{x+1}}$, (b) $q_x = \dfrac{(1 + i)A_x - A_{x+1}}{1 - A_{x+1}}$.

8. (20) agrees to deposit $100 at the start of each year for five years. At the end of the fifth year, the accumulation is to be used as a net single premium to purchase a whole life insurance benefit at the attained age. What will be the size of this benefit if: (a) the accumulation to date of death will be paid to the man's estate if he dies before reaching age 25; (b) the accumulation is to be forfeited in the event of his death before reaching age 25?

3.3 RELATIONS BETWEEN SINGLE PREMIUMS

Certain fundamental relations exist between the two sets of commutation symbols and also between A_x and $\ddot{a}_x$. Since

$$d_x = l_x - l_{x+1},$$
$$v^{x+1}d_x = v \cdot v^x l_x - v^{x+1}l_{x+1},$$

from the definitions of C_x and D_x it follows that

$$C_x = v \cdot D_x - D_{x+1}. \qquad (3.2)$$

Likewise,

$$C_{x+1} = vD_{x+1} - D_{x+2},$$
$$C_{x+2} = vD_{x+2} - D_{x+3},$$

and so on, to the end of the table. Adding these results by columns, we obtain

$$M_x = v \cdot N_x - N_{x+1}. \tag{3.3}$$

Dividing both members of equation (3.3) by D_x, we have immediately

$$A_x = v\ddot{a}_x - a_x. \tag{3.4}$$

If we replace a_x by its equivalent, $\ddot{a}_x - 1$, equation (3.4) becomes

$$A_x = 1 - (1 - v)\ddot{a}_x.$$

In Exercise 5 of Section 2.2 we defined d, the *rate of discount*, as equal to iv, and it was to be shown in that exercise that $d = 1 - v$. Substituting in the above equation for $1 - v$, we have

$$A_x = 1 - d\ddot{a}_x. \tag{3.5}$$

It is evident from these relations that values of C_x and M_x could, if necessary, be obtained directly from a table of values of D_x and N_x without recourse to the original mortality table, and values of A_x could be obtained from a table of values of either $\ddot{a}_x$ or a_x.

Formulas (3.4) and (3.5) can be given verbal interpretations which are highly instructive. Thus equation (3.4) may be substantiated as follows: Consider an annuity of v payable at the beginning of each year which (x) enters, and a second annuity of 1 payable at the end of each year which (x) completes. The first annuity contains one payment more than the second annuity, namely, the payment of v at the beginning of the year in which (x) dies. Since a payment of v at the beginning of any year is equivalent to a payment of 1 at the end of that year, the difference between these two annuities is represented by the payment of v at the beginning of the year in which (x) dies. This payment of v will accumulate to 1 at the end of the year in which (x) dies; hence the difference between the present values of the two annuities is the present value of 1 payable at the end of the year in which (x) dies, or A_x.

Similarly equation (3.5) can be verbally interpreted as follows: Suppose that one dollar were invested for the lifetime of (x) at the rate i. The interest of i payable at the end of any year is equivalent to iv or d payable at the beginning of that year. Thus the original investment of \$1 produces an annuity due of d for the lifetime of

(x) and returns the principal of $1 at the end of the year in which (x) dies. Upon equating present values, equation (3.5) results.

Exercises

Prove and interpret each of the first three equations verbally:

1. $v^n = 1 - d \cdot \ddot{a}_{\overline{n}|}$.
2. $v^n = v \cdot \ddot{a}_{\overline{n}|} - a_{\overline{n-1}|}$.
3. $l_x(1 + i)A_x = d_x + l_{x+1}A_{x+1}$.
4. Show that $M_x = D_x - dN_x$.
5. Prove $A_x = v(1 - ia_x) = v - (1 - v)a_x = v - da_x$.
6. Find the rate of interest if $\ddot{a}_x = 14.260$ and $A_x = 0.19283$.
7. Find the value of a_x if $A_x = 0.21000$ and $i = 4\%$.
8. Show that

$$l_{x+1} \cdot A_{x+1} + l_{x+2} \cdot A_{x+2} + \cdots + l_{\omega-1} A_{\omega-1} = l_x \cdot a_x.$$

3.4 ANNUAL PREMIUMS

Policies commonly issued by life insurance companies frequently provide for the payment of premiums in equal annual installments. These annual premiums are payable at the beginning of each policy year and may continue throughout the entire lifetime of the insured or they may be limited to a specified period of years, called the *premium payment period*. Thus, a policy containing a whole life insurance benefit may be classified as: (a) *ordinary life*, where the annual premium is payable throughout the entire lifetime of the insured, or (b) *limited payment life*, in which the annual premium is payable only for a limited number of years, such as ten, fifteen or twenty years. Premiums for limited payment life policies are, of course, larger than those for ordinary life policies. A single premium life policy is a special case of a limited payment life policy, that is, a limited payment life policy with just one premium.

Let P_x denote the net level annual premium for an ordinary life policy issued at age x. These annual premiums form a life annuity due, whose present value is $P_x \cdot \ddot{a}_x$. Since the present value of these premiums is, by definition, equal to the net single premium for the benefit provided by the policy, we have

$$P_x \cdot \ddot{a}_x = A_x,$$

and hence

$$P_x = \frac{A_x}{\ddot{a}_x}, \tag{3.6}$$

or substituting values in commutation symbols for A_x and $\ddot{a}_x$, we have

$$P_x = \frac{M_x}{N_x}. \tag{3.7}$$

Another form for P_x can be found by replacing A_x by $1 - d\ddot{a}_x$ in equation (3.6). In this manner, we find

$$P_x = \frac{1 - d\ddot{a}_x}{\ddot{a}_x} = \frac{1}{\ddot{a}_x} - d. \tag{3.8}$$

Let $_nP_x$ denote the net level annual premium for a limited payment life policy, with a premium payment period of n years. Such a policy is usually referred to as an n-payment life policy. In this case the premiums form a temporary life annuity. Equating their present value to the net single premium, A_x, we have

$$_nP_x \, \ddot{a}_{x:\overline{n}|} = A_x.$$

and hence

$$_nP_x = \frac{A_x}{\ddot{a}_{x:\overline{n}|}}, \tag{3.9}$$

or

$$_nP_x = \frac{M_x}{N_x - N_{x+n}} \tag{3.10}$$

It should be noted that all formulas for premiums which have been considered are net premiums providing for a benefit of $1. Premiums for other amounts of insurance are found by multiplying the premium for a benefit of one dollar by the face amount of insurance. Table V shows the numerical values of the net premiums for the ordinary life, nineteen-payment life, and twenty-payment life policies.

Exercises

1. Find to the nearest cent the numerical value of the net annual premium for each of the following policies issued at age 30, the amount of insurance in each case to be $1000:
   (a) five-payment life,
   (b) ten-payment life,
   (c) thirty-payment life.
2. Check the numerical value of P_{45} given in Table V, by means of (3.8).

3. What is the net annual premium for a twenty-payment life policy for $5000 issued at age 60? Age 20? Age 15?

4. Prove that

   (a) $\quad A_x = \dfrac{P_x}{P_x + d}$,   (b) $\quad P_x = \dfrac{dA_x}{1 - A_x}$.

5. Show that

$$P_x = \frac{vq_x + P_{x+1}\cdot a_x}{\ddot{a}_x}.$$

6. How much whole life insurance at age 40 can be purchased by 25 net annual premiums of $100 each?

7. What is the net annual premium for a whole life insurance policy issued to (35) which provides for a death benefit of $1000 at the end of the year of death and $1000 at the end of each of the following nine years?

8. Find the rate of interest if $P_x = 0.010809$ and $A_x = 0.18500$.

9. Prove that

$$P_x = \frac{dP_x}{\dfrac{1}{\ddot{a}_x} - P_x}.$$

3.5   TERM INSURANCE

A term insurance may be defined as the benefit consisting of a fixed sum to be paid to the beneficiary at the death of the insured, provided that death occurs within a limited period. It should be noted that no payment is made by the company in event that the insured survives the limited period. Thus, a ten-year term insurance gives no benefit unless the insured dies within ten years. Let $A^1_{x:\overline{n}|}$ denote the net single premium for an n-year term insurance of $1 on the life of (x). The first subscript in the symbol indicates the present age (age at issue) of the insured, while the second subscript indicates the temporary period during which the insurance is effective. The mark "1" above the age indicates that the benefit is payable only if the insured dies before the n years expire.*

If a company were to issue n-year term policies to each of l_x individuals, all of age x, the total net single premiums collected im-

---

*The supplementary symbol $A_{x:\overline{n}|}^{1}$ is often used to denote the present value of an n-year pure endowment of $1, since the mark "1" indicates that the benefit is payable only if the n-year period expires before (x) dies, that is, only if (x) survives n years.

Except for this one instance the capital "A" with proper subscripts is invariably used to denote the present value of payments to be made upon the death of an individual, while the small "a" with proper subscripts is always used to represent the present value of an annuity, that is, a series of payments contingent upon the *life* of an individual.

mediately by the company would aggregate $l_x \cdot A^1_{x:\overline{n}|}$. As in the case of whole life insurance, vd_x would be needed immediately to pay death claims to beneficiaries on account of deaths in the first policy year, $v^2 d_{x+1}$ would be needed to pay beneficiaries on account of deaths in the second policy, and so on, until $v^n d_{x+n-1}$ would be needed to pay beneficiaries on account of deaths in the nth year, after which all the remaining policies would expire. Hence, equating the present value of the total net premiums to the total present value of the benefit, we find

$$l_x \cdot A^1_{x:\overline{n}|} = vd_x + v^2 d_{x+1} + v^3 d_{x+2} + \cdots + v^n d_{x+n-1}.$$

The net single premium for each policy is found by dividing both members of this equation by l_x; thus we have

$$A^1_{x:\overline{n}|} = \frac{vd_x + v^2 d_{x+1} + v^3 d_{x+2} + \cdots + v^n d_{x+n-1}}{l_x}.$$

Multiplying numerator and denominator by v^x and inserting the commutation symbols, we obtain

$$A^1_{x:\overline{n}|} = \frac{C_x + C_{x+1} + C_{x+2} + \cdots + C_{x+n-1}}{D_x}.$$

Since

$$M_x = C_x + C_{x+1} + C_{x+2} + \cdots + C_{x+n-1} + C_{x+n} + \cdots + C_{\omega-1}$$

and

$$M_{x+n} = \qquad\qquad\qquad\qquad\qquad C_{x+n} + \cdots + C_{\omega-1},$$

we have, upon subtraction,

$$M_x - M_{x+n} = C_x + C_{x+1} + C_{x+2} + \cdots + C_{x+n-1},$$

and hence

$$A^1_{x:\overline{n}|} = \frac{M_x - M_{x+n}}{D_x}. \tag{3.11}$$

The net single premium for a one-year term insurance on the life of (x) is called the *natural premium* at age x and is denoted by c_x. Upon setting $n = 1$ in expression (3.11), we find

$$c_x = A^1_{x:\overline{1}|} = \frac{M_x - M_{x+1}}{D_x} = \frac{C_x}{D_x}, \tag{3.12}$$

since $C_x = M_x - M_{x+1}$.

If $_mP^1_{x:\overline{n}|}$ denotes* the net annual premium payable for m years $(m \leq n)$ to provide an n-year term insurance of $1, it follows that

$$_mP^1_{x:\overline{n}|} \cdot \ddot{a}_{x:\overline{m}|} = A^1_{x:\overline{n}|},$$

and hence

$$_mP^1_{x:\overline{n}|} = \frac{A^1_{x:\overline{n}|}}{\ddot{a}_{x:\overline{m}|}} = \frac{M_x - M_{x+n}}{N_x - N_{x+m}}. \tag{3.13}$$

When the premium payment period coincides with the term insurance period, $m = n$, the notation $_nP^1_{x:\overline{n}|}$ is shortened to $P^1_{x:\overline{n}|}$; hence we have

$$P^1_{x:\overline{n}|} = \frac{A^1_{x:\overline{n}|}}{\ddot{a}_{x:\overline{n}|}} = \frac{M_x - M_{x+n}}{N_x - N_{x+n}}. \tag{3.14}$$

Numerical values of c_x are shown in Table V, whereas values of the single premiums, $A^1_{x:\overline{n}|}$, for selected values of n, are given in Table XI. Unless otherwise stated, the phrase *net premium for an n-year term insurance* will mean the net annual premium for an n-payment n-year term insurance given by equation (3.14).

Exercises

1. Show that

   (a) $A_x = A^1_{x:\overline{n}|} + _nE_x \cdot A^1_{x+n:\overline{n}|} + _{2n}E_x \cdot A^1_{x+2n:\overline{n}|} + \cdots,$

   (b) $A_x = c_x + _1E_x\, c_{x+1} + _2E_x\, c_{x+2} + \cdots,$
   and interpret each of these formulas verbally.

2. Prove that

   (a) $c_x = vq_x = v \cdot \dfrac{d_x}{l_x};$ (b) $A^1_{x:\overline{n}|} = v\ddot{a}_{x:\overline{n}|} - a_{x:\overline{n}|};$

   (c) $P^1_{x:\overline{n}|} = v - \dfrac{a_{x:\overline{n}|}}{\ddot{a}_{x:\overline{n}|}}.$

3. Compute to the nearest cent the numerical value of the net annual premium for each of the following policies issued at age 30, the amount of insurance in each case to be $1000:

   (a) ten-year term; (b) ten-payment twenty-year term; (c) fifty-year term.

*For a given type of policy it should be noted that the prefix on the symbol for the annual premium denotes the number of premiums to be paid, while the subscripts on the right have the same meaning as those on the symbol for the net single premium.

4. Derive by the mutual fund method the net single premium in terms of commutation symbols for a ten-year term insurance policy for an amount R issued at age 45.

5. (a) Find the net single premium for a five-year term policy for $1000 issued to a man aged 50. (b) Find the natural premiums for a $1000 insurance at each of the ages 50, 51, 52, 53, and 54. (c) Why is the sum of the five results in (b) not equal to the result of (a)?

6. Find the net annual premium payable for life for a policy issued at age 29 which provides for a death benefit of $2000 if death occurs before age 65 but only $1000 if death occurs thereafter.

7. Find the net annual premium for a five-payment, twelve-year term insurance for $7500 issued at age 43.

8. (30) has a policy which provides him with $10,000 of insurance for the first ten years, $7500 for the next ten years, and $5000 for the remainder of his life. He is to pay for this by means of twenty net annual premiums. Find their size.

9. How much term insurance expiring at age 65 can (33) buy for a net annual premium of $150?

3.6   ENDOWMENT INSURANCE

An endowment insurance provides for the payment of a benefit in event of the death of the insured within a certain period, called the *endowment period,* and also provides for the payment of an equal benefit at the end of the endowment period, provided the insured be then living. Hence, an n-year endowment insurance may be considered as an n-year term insurance plus an n-year pure endowment.

If the net single premium for an n-year endowment insurance of $1 be denoted* by $A_{x:\overline{n}|}$, one has immediately

$$A_{x:\overline{n}|} = A^1_{x:\overline{n}|} + {}_nE_x,$$

by means of which the numerical value of $A_{x:\overline{n}|}$ can be computed from Tables XI and VII. Expressing each term of the right member by commutation symbols, we have

$$A_{x:\overline{n}|} = \frac{M_x - M_{x+n}}{D_x} + \frac{D_{x+n}}{D_x},$$

and hence

$$A_{x:\overline{n}|} = \frac{M_x - M_{x+n} + D_{x+n}}{D_x}. \tag{3.15}$$

---

*The double subscript on the symbol $A_{x:\overline{n}|}$ indicates that the benefit is payable either (a) if (x) dies before the n-year endowment period expires, or (b) if the n-year period expires before (x) dies. Thus $A_{x:\overline{n}|} = A^1_{x:\overline{n}|} + A^{\ 1}_{x:\overline{n}|}$.

The single premium $A_{x:\overline{n}|}$ for an endowment insurance may be also derived in a form similar to that shown in equation (3.5). We have by equation (3.3)

$$M_x = vN_x - N_{x+1} = (1 - d)\,N_x - (N_x - D_x),$$

and hence

$$M_x = D_x - dN_x,$$

and

$$M_{x+n} = D_{x+n} - dN_{x+n}.$$

Subtracting these two equations and adding D_{x+n} to each member of the result, we find

$$M_x - M_{x+n} + D_{x+n} = D_x - D_{x+n} - d(N_x - N_{x+n}) + D_{x+n},$$

and hence, after dividing by D_x,

$$A_{x:\overline{n}|} = \frac{D_x - d(N_x - N_{x+n})}{D_x},$$

or

$$A_{x:\overline{n}|} = 1 - d\ddot{a}_{x:\overline{n}|}. \tag{3.16}$$

The symbol $_mP_{x:\overline{n}|}$ is used to denote the net annual premium payable for m years ($m \leq n$) for an n-year endowment insurance of $\$1$. Upon equating the present value of the net annual premiums to the net single premium for the benefit, one has

$$_mP_{x:\overline{n}|} \cdot \ddot{a}_{x:\overline{m}|} = A_{x:\overline{n}|},$$

or

$$_mP_{x:\overline{n}|} = \frac{A_{x:\overline{n}|}}{\ddot{a}_{x:\overline{m}|}} = \frac{M_x - M_{x+n} + D_{x+n}}{N_x - N_{x+m}}. \tag{3.17}$$

When the premium payment period coincides with the endowment period, $m = n$, the notation $_nP_{x:\overline{n}|}$ is shortened to $P_{x:\overline{n}|}$, and hence one has

$$P_{x:\overline{n}|} = \frac{M_x - M_{x+n} + D_{x+n}}{N_x - N_{x+n}}. \tag{3.18}$$

Unless otherwise specified, the net annual premium for an endowment insurance will be considered as payable for the entire endowment period, and the word *endowment* will mean *endowment insurance*, rather than *pure endowment*. The net annual premium for an n-year endowment insurance can be derived in a form similar to that shown for the ordinary life net annual premium in equation (3.8). After dividing equation (3.16) by $\ddot{a}_{x:\overline{n}|}$, one obtains

$$P_{x:\overline{n}|} = \frac{A_{x:\overline{n}|}}{\ddot{a}_{x:\overline{n}|}} = \frac{1}{\ddot{a}_{x:\overline{n}|}} - d. \tag{3.19}$$

Exercises

1. Show that

$$A_{x:\overline{n}|} = v\ddot{a}_{x:\overline{n}|} - a_{x:\overline{n-1}|}$$

and interpret this formula verbally.

2. Compute the net annual premium for a $1000 twenty-year endowment insurance policy issued at age 20. Age 40. Age 60.

3. Compute the net annual premium at age 35 for each of the following policies (amount of insurance $1000):
    (a) ten-year endowment;
    (b) ten-payment endowment at age 65 (maturing at age 65);
    (c) twenty-payment thirty-year endowment.

4. How large an endowment insurance policy maturing in fifteen years can be purchased by a net annual premium, payable for ten years, of $100, if the policy is issued at age 40?

5. Find the net annual premium payable for twenty years for a policy issued at age 35 which provides for a death benefit of $2000 if death occurs before age 60, $1000 if death occurs between age 60 and 70, and a pure endowment of $500 if the insured survives to age 70.

6. Show that

$$a_{x:\overline{n}|} = \frac{v - A_{x:\overline{n+1}|}}{d}.$$

7. Show that

$$\frac{1 - ia_{x:\overline{t-1}|}}{1 + i} = \frac{M_x - M_{x+t} + D_{x+t}}{D_x}.$$

8. An insurance policy issued at age 25 provides for the payment of $10,000 in the event of the death of the insured prior to age 65. If the insured is living at that age, he is to receive a whole life annuity of $500 per year, first payment to be made at 65. Find the net annual premium payable up to (but not including) age 65.

9. Find the net annual premium for a "double endowment" policy issued to (32), which provides a death benefit of $1000 for twenty years and a payment of $2000 if the insured survives the period.

3.7   DEFERRED INSURANCE

The symbol $_r|A_{x:\overline{n}|}^1$ is used to denote the net single premium for an

n-year term insurance of \$1, deferred r years, that is, the present value of \$1 to be paid at the end of the year in which (x) dies, provided he dies after attaining age $x + r$ and before attaining age $x + r + n$. Obviously, this single premium may be considered as the difference between the single premium for an $(n + r)$-year term insurance and the single premium for an r-year term insurance. Thus

$$_r|A^1_{x:\overline{n}|} = A^1_{x:\overline{r+n}|} - A^1_{x:\overline{r}|} = \frac{M_x - M_{x+r+n}}{D_x} - \frac{M_x - M_{x+r}}{D_x},$$

and hence

$$_r|A^1_{x:\overline{n}|} = \frac{M_{x+r} - M_{x+r+n}}{D_x}. \tag{3.20}$$

Similarly, if $_r|A_x$ denotes the net single premium for a whole life insurance of \$1 deferred r years, then

$$_r|A_x = A_x - A^1_{x:\overline{r}|} = \frac{M_x}{D_x} - \frac{M_x - M_{x+r}}{D_x},$$

and hence

$$_r|A_x = \frac{M_{x+r}}{D_x}. \tag{3.21}$$

Similarly, if $_r|A_{x:\overline{n}|}$ denotes the net single premium for an n-year endowment insurance of \$1 deferred r years, then

$$_r|A_{x:\overline{n}|} = A_{x:\overline{r+n}|} - A^1_{x:\overline{r}|}$$
$$= \frac{M_x - M_{x+r+n} + D_{x+r+n}}{D_x} - \frac{M_x - M_{x+r}}{D_x},$$

and hence

$$_r|A_{x:\overline{n}|} = \frac{M_{x+r} - M_{x+r+n} + D_{x+r+n}}{D_x}. \tag{3.22}$$

The above three formulas could, of course, have been derived by the use of the mutual fund method as employed in Section 3.2.

3.8 ACCUMULATED COST OF INSURANCE

The symbol* $_nk_x$ is used to denote the net single premium payable at the end of the term for an n-year term insurance of \$1. A life insurance policy based upon the plan of paying the premium after the insurance has expired would have no practical value for an insurance company, inasmuch as those who die in the period of n years pay no

---

*There is no internationally adopted symbol for the accumulated cost of insurance, but $_nk_x$ has been in wide use in the United States for many years.

premium and the company would have difficulty in collecting premiums from those alive at the end of the term. The notion of the accumulated cost of insurance is valuable, however, in the consideration of reserves on life insurance policies and will be used extensively in · the succeeding chapter.

Since the premium $_nk_x$ is payable at the end of the n years only if the insured survives the period, the present value of the premium is $_nk_x \cdot {}_nE_x$. Equating this value to the present value of the term insurance benefit, we obtain

$$_nk_x \cdot {}_nE_x = A^1_{x:\overline{n}|},$$

and hence

$$_nk_x = \frac{A^1_{x:\overline{n}|}}{{}_nE_x},$$

or

$$_nk_x = \frac{M_x - M_{x+n}}{D_{x+n}}. \tag{3.23}$$

When $n = 1$, the notation k_x is usually used instead of $_1k_x$; hence we write

$$k_x = {}_1k_x = \frac{M_x - M_{x+1}}{D_{x+1}} = \frac{C_x}{D_{x+1}}. \tag{3.24}$$

Numerical values of $_nk_x$ and k_x may be found in Table XIII and VI, respectively.

3.9   GENERAL INSURANCE FORMULA

In a manner similar to that of Section 2.9 it is now possible to set up a general expression for the value, at any time, of an insurance benefit. Thus

$$R \cdot \frac{M_a - M_b}{D_c}, \tag{3.25}$$

represents the value at age c of an insurance benefit of $\$R$ payable at the end of the year of death of a designated individual, provided he dies after age a and before age b. Whenever the age b is beyond the limiting age of the table the second term in the numerator disappears. The difference $(b - a)$ indicates the temporary period during which the insurance is effective. By properly choosing the ages a, b, and c, the expression (3.25) may be adapted to reproduce the formulas for A_x, $A^1_{x:\overline{n}|}$, $_r|A^1_{x:\overline{n}|}$, $_nk_x$, k_x, and others.

Exercises

1. A certain life insurance policy issued at age 30 provides for twenty annual premiums. In event of death of the insured between ages 30 and 40 the policy pays $1000, in event of death between ages 40 and 50 the policy pays $2000, and in event of the death of the insured after reaching age 50 the policy pays $3000. Find the net annual premium.

Solution. Let P denote the net annual premium. Upon equating the present value of the net premiums to the present value of the benefits, one finds

$$P \cdot a_{30:\overline{20}|} = 1000 A^1_{30:\overline{10}|} + 2000_{10|}A^1_{30:\overline{10}|} + 3000_{20|}A_{30},$$

or

$$P = \frac{1000(M_{30} - M_{40}) + 2000(M_{40} - M_{50}) + 3000 M_{50}}{N_{30} - N_{50}},$$

$$= 1000 \frac{M_{30} + M_{40} + M_{50}}{N_{30} - N_{50}}.$$

Inserting the numerical values of the commutation symbols, we have, by Table III,

$$P = 1000 \frac{3,415,797}{58,403,511} = 58.49$$

2. A certain life insurance policy issued at age 20 provides for thirty annual premiums. The benefits provided are $1000 in event of death during the first twenty years and $3000 in event of death thereafter. Compute the net annual premium.

3. A certain life insurance policy provides for $2000 in event of death before age 65 with $1000 cash payment if the insured survives to age 65. Assuming the policy is issued at age 30 and provides for ten annual premiums, compute the net annual premium.

4. The so-called "modified" life policy provides for the payment of $1000 in event of the death of the insured now aged 50. The premiums payable for the first five years are exactly one-half of the ultimate premium payable for life thereafter. Compute the ultimate net premium.

5. Prove algebraically the following identities:

(a) $A_x \cdot u_x = k_x + A_{x+1}$; $\qquad$ (b) $A^1_{x:\overline{n}|} \cdot u_x = k_x + A^{\ 1}_{x+1:\overline{n-1}|}$;

$\qquad\qquad$ (c) $A_{x:\overline{n}|} \cdot u_x = k_x + A_{x+1:\overline{n-1}|}$.

6. Show that

(a) $A_x = (_m k_x + A_{x+m})_m E_x$; $\qquad$ (b) $A^1_{x:\overline{n}|} = (_m k_x + A^{\ \ 1}_{x+m:\overline{n-m}|})_m E_x$;

$\qquad\qquad$ (c) $A_{x:\overline{n}|} = (_m k_x + A_{x+m:\overline{n-m}|})_m E_x$.

7. Show that

(a) $c_x \cdot u_x = k_x$;

(b) $P_{x+1} = P_x + \dfrac{P_{x+1} - c_x}{\ddot{a}_x}$;

(c) $P^1_{x:\overline{n}|} = \dfrac{n k_x}{\ddot{s}_{x:\overline{n}|}}$.

8. Prove the identities

(a) $\ddot{s}_{x:\overline{t}|} = \ddot{s}_{x+1:\overline{t-1}|} + \dfrac{1}{{}_t E_x}$.

(b) $_t k_x = {}_{t-1} k_{x+1} + \dfrac{c_x}{{}_t E_x}$.

9. The members of a society agree that for a period of twenty years the society will pay \$1000 to the beneficiary of each member who dies during that period. Payments are to be made at the end of the contract year in which death occurs. The surviving members are to share the accumulated cost equally. If all of the members were aged 25 at the start of this agreement, what will it cost each survivor?

10. Given that $P_{40:\overline{20}|} = 0.0400$, $_{20}P_{40} = 0.0300$, and $A_{60} = 0.6000$, find the value of $P^1_{40:\overline{20}|}$.

11. A special ten-payment life insurance policy issued at age 26 provides a death benefit of \$1000 for the first fifteen years and \$2000 thereafter for the remainder of life. Find the size of the net annual premiums.

3.10   INCREASING INSURANCE

Consider a whole life insurance policy in which the benefit increases annually so that \$1 is payable if the insured dies in the first policy year, \$2 are payable if the insured dies in the second year, \$3 are payable if the insured dies in the third year, and so on. Such a benefit may be considered as the sum of several level whole life benefits of \$1 each, the first to begin immediately, the second deferred one year, the third deferred two years, and so on. If the net single premium for such an increasing insurance benefit issued at age x is denoted by $(IA)_x$, we have

$$(IA)_x = A_x + {}_1|A_x + {}_2|A_x + \cdots + {}_{\omega-x-1}|A_x$$
$$= \frac{M_x}{D_x} + \frac{M_{x+1}}{D_x} + \frac{M_{x+2}}{D_x} + \cdots + \frac{M_{\omega-1}}{D_x},$$

and hence

$$(IA)_x = \frac{M_x + M_{x+1} + M_{x+2} + \cdots + M_{\omega-1}}{D_x},$$

Define the commutation symbol R_x, such that

$$R_x = M_x + M_{x+1} + M_{x+2} + \cdots + M_{\omega-1}.$$

The net single premium for the increasing whole life insurance policy can now be written

$$(IA)_x = \frac{R_x}{D_x}. \tag{3.26}$$

Values of the commutation symbol R_x are given in Table III.

It is not difficult to develop formulas for increasing term insurances and for policies under which the protection increases regularly for a period and then remains level for the balance of life. Procedures analogous to those suggested in Section 2.10 may be followed. Similarly, decreasing insurances may be handled by considering such a policy as the difference between a level insurance and an increasing insurance.

3.11 RETURN OF PREMIUM POLICY

A life insurance contract may provide for the return, at the time of death of the insured, of all the net premiums which he has paid. This special benefit is given in addition to the payment of the face amount of insurance.

Consider an ordinary life policy which provides for the payment, at the death of the insured, of the face amount $1 together with the return, without interest, of all the net premiums paid by the insured prior to his death. Let P denote the net annual premium for this contract. In event of the death of the insured during the first policy year the company agrees to pay the face amount $1 and return the first premium P. Hence the total amount payable in event of death in the first policy year is $(1 + P)$. In event of the death of the insured during the second policy year the company pays the face amount $1 in addition to the return of two net premiums, which the insured paid at the beginning of the first and second policy years. Thus the total amount of insurance during the second policy year is $(1 + 2P)$. Similarly, the total amount of insurance during the third policy year is $(1 + 3P)$ the fourth year $(1 + 4P)$, and so on, increasing by P per year. The return of the net premiums forms an increasing insurance and, since the present value of the net premiums must equal the present value of the benefits, it follows that

$$P \cdot \ddot{a}_x = A_x + P \cdot (IA)_x.$$

Solving for the net premium P and inserting commutation symbols, we obtain

$$P = \frac{A_x}{\ddot{a}_x - (IA)_x} = \frac{M_x}{N_x - R_x}. \tag{3.27}$$

Exercises

1. Calculate the net single premium for an increasing whole life insurance which begins with a death benefit of $500 in the first policy year and increases by $100 per year, assuming the age at issue is age 30.

Solution. The single premium for this increasing benefit may be written

$$A = \frac{500v \cdot d_{30} + 600v^2 \cdot d_{31} + 700v^3 d_{32} + \cdots}{l_{30}}$$

$$= \frac{500C_{30} + 600C_{31} + 700C_{32} + \cdots}{D_{30}}$$

$$= \frac{500(C_{30} + C_{31} + C_{32} + \cdots) + 100(C_{31} + C_{32} + \cdots) + 100(C_{32} + C_{33} + \cdots) + \cdots}{D_{30}}$$

$$= \frac{500M_{30} + 100(M_{31} + M_{32} + \cdots)}{D_{30}}$$

$$= \frac{500M_{30} + 100R_{31}}{D_{30}}.$$

Since $M_{30} = R_{30} - R_{31}$, the single premium A may be written

$$A = \frac{400M_{30} + 100R_{30}}{D_{30}}.$$

After inserting the numerical values of the commutation symbols, we find by Table III,

$$A = \frac{4{,}933{,}357{,}900}{3{,}905{,}782.0} = 1{,}263.09.$$

2. Show that if the term of the insurance described in Section 3.10 be limited to n years, the net single premium becomes

$$(IA)^1_{x:\overline{n}|} = \frac{R_x - R_{x+n} - n \cdot M_{x+n}}{D_x}.$$

3. Show that the net single premium for an increasing insurance on the life of (x) is

$$\frac{hM_x + kR_{x+1}}{D_x},$$

if the death benefit in the first year is h, and the death benefit increases by k per year.

4. A certain policy issued at age 45 provides for the following schedule of amounts payable in event of death:

Year	1	2	3	4	5	6	7	8	9	thereafter
Amount	1000	1200	1400	1600	1800	2000	1500	1000	500	0

(a) Compute the net single premium for the above policy.
(b) What net annual premium payable for five years will purchase the above policy?

5. A child's endowment policy issued at age 1 provides for a death benefit of $100 in event of death the first year, $200 in event of death the second year, and so on, increasing by $100 per year until a maximum of $1000 is reached. The policy matures at age 21 with an endowment of $1000. Show that the net annual premium payable for twenty years is

$$1000\frac{0.1(R_1 - R_{11}) - M_{21} + D_{21}}{N_1 - N_{21}}.$$

6. A certain life insurance policy provides for $10,000 payable in event of death between age x and age 41, $9700 in event of death between ages 41 and 42, $9400 in event of death between ages 42 and 43, and so on, decreasing $300 each year until the amount of insurance reaches $1000 at age 70, after which it remains constant. Premiums are payable from age x to age 64, inclusive.

(a) Show that the net annual premium for this policy may be expressed in the form

$$\frac{10,000M_x - 300(R_{41} - R_{71})}{N_x - N_{65}}.$$

(b) Compute the net annual premium for age 25 at issue.

7. Describe the type of insurance whose net single premium is given by each of the following:

(a) $\dfrac{1000}{D_x}(M_x + 3R_{x+1})$;   (b) $\dfrac{1000}{D_{25}}[M_{25} + 2(R_{30} - R_{35})]$;

(c) $\dfrac{100}{D_x}(M_x + 3R_{x+2} + 3R_{x+3})$.

8. Describe the type of policy whose net annual premium is given by each of the following:

(a) $1000\dfrac{M_x + R_{x+1}}{N_x - N_{x+10}}$;   (b) $1000\dfrac{R_x}{N_x}$;   (c) $\dfrac{1000(M_x - M_{x+15})}{N_x}$.

(d) Would the policy whose net annual premium is given by (c) be practical for issue by a life insurance company?

9. Show that

(a) $R_x = vS_x - S_{x+1}$;   (b) $R_x = N_x - d \cdot S_x$;
(c) $\ddot{a}_x = (IA)_x + d \cdot (I\ddot{a})_x$.

10. A certain whole life policy provides for a death benefit in the nth year of $(1.01)^n$. Assuming that the company operates upon a three and one-half per cent interest basis, show that the net annual premium for the policy is approximately

$$\frac{A_x}{\ddot{a}_x},$$

in which the numerator is computed at $2\frac{1}{2}\%$ and the denominator at $3\frac{1}{2}\%$.

11. A special twenty-year endowment policy issued at age x provides, in event of the death of the insured during the twenty-year period, for a benefit of $1 and the return, without interest, of all net premiums paid. If the insured survives the twenty-year period the policy matures, the insured receiving only the face amount $1. Show that the net annual premium may be written in the form

$$\frac{M_x - M_{x+20} + D_{x+20}}{N_x - N_{x+20} - R_x + R_{x+20} + 20 M_{x+20}}.$$

12. Express in terms of commutation symbols the net annual premium for a twenty-payment life policy issued at age x which provides, in event of the death of the insured during the first twenty policy years, for the return, without interest, of all net premiums paid in addition to the face amount of $1.

13. A single premium whole life policy issued at age x provides for the return, without interest, of the net single premium together with the payment of the face amount $1 at the death of the insured.
    (a) Express the net single premium in terms of commutation symbols.
    (b) Compute the net single premium for $x = 35$.

14. A life annuity contract, issued at age 30, provides for the payment of $1000 a year, first payment at age 60. The annuity is to be purchased by annual premiums payable for thirty years. In event of the death of the policyholder prior to age 60, the net premiums already paid are to be returned, without interest. Compute the net premium.

Review Exercises

1. What is the difference between the net annual premium for a $1000 ordinary life policy issued at age 30 and the net annual premium for a 55-year endowment issued for the same amount at the same age? (The latter policy, endowing at age 85, is frequently issued by life insurance companies in place of the ordinary life.)

2. What are the two principal reasons why an individual should not delay in purchasing his insurance?

3. Express in commutation symbols the net single premium for a whole life insurance policy which provides that the beneficiary receive $1000 at the death of the insured and $1000 per year for the subsequent nine years.

4. Draw a graph showing the values of the natural premiums for ages above 50 and indicate thereon the value of the ordinary life net annual premium for age 50.

5. A certain single premium contract provides for a pure endowment of $1000 payable if (x) survives n years. In event of the death of (x) before age $x + n$ the single premium is to be returned without interest. Express the net single premium in terms of commutation symbols.

6. Complete the following table expressing each of the symbols $\ddot{a}_x$, A_x, and P_x entirely in terms of each of the others and the discount factor d.

	$\ddot{a}_x$	A_x	P_x
$\ddot{a}_x$	$\ddot{a}_x$		
A_x	$1 - d\ddot{a}_x$	A_x	
P_x	$\dfrac{1}{\ddot{a}_x} - d$		P_x

7. Complete the following table expressing each of the symbols $\ddot{a}_{x:\overline{n}|}$, $A_{x:\overline{n}|}$, and $P_{x:\overline{n}|}$ entirely in terms of each of the others and the discount factor d

	$\ddot{a}_{x:\overline{n}|}$	$A_{x:\overline{n}|}$	$P_{x:\overline{n}|}$
$\ddot{a}_{x:\overline{n}|}$	$\ddot{a}_{x:\overline{n}|}$		
$A_{x:\overline{n}|}$	$1 - d\ddot{a}_{x:\overline{n}|}$	$A_{x:\overline{n}|}$	
$P_{x:\overline{n}|}$	$\dfrac{1}{\ddot{a}_{x:\overline{n}|}} - d$		$P_{x:\overline{n}|}$

8. Express each of the following entirely in terms of whole life and temporary life annuity symbols and the rate of interest.
   (a) Annual premium for 20-year term insurance.
   (b) Annual premium for 20-year pure endowment.

9. Use commutation symbols to prove that

$$\frac{A_{x+n} - A_x}{1 - A_x} + \frac{\ddot{a}_{x+n}}{\ddot{a}_x} = 1.$$

10. Compute the net single premium to provide an annuity of $100 per year payable in equal installments at the beginning of each quarter for as long as (50) survives, with the condition that if death occurs in the first policy year, four-fifths of the premium will be refunded; this death benefit to decrease by one-fifth of the premium each year until it disappears.

11. A man aged x offers to pay a lump sum of $_nE_x$ and also an annual premium of $P^1_{x:\overline{n}|}$ for an endowment policy maturing at age $x + n$. Find the amount of the policy.

12. Show that:
   (a) $$P^1_{x:\overline{n}|} = v - a_{x:\overline{n}|}(P_{x:\overline{n}|} + d);$$

   (b) $$a_{x:\overline{n}|} = \frac{1 - A_{x:\overline{n+1}|}}{d} - 1.$$

13. Under a certain mortality table $A_x = 0.01 \cdot x$ for all values of x when the rate of interest is 4%. Find expressions for $\ddot{a}_x$ and P_x.

14. A certain t-year endowment policy issued at age x provides for the payment of $\ddot{a}_{\overline{m}|}$ in event death occurs during the first policy year, $\ddot{a}_{\overline{2m}|}$ in

event death occurs during the second policy year, and so forth, and $\ddot{a}_{\overline{tm}|}$ in event death occurs during the tth policy year or in event (x) survives the t-year period. Show that the net single premium at rate i for this policy can be expressed as

$$\frac{A_{x:\overline{t}|} - \acute{A}_{x:\overline{t}|}}{d},$$

where $A_{x:\overline{t}|}$ is calculated at rate i and $\acute{A}_{x:\overline{t}|}$ is calculated at a different rate of interest.

CHAPTER 4

Net Level Reserve

4.1 RESERVES

All mortality tables show a rate of mortality which, except at the very low ages, is increasing from age to age. Thus, if the amount of insurance provided by a given policy is the same year after year, the current cost of the insurance benefit (as indicated by the natural premium c_x) will increase from policy year to policy year. Under these conditions the net level premium for the policy is, in the early policy years, more than sufficient to cover the current cost of the insurance and, in the later policy years, the level premium is insufficient to pay the increased cost current in these later years. The significance of this statement may be readily understood by considering a numerical example. Under the 1958 CSO Table, with 3% interest, the net level premium for a $1000 ordinary life policy issued at age 40 is $19.96. The cost of insurance in the first policy year is $1000c_{40}$, or $3.43 as given by Table VI. In the second policy year the net level premium is the same, $19.96, while the cost of insurance is now $1000c_{41}$, or $3.73. The cost of the insurance gradually rises from year to year, reaching $19.75 at age 60 and $106.78 at age 80, whereas the net level premium remains constant at the original amount, $19.96. The diagram shown on page 72 compares graphically the net level premium $19.96 with the increasing annual cost of the insurance benefit provided by an ordinary life policy issued at age 40.

It should be noted that at the older ages the cost of insurance greatly exceeds the net level premium. If the insurance company is to continue upon a solvent basis, it is necessary that the company accumulate a fund from the excess of the net level premium over the current cost during the early policy years in order to be able to

provide for the increased cost in the later policy years. The accumulation of this "excess" is called the *reserve*.

GRAPHICAL COMPARISON OF NET LEVEL PREMIUM
FOR ORDINARY LIFE WITH ONE-YEAR PREMIUMS
AGE AT ISSUE 40   1958 CSO 3%

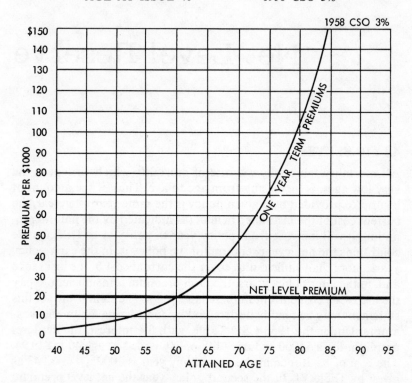

The necessity of accumulating reserves may also be seen from another point of view. When a policy is issued, the net level premium is
so calculated as to make the present value of the net premiums equal
to the present value of the benefits. This equation holds only at the
date of issue of the policy. At any time thereafter the present value of
the remaining net premiums is less than upon the date of issue since
a fewer number of premiums remain to be received, while the present value of the insurance has increased because the date of payment has drawn nearer. The difference between the increased value
of the insurance benefits and the decreased value of the future net
premiums must be represented by funds which the company has on
hand in its reserve fund.

The first point of view deals exclusively with the past history of the policy and is "retrospective," while the second point of view is concerned with the future of the policy and is "prospective." It is natural to suppose that these two methods will give identical amounts of reserve; this equality will be shown later.

4.2 NUMERICAL ILLUSTRATION

Suppose that a life insurance company issues a three-payment six-year endowment policy for an amount of $1 to each of l_{40} individuals at age 40. Assume that the company has available, after expenses have been met, a net level premium from each policy based upon the 1958 CSO 3% table. Under this assumption the company would have

$$_3P_{40:\overline{6}|} = \frac{M_{40} - M_{46} + D_{46}}{N_{40} - N_{43}} = 0.289011$$

available from each policy to meet the current costs of insurance and maintain the reserve fund. At the beginning of the first year l_{40}, or 9,241,359, premiums of $0.289011 are collected, producing an initial fund of $2,670,854. At the end of the year interest at 3% is added, giving a total of $2,750,980. At the end of the year d_{40}, or 32,622, death claims of $1 each are paid, leaving a balance of $2,718,358. There are $l_{41} = 9,208,737$ survivors, so that the total fund, $2,718,358 divided by 9,208,737, gives $0.29519 as the share, or reserve, per policy. At the beginning of the second year $2,661,426 in premiums is collected from 9,208,737 policyholders, and this amount is added to the balance remaining from the previous year, and so on. The table below shows the result of the numerical calculations:

Year	Total Premiums Received	Total Fund Beginning of Year	Fund with Interest	Death Claims	Fund at End of Year	Number of Survivors	Reserve per Policy
1	2,670,854	2,670,854	2,750,980	32,622	2,718,358	9,208,737	0.29519
2	2,661,426	5,379,784	5,541,178	35,362	5,505,816	9,173,375	0.60020
3	2,651,206	8,157,022	8,401,733	38,253	8,363,480	9,135,122	0.91553
4		8,363,480	8,614,384	41,382	8,573,002	9,093,740	0.94274
5		8,573,002	8,830,192	44,741	8,785,451	9,048,999	0.97088
6		8,785,451	9,049,015	48,412	9,000,603	9,000,587	1.00000

It should be noted that in accordance with the provisions of the policy no premiums are collected after the third year, and that the reserve at the end of the sixth year is just sufficient to provide the endowment payment of $1 at that time.

The reserves, as exhibited in the table, are those which are on hand at the end of the various policy years and are known as *terminal reserves*. Thus, the figure, 0.60020 appearing in the last column of the second line, is called the second terminal reserve, and represents the amount on hand for each policy remaining in force at the end of the second policy year just before the third premium is paid. In the formation of the table it was tacitly assumed that all of the living policyholders continue their policies by paying premiums as they come due. In a practical situation, some of the living policyholders may fail to pay one or more premiums, and in this event the terminal reserve would furnish a rough criterion as to the company's liability to the withdrawing policyholder.

Exercises

1. Assume that 100,000 lives aged 40 each purchase an ordinary life insurance policy for \$1 for a net annual premium of 0.02. If interest is at 3% and if the mortality table shows 400 deaths at age 40, compute the first year terminal reserve for this policy.
2. Make a table similar in form to that of Section 4.2, showing the accumulation of the reserves for a five-year endowment policy issued at age 50.
3. Make a table similar in form to that of Section 4.2, showing the accumulation of the reserves for a five-year term policy issued at age 20.

4.3 RETROSPECTIVE RESERVE

The method given by the table in Section 4.2 is too long and cumbersome to be of much practical use in the calculation of terminal reserves. Attention will now be given to more convenient methods. From the retrospective point of view the terminal reserve for a given policy is defined as the difference betweeen the accumulated value of past net premiums and the accumulated value of past insurance benefits. Hence, for a policy issued at age x, the tth terminal reserve represents this difference at the end of the tth policy year, when the insured attains age $x + t$, so that

$$\begin{pmatrix} t\text{th Terminal} \\ \text{reserve} \end{pmatrix} = \begin{pmatrix} \text{Accumulated value at} \\ \text{age } x + t \text{ of} \\ \text{past net premiums} \end{pmatrix} - \begin{pmatrix} \text{Accumulated value at} \\ \text{age } x + t \text{ of past} \\ \text{insurance benefits} \end{pmatrix}.$$

Let us apply this definition to obtain an expression for the tth terminal reserve for an ordinary life policy issued at age x. By the end of the t-year period following the date of issue the company has received t premiums of P_x each, paid at the beginning of each year throughout this period. The accumulated value at age $x + t$ of these net premiums is $P_x \cdot \ddot{s}_{x:\overline{t}|}$. The accumulated cost of the insurance in force over the temporary period of t years is $\$1 \cdot {}_t k_x$. Denoting the tth terminal reserve for a $\$1$ ordinary life policy issued at age x by the symbol ${}_t V_x$, we have

$$ {}_t V_x = P_x \cdot \ddot{s}_{x:\overline{t}|} - {}_t k_x \tag{4.1} $$

and hence

$$ {}_t V_x = \frac{1}{D_{x+t}} [P_x (N_x - N_{x+t}) - (M_x - M_{x+t})]. $$

Similarly, if the tth terminal reserve for an n-payment life be denoted by ${}_t^n V_x$, then if $t \leq n$, we find

$$ {}_t^n V_x = {}_n P_x \cdot {}_t u_x - {}_t k_x, \tag{4.2} $$

following the common American custom of using ${}_t u_x$ in place of $\ddot{s}_{x:\overline{t}|}$.

In considering the tth terminal reserve for an n-payment life policy with $t > n$, it should be noted that no premiums are paid for the interval of time elapsing from the end of the nth policy year to the end of the tth policy year. The accumulated value of past net premiums is ${}_n P_x \cdot {}_n u_x$ at the end of the premium payment period, and this amount is then accumulated, with the benefit of interest and survivorship, to the end of the tth policy year. The accumulation factor for this latter interval is

$$ \frac{1}{{}_{t-n} E_{x+n}}, $$

since $x + n$ is the age attained by the insured at the beginning of the interval and $(t - n)$ is the number of years for which this accumulation is to be made. Thus, for values of $t > n$, the retrospective formula becomes

$$ {}_t^n V_x = \frac{{}_n P_x \cdot {}_n u_x}{{}_{t-n} E_{x+n}} - {}_t k_x = \frac{1}{D_{x+t}} [{}_n P_x (N_x - N_{x+n}) - (M_x - M_{x+t})]. \tag{4.3} $$

Similarly, for an n-year endowment* of $\$1$ issued at age x, the retrospective method yields

---

*It should be noted that the subscript at the left in the symbol for the terminal reserve for a given policy indicates the policy year at the end of which the reserve is to be taken, while the other subscripts have the same meaning as the subscripts in the symbol for the net annual premium.

$$_tV_{x:\overline{n}|} = P_{x:\overline{n}|} \cdot {_tu_x} - {_tk_x} = \frac{1}{D_{x+t}}\left[P_{x:\overline{n}|}(N_x - N_{x+t}) - (M_x - M_{x+t})\right].$$

(4.4)

Exercises

1. Compute by the retrospective method the third terminal reserve for the three-payment six-year endowment policy of Section 4.2.

Solution. Applying the retrospective definition of the third terminal reserve, we obtain immediately

$$_3^3V_{40:\overline{6}|} = {_3P_{40:\overline{6}|}} \cdot {_3u_{40}} - {_3k_{40}}.$$

Using Tables XII and XIII, we find

$$_3^3V_{40:\overline{6}|} = (0.289011)(3.20920) - 0.011963 = 0.91553,$$

which checks with the numerical value found in Section 4.2.

2. By the retrospective method obtain a simple form for the nth terminal reserve for each of the following policies: (a) an n-year term insurance policy; (b) an n-payment life policy; (c) an n-year endowment policy.

3. Express in terms of commutation symbols the twenty-fifth terminal reserve for a twenty-payment thirty-year endowment policy issued at age 35. Show that this expression is equal to $A_{60:\overline{5}|}$.

4. Find numerical values for the fifth terminal reserves for the following $1000 policies issued at age 25: (a) ordinary life; (b) twenty-payment life; (c) twenty-year endowment; (d) ten-year term.

5. Find numerical values for the tenth terminal reserves for the following policies issued at age 25: (a) ordinary life: (b) twenty-payment life; (c) twenty-year endowment; (d) five-payment life.

6. Compute the fifteenth terminal reserve for each of the following $1000 policies issued at age 40: (a) ten-payment life; (b) ten-payment twenty-year endowment; (c) twenty-payment thirty-year endowment.

7. Compute the twentieth year terminal reserve for a $1000 policy issued to (29) on each of the following plans: (a) term to age 65; (b) ordinary life; (c) ten-payment whole life; (d) fifteen-payment whole life.

8. (a) Compute the tenth year terminal reserve for a $1000 ten-payment whole life policy issued at age 32. (b) Compute the twentieth year terminal reserve on a twenty-payment whole life policy issued at age 22. Compare the answers to (a) and (b) and explain.

4.4 PROSPECTIVE RESERVE

From the prospective point of view the terminal reserve for a given policy is defined as the difference between the value of the future benefits of the policy and the value of the future net premiums. Hence, for a policy issued at age x, the tth terminal reserve represents this difference in values at the end of the tth policy year when the insured attains age $x + t$, so that

$$\left(\begin{array}{c} t\text{th Terminal} \\ \text{reserve} \end{array}\right) = \left(\begin{array}{c} \text{Value at age } x + t \\ \text{of} \\ \text{future benefits} \end{array}\right) - \left(\begin{array}{c} \text{Value at age } x + t \\ \text{of} \\ \text{future net premiums} \end{array}\right).$$

Consider an ordinary life policy issued at age x for a face amount of insurance of $1. At the end of the tth policy year, the future premiums constitute a life annuity due of P_x, payable at the beginning of each year for the lifetime of an individual age $x + t$. Since the value of these future premiums is $P_x \cdot \ddot{a}_{x+t}$ and the value of the future benefits to be provided by the ordinary life policy is A_{x+t}, the prospective method gives

$$_tV_x = A_{x+t} - P_x \cdot \ddot{a}_{x+t}, \tag{4.5}$$

or

$$_tV_x = \frac{1}{D_{x+t}}[M_{x+t} - P_x \cdot N_{x+t}].$$

Similarly, for the tth terminal reserve upon a one-dollar n-payment life policy issued at age x, $t \leq n$, we have

$$_t^nV_x = A_{x+t} - {_nP_x} \cdot \ddot{a}_{x+t:\overline{n-t}|}, \tag{4.6}$$

since the future premiums constitute in this case a temporary life annuity for $(n - t)$ years, which is the balance of the premium payment period. When the terminal reserve is required at the end of a policy year subsequent to the end of the premium payment period, $t > n$, the value of the future premiums is zero; consequently we have

$$_t^nV_x = A_{x+t}.$$

In considering the tth terminal reserve for a one-dollar n-year endowment policy, the future benefits consist of endowment insurance for $(n - t)$ years, while the future premiums constitute a temporary annuity due payable for $(n - t)$ years. Applying the prospective definition for the reserve, we have

$$_tV_{x:\overline{n}|} = A_{x+t:\overline{n-t}|} - P_{x:\overline{n}|} \cdot \ddot{a}_{x+t:\overline{n-t}|}, \tag{4.7}$$

and hence

$$_tV_{x:\overline{n}|} = \frac{1}{D_{x+t}}[M_{x+t} - M_{x+n} + D_{x+n} - P_{x:\overline{n}|}(N_{x+t} - N_{x+n})].$$

It will be shown in the next section that the two definitions, retrospective and prospective, for the terminal reserve are equivalent.

Exercises

1. Compute by the prospective method the first terminal reserve for the three-payment six-year endowment policy of Section 4.2.

   Solution.   Upon applying the prospective definition of the first terminal reserve, we obtain immediately

   $$\substack{3\\1}V_{40:\overline{6}|} = A_{41:\overline{5}|} - {}_3P_{40:\overline{6}|}\,\ddot{a}_{41:\overline{2}|}.$$

   Using Tables VII, XI, and IX, we find

   $$\substack{3\\1}V_{40:\overline{6}|} = 0.863719 - (0.289011)(1.967146) = 0.29519,$$

   which checks with the numerical value found in Section 4.2.

2. Find the numerical values for the fifth terminal reserve by the prospective method for the following $1000 policies issued at age 25: (a) ordinary life; (b) twenty-payment life; (c) twenty-year endowment; (d) ten-year term.

3. Express in terms of commutation symbols the twenty-fifth terminal reserve for a twenty-payment thirty-year endowment policy issued at age x.

4. Compute the tenth terminal reserve by the prospective method for a $1000 twenty-payment endowment insurance maturing at age 65, the policy having been issued at age 35.

5. Compute by the prospective method the fifteenth terminal reserve for each of the following $1000 policies issued at age 25: (a) ordinary life; (b) ten-payment life; (c) ten-payment twenty-year endowment; (d) thirty-year endowment.

6. Show algebraically that the retrospective and prospective methods give identical values for the tth terminal reserve for an ordinary life policy issued at age x.

7. Same as Exercise 6 for a twenty-payment life policy, (a) for $t \leqq 20$, (b) for $t > 20$.

8. A man now aged 40 has carried a $1000 ordinary life policy for the past ten years. He now wishes to change this to a twenty-payment whole life policy as of his original age at issue, paying for the next ten years the regular twenty-payment life premium. How much must he pay to the insurance company now in order to bring the reserve on his present policy up to the tenth year reserve on a twenty-payment life policy issued at age 30?

4.5 EQUIVALENCE OF THE RETROSPECTIVE AND PROSPECTIVE DEFINITIONS

In order to show that the retrospective and prospective methods of obtaining a given reserve always produce identical results consider the fundamental equation used in determining the net premium, namely,

$$\left(\begin{array}{c}\text{Value at age of issue}\\ \text{of all net premiums}\end{array}\right) = \left(\begin{array}{c}\text{Value at age of issue}\\ \text{of all policy benefits}\end{array}\right).$$

Accumulating both sides of this equation with the benefit of interest and survivorship to the date at which the reserve is to be taken, we have

$$\left(\begin{array}{c}\text{Value at reserve date}\\ \text{of all net premiums}\end{array}\right) = \left(\begin{array}{c}\text{Value at reserve date}\\ \text{of all policy benefits}\end{array}\right).$$

The value of all net premiums at the reserve date may be separated into two parts, (a) the accumulated value of all net premiums paid before the reserve date, and (b) the value of all future premiums. Similarly, the value of all policy benefits at the reserve date may be divided into two parts, (a) the accumulated value of the temporary insurance provided by the policy prior to the reserve date, and (b) the value of all future policy benefits. Hence, it follows that (all values refer to the reserve date)

$$\left(\begin{array}{c}\text{Accumulated value}\\ \text{of past premiums}\end{array}\right) + \left(\begin{array}{c}\text{Value of}\\ \text{future premiums}\end{array}\right).$$

$$= \left(\begin{array}{c}\text{Accumulated value}\\ \text{of past benefits}\end{array}\right) + \left(\begin{array}{c}\text{Value of}\\ \text{future benefits}\end{array}\right).$$

Transposing the second term and the third term of this equation, we obtain immediately

$$\left(\begin{array}{c}\text{Retrospective}\\ \text{reserve}\end{array}\right) = \left(\begin{array}{c}\text{Prospective}\\ \text{reserve}\end{array}\right).$$

Exercises

1. A twenty-payment insurance policy provides for the following death benefits:

   $1000 in event of death during the first five years;
   $2000 in event of death during the next five years; and
   $3000 in event of death thereafter.
   Give in terms of commutation symbols formulas for:

   (a) the net annual premium;
   (b) the seventh terminal reserve by the retrospective method;
   (c) the seventh terminal reserve by the prospective method;
   (d) Show that the expressions found under (b) and (c) are equal.

Solution.   (a) Equating the present value of the net premiums to the present value of the benefits, we obtain

$$P \cdot \ddot{a}_{x:\overline{20|}} = 1000A_x + 1000_5|A_x + 1000_{10}|\mathrm{A}_x.$$

Inserting commutation symbols and solving for *P*, we have

$$P = \frac{1000(M_x + M_{x+5} + M_{x+10})}{N_x - N_{x+20}}.$$

(b) In considering the accumulated cost of insurance under this policy at the end of the seventh year, one must bear in mind that the insurance benefit increased at the end of the fifth year from $1000 to $2000. By the end of the seventh year, the insured has had the benefit of $1000 insurance for seven years and an additional $1000 for the last two years. Hence the accumulated cost of insurance is $1000(_7k_x + _2k_{x+5})$. Applying the retrospective definition of the seventh reserve, we obtain

$$_7V = P \cdot _7u_x - 1000(_7k_x + _2k_{x+5})$$
$$= P\frac{N_x - N_{x+7}}{D_{x+7}} - 1000\frac{M_x + M_{x+5} - 2M_{x+7}}{D_{x+7}}.$$

(c) The future benefits of this policy, valued at the end of seven years, consist of a whole life insurance of $2000 and an additional $1000 whole life insurance deferred three years. Hence, applying the prospective definition, we find

$$_7V = 2000A_{x+7} + 1000_3|A_{x+7} - P \cdot \ddot{a}_{x+7:\overline{13|}}$$
$$= 1000\frac{2M_{x+7} + M_{x+10}}{D_{x+7}} - P\frac{N_{x+7} - N_{x+20}}{D_{x+7}}.$$

(d) The following method of proving that the seventh terminal reserves found by the prospective and retrospective methods are identical is patterned after Section 4.5. From (a), we have

$$\frac{P}{D_x}(N_x - N_{x+20}) = \frac{1000}{D_x}(M_x + M_{x+5} + M_{x+10}).$$

Multiplying both sides of this equation by D_x/D_{x+7} and transposing, we find

$$\frac{P}{D_{x+7}}N_x - 1000\frac{M_x + M_{x+5}}{D_{x+7}} = \frac{1000M_{x+10}}{D_{x+7}} + P\frac{N_{x+20}}{D_{x+7}}.$$

Subtracting the expression

$$\frac{P \cdot N_{x+7} - 2000M_{x+7}}{D_{x+7}}$$

from both members of the preceding equation, we have

$$P \frac{N_x - N_{x+7}}{D_{x+7}} - 1000 \frac{M_x + M_{x+5} - 2M_{x+7}}{D_{x+7}}$$

$$= 1000 \frac{2M_{x+7} + M_{x+10}}{D_{x+7}} - P \frac{N_{x+7} - N_{x+20}}{D_{x+7}},$$

or

$$\text{7th retrospective reserve} = \text{7th prospective reserve.}$$

2. Show that the retrospective and prospective formulas for the tth year terminal reserve for an ordinary life policy issued at age x are equivalent.

3. Demonstrate the equivalence of the prospective and retrospective formulas for the tth year terminal reserve for an n-payment whole life policy issued at age x if: (a) t is less than n; (b) t is greater than n.

4. Show that the retrospective and prospective formulas for the tth policy year terminal reserve for an n-year endowment insurance policy issued at age x are equivalent

5. Express in terms of commutation symbols the third and tenth year terminal reserves, respectively, by both the prospective and retrospective methods for the modified life policy described in Exercise 4 of Section 3.9.

6. (a) Give in terms of commutation symbols the prospective formula for the eighth terminal reserve on a ten-payment 25-year endowment insurance issued to (x).
   (b) As in (a), using the retrospective formula.
   (c) Prove algebraically that the formulas found in (a) and (b) are equivalent.

7. (a) Give in terms of commutation symbols the prospective formula for the twenty-third terminal reserve on a ten-payment 25-year endowment issued at age x.
   (b) Give in terms of commutation symbols the retrospective formula for the same reserve.
   (c) Prove algebraically that the formulas found in (a) and (b) are equivalent.

8. A certain life insurance policy provides for $100 payable in event of death the first year, $200 payable in event of death the second year, $300 payable in event of death the third year, and so on. Level premiums are payable for life. Assuming that the policy is issued at age 30, compute (a) the net annual premium, (b) the tenth terminal reserve by the prospective method, and (c) the tenth terminal reserve by the retrospective method.

9. A certain life insurance policy provides for $10,000 payable in event of death between age 30 and age 41, $9700 in event of death between ages 41 and 42, $9400 in event of death between ages 42 and 43, and so on, decreasing $300 each year until the amount of insurance reaches $1000 at age 70, after which it remains constant. The policy is issued at age

30, and provides for annual premiums for 35 years. Compute the twentieth terminal reserve
   (a) by the prospective method,
   (b) by the retrospective method.
(See Exercise 6, Section 3.11.)

4.6 OTHER FORMULAS

It is evident that the terminal reserve for a given policy may be expressed in many different forms. Some of these forms are interesting because they afford verbal interpretations, others because of their adaptability in computing. As an illustration, replacing in formula (4.5) the symbol A_{x+t} by $P_{x+t} \cdot \ddot{a}_{x+t}$, we obtain

$$_tV_x = (P_{x+t} - P_x) \cdot \ddot{a}_{x+t}.$$

A verbal interpretation of this form is as follows: An ordinary life insurance policy issued at age x provides for a premium payment annually of P_x. If, after reaching age $x + t$, the insured desires to duplicate the benefits afforded by this policy, he must purchase a new ordinary life policy issued at age $x + t$ and providing for annual premiums of P_{x+t}. Thus, the deficit in future premiums, which must be made up by the reserve fund is $(P_{x+t} - P_x) \ddot{a}_{x+t}$.
   Making use of the identities

$$A_x = 1 - d \cdot \ddot{a}_x, \qquad P_x + d = \frac{1}{\ddot{a}_x},$$

we may write formula (4.5) in the form

$$_tV_x = 1 - \frac{\ddot{a}_{x+t}}{\ddot{a}_x}. \tag{4.8}$$

This form is particularly useful in the computation of reserves.

Exercises

1. Show that the tth terminal reserve for an ordinary life policy issued at age x can be written in each of the following forms.

   (a) $\dfrac{A_{x+t} - A_x}{1 - A_x}.$ (b) $1 - \dfrac{1 - A_{x+t}}{1 - A_x}.$

   (c) $\dfrac{a_x - a_{x+t}}{1 + a_x}.$ (d) $A_{x+t}\left(1 - \dfrac{P_x}{P_{x+t}}\right).$

2. Given that $\ddot{a}_x + \ddot{a}_{x+2t} = 2\ddot{a}_{x+t}$, find $_tV_{x+t}$ and $_{2t}V_x$ in terms of $_tV_x$.

3. If $1 - A_{x+2t} = A_{x+2t} - A_{x+t} = A_{x+t} - A_x$, express $_tV_{x+t}$ in terms of $_tV_x$ and find the numerical values of $_tV_{x+t}$ and $_tV_x$.

4. Prove the identity
$$_{t+r}V_x = 1 - (1 - _rV_x)(1 - _tV_{x+r}).$$

5. Employ the result of Exercise 4 to prove that
$$_tV_x = 1 - (1 - _1V_x)(1 - _1V_{x+1}) \cdots (1 - _1V_{x+t-1}).$$

6. Show that the tth terminal reserve for an n-year endowment policy can be written in each of the following forms:

(a) $\dfrac{A_{x+t:\overline{n-t}|} - A_{x:\overline{n}|}}{1 - A_{x:\overline{n}|}}.$

(b) $1 - \dfrac{\ddot{a}_{x+t:\overline{n-t}|}}{\ddot{a}_{x:\overline{n}|}}.$

(c) $(P_{x+t:\overline{n-t}|} - P_{x:\overline{n}|})\,\ddot{a}_{x+t:\overline{n-t}|}.$

(d) $A_{x+t:\overline{n-t}|}\left(1 - \dfrac{P_{x:\overline{n}|}}{P_{x+t:\overline{n-t}|}}\right).$

7. Show that the tth terminal reserve for an n-payment life policy issued at age x can be written, for $t \leqq n$, in the form
$$_t^nV_x = (_{n-t}P_{x+t} - {}_nP_x)\ddot{a}_{x+t:\overline{n-t}|},$$

and give a verbal interpretation of this form.

8. Show that the tth terminal reserve for an n-year term policy issued at age x can be written in the form
$$_tV^1_{x:\overline{n}|} = (P^1_{x+t:\overline{n-t}|} - P^1_{x:\overline{n}|})\ddot{a}_{x+t:\overline{n-t}|},$$

and give a verbal interpretation of this form.

4.7   FACKLER'S ACCUMULATION FORMULA

A useful formula for obtaining sequentially the reserves upon a given policy may be derived by simplifying the method used in building the table shown in Section 4.2. Explicit notation is omitted in the derivation, since the method is entirely general and the formula may be used for any policy. Consider a life insurance company issuing the same policy in amount of $1 to each of l_x persons at age x. After t years the total reserve fund held by the company for the survivors of this group is $l_{x+t} \cdot {}_tV$. The net premiums collected by the company at the beginning of the succeeding year total $l_{x+t} \cdot P$. During this succeeding year interest at the assumed rate i is earned and at the end of the year d_{x+t} death claims of $1 each are payable. The balance left at the end of the year represents the total reserve fund held for the l_{x+t+1} policyholders who survive this year, or $l_{x+t+1} \cdot {}_{t+1}V$. From the preceding argument it follows that

$$(l_{x+t} \cdot {}_tV + l_{x+t} \cdot P)\,(1 + i) - d_{x+t} = l_{x+t+1} \cdot {}_{t+1}V. \qquad (4.9)$$

Dividing this equation by l_{x+t+1} and multiplying the numerator and denominator of each term of the first member by v^{x+t+1}, we have

$$({}_tV + P)\frac{D_{x+t}}{D_{x+t+1}} - \frac{C_{x+t}}{D_{x+t+1}} = {}_{t+1}V,$$

and hence

$$({}_tV + P)\, u_{x+t} - k_{x+t} = {}_{t+1}V. \tag{4.10}$$

Equation (4.10), known as *Fackler's Accumulation Formula,* affords an effective means of calculating sequentially the respective terminal reserves on a policy. For $t = 0$, since ${}_0V = 0$, equation (4.10) becomes

$$P \cdot u_x - k_x = {}_1V, \tag{4.11}$$

and for $t = 1$,

$$({}_1V + P)\, u_{x+1} - k_{x+1} = {}_2V, \tag{4.12}$$

and so on. In applying the formula the first terminal reserve is computed by means of (4.11) and the result inserted in equation (4.12) to obtain the second reserve, and so on. For policy years after the expiration of the premium payment period the net premium is omitted from the formula.

Exercises

1. Use Fackler's Accumulation Formula to compute the first five terminal reserves for a \$1000 ten-year endowment policy issued at age 25. Check the fifth terminal reserve by means of the prospective method.

   Solution.   Employing formula (3.17) with $m = n = 10$, we have

   $$P = \frac{1000A_{25:\overline{10|}}}{\ddot{a}_{25:\overline{10|}}} = \frac{1000A^{1}_{25:\overline{10|}} + 1000\,{}_{10}E_{25}}{\ddot{a}_{25:\overline{10|}}}.$$

   The values of $1000A^{1}_{25:\overline{10|}}$, $1000\,{}_{10}E_{25}$, and $\ddot{a}_{25:\overline{10|}}$ are found in Tables XI, VII, and IX, respectively; hence we have immediately

   $$P = \frac{17.8822 + 728.4104}{8.71062} = 85.6762.$$

   Equation (4.11) gives

   $${}_1V = Pu_{25} - 1000k_{25},$$

   and, employing Table VI, we find

   $${}_1V = (85.6762)(1.031992) - 1.93373 = 86.4834.$$

Using Equation (4.12) to compute the second terminal reserve, we obtain

$$_2V = (_1V + P)u_{26} - 1000k_{26}$$
$$= (86.4834 + 85.6762)(1.032023) - 1.96385 = 175.7088.$$

Similarly, we find

$$_3V = (175.7088 + 85.6762)(1.032054) - 1.99392 = 267.7695,$$
$$_4V = (267,7695 + 85.6762)(1.032095) - 2.03408 = 362.7555,$$

and, finally,

$$_5V = (362.7555 + 85.6762)(1.032147) - 2.0843 = 460.7630.$$

As a check, by the prospective method, there results

$$_5V = 1000A^1_{30:\overline{5}|} + 1000_5E_{30} - P\ddot{a}_{30:\overline{5}|}$$
$$= 10.2777 + 852.9138 - (85.6762)(4.69709)$$
$$= 460.7626.$$

2. Show that Fackler's Accumulation Formula can be written in the form

$$_{t+1}V = (_tV + P - c_{x+t})u_{x+t}.$$

3. Verify the six terminal reserves shown in the table in Section 4.2 by a computation employing Fackler's Accumulation Formula.
4. Use Fackler's Accumulation Formula to compute the first ten terminal reserves for a $1000 ordinary life policy issued at age 20.
5. Use Fackler's Accumulation Formula to compute the ten terminal reserves for a $1000 ten-year term policy issued at age 30.
6. (a) Develop by the method of Section 4.7 the equation

$$_{r+t}V = {_t}V \cdot \frac{1}{_rE_{x+t}} + P_ru_{x+t} - {_r}k_{x+t}.$$

Give a verbal interpretation of this formula.
(b) Given that the fifth terminal reserve for a $1000 ordinary life policy issued at age 30 is $62.12 and the net premium is $13.47, use equation in (a) to compute the fifteenth terminal reserve for the same policy.

4.8   CHANGES IN THE INTEREST RATE

It will be observed from the following tables that an increase in the rate of interest produces a decrease in the net premium and in the reserve. Thus, a life insurance company which operates upon the basis of an interest rate of $2\frac{1}{2}\%$, for example, maintains a larger reserve than a company operating upon a 3% or $3\frac{1}{2}\%$ interest basis. One also notes from the tables that the relative variation in premiums, resulting from a change in the interest rate, is larger at younger ages than at older ages.

NET LEVEL PREMIUMS
1958 CSO
$1000

	2½%	3%	3½%
Ordinary life age 20	10.75	9.56	8.51
Ordinary life age 40	21.38	19.96	18.65
Ordinary life age 60	51.50	50.02	48.61
Twenty-payment life age 20	19.48	16.40	13.90
Twenty-payment life age 40	30.84	27.95	25.43
Twenty-payment life age 60	56.66	54.64	52.75
Twenty-year endowment age 20	39.28	37.25	35.30
Twenty-year endowment age 40	41.62	39.62	37.71
Twenty-year endowment age 60	59.10	57.33	55.63

The percentage change in the reserve due to a change in the rate of interest is found to be greater for the earlier policy years. The table below shows the net level reserves on an ordinary life policy issued at age 25 for $1000 on the 1958 CSO Table.

Years in Force	2½%	3%	3½%
5	57.45	51.40	45.97
10	121.87	110.32	99.83
20	269.31	249.37	230.79
30	431.45	407.68	385.01
40	592.35	569.58	547.39
50	729.67	711.17	692.81
60	834.35	821.28	808.10
70	916.98	909.61	902.07

4.9   INITIAL RESERVE, NET AMOUNT AT RISK

The *initial* reserve for a given policy is defined as the reserve at the beginning of a policy year just after the premium has been received. Thus, the initial reserve at the beginning of the tth policy year is the terminal reserve at the end of the previous year increased by the net premium paid at the beginning of the tth year. Hence, if the tth initial reserve on a given policy issued at age x be denoted by $_tI$, we have

$$_tI = _{t-1}V + P.$$

Explicit notation denoting the type of policy has been omitted from this equation, since it is valid for all plans of insurance. It should be noted that, after the premium payment period has expired, no further premiums are received and the initial reserve for any year is the terminal reserve for the previous year.

The *net amount at risk* for a given policy in the tth policy year is de-

fined as the difference between the face amount of insurance provided in event of the death of the insured and the terminal reserve at
the end of that year. If the policy provides for a payment of $1 in
event of death in the tth year, the net amount at risk in this policy
year is

$$1 - {}_tV.$$

Equation (4.9) of the previous section may be reduced to an interesting relationship connecting the initial and terminal reserves
and the net amount at risk. Dividing equation (4.9) by l_{x+t}, we
obtain

$$({}_tV + P)(1 + i) - \frac{d_{x+t}}{l_{x+t}} = \frac{l_{x+t+1}}{l_{x+t}} \cdot {}_{t+1}V;$$

hence

$$({}_tV + P)(1 + i) - q_{x+t} = p_{x+t} \cdot {}_{t+1}V = (1 - q_{x+t}) \, {}_{t+1}V.$$

Transposing the term $q_{x+t} \cdot {}_{t+1}V$, we find

$$({}_tV + P)(1 + i) - q_{x+t}(1 - {}_{t+1}V) = {}_{t+1}V. \tag{4.13}$$

The term $q_{x+t}(1 - {}_{t+1}V)$ is called the *cost of insurance based upon
the net amount at risk*. A verbal interpretation of equation (4.13)
shows that the terminal reserve at the end of a given year consists of
the difference between the initial reserve, accumulated with interest,
and the cost of insurance based upon the net amount at risk.

After equation (4.13) is solved for the net premium P, we have

$$P = v q_{x+t}(1 - {}_{t+1}V) + (v \cdot {}_{t+1}V - {}_tV). \tag{4.14}$$

Equation (4.14) implies that the net premium P for any policy must
be sufficient to cover (a) the cost of insurance based upon the net
amount at risk, and (b) the difference in the values of the two terminal reserves discounted to the beginning of the year. For most
policies the quantity (a) decreases as t increases, whereas the second quantity (b) increases. The net premium, however, is constant
from year to year. Thus, any endowment policy may be considered,
upon applying equation (4.14), as consisting of two parts: (a) a
term policy upon which the amount of insurance varies from year
to year, being always equal to the net amount at risk for the endowment policy, and (b) a savings fund invested at rate i into
which the balance of the net premium, not needed to purchase the
term policy described in (a), is invested at the beginning of each
year.

4.10   MEAN RESERVE

The term *mean reserve* is applied to the average of the initial and terminal reserves in any policy year. Thus the tth mean reserve is the average of the initial reserve for the tth policy year and the tth terminal reserve, and is equal to

$$\frac{_{t-1}V + P + {_t}V}{2}. \tag{4.15}$$

Life insurance companies are required, by the various state insurance departments, to file at the end of each calendar year a statement showing, in addition to other information, the total reserves on all outstanding policies. For convenience in the preparation of this statement, all policies issued in the same calendar year are assumed to have been issued at the middle of that calendar year (on July 1). This assumption supposes that the policy year begins on July 1 of a calendar year and terminates on the succeeding July 1. Since the date of valuation (December 31) is midway between the beginning and end of the policy year, the reserve used is the average of the initial and terminal reserves, that is, the mean reserve. Thus, in a financial statement as of December 31, 1964, the first mean reserve would be used for all policies issued in 1964, the second mean reserve would be used for all policies issued in 1963, the third mean reserve for all policies issued in 1962, and so on. It should be observed that whenever the difference between the year of valuation and the year of issue is t, the $(t + 1)^{th}$ mean reserve is used.

Exercises

1. An individual aged 20, whose health is impaired, purchases a $1000 ordinary life policy by the payment of net annual premiums which are $5 greater than the normal net premium for that age. (a) If the 3% 1958 CSO first-year terminal reserve for the policy is $8.07, for what rate of mortality does this total net premium provide in the first policy year? (b) If the fifth-year terminal reserve is $42.65, for what rate of mortality does it provide in the fifth policy year?

   Solution.   (a) From Table V we find $1000P_{20} = 9.56$. Dividing this net premium and also the terminal reserve by 1000 to get the corresponding figures for a $1 policy, we find

   $$P_{20} = 0.00956, \quad _1V_{20} = 0.00807.$$

   Inasmuch as the individual is paying a premium of $5 per 1,000 greater than the normal premium, the total net premium on a $1 policy is

   $$P'_{20} = 0.01456.$$

Solving equation (4.13) for the rate of mortality, q_{x+t}, we obtain

$$q_{x+t} = \frac{({}_tV + P)(1 + i) - {}_{t+1}V}{1 - {}_{t+1}V}.$$

Inserting the numerical values in this equation with $t = 0$, we obtain

$$q'_{20} = \frac{(0 + 0.01456)(1.03) - 0.00807}{1 - 0.00807} = 0.00698.$$

(b) Similarly, for the fifth policy year, with $t = 4$, we may write

$$q'_{24} = \frac{(0.03363 + 0.01456)(1.03) - 0.04265}{1 - 0.04265} = 0.00730.$$

2. For a twenty-year endowment policy issued at age 25, compute:
   (a) the first, second, and third terminal reserves;
   (b) the net amount at risk in each of the first three years;
   (c) the cost of insurance based upon the net amount at risk for each of these years, and verify equation (4.13) for $t = 0$, 1, and 2.
3. The sixteenth terminal reserve on an ordinary life policy issued at age 25 for a face amount of $1 is 0.17512. If the net premium is 0.01016, the rate of mortality in the seventeenth year 0.00384, and the interest rate $3\frac{1}{2}$%, find the seventeenth terminal reserve.
4. In some old records you find the net premium and the terminal reserves for the first twenty policy years on a $1000 policy issued at age 20. If the rate of interest is known to be 3%, how much of the mortality table could you reproduce and what would be your method?
5. On a 4% table the tenth and eleventh terminal reserves for a $1000 twenty year endowment policy issued at age 35 are $384.69 and $433.64, respectively. If the rate of mortality at age 45 is 0.01116, find the net premium for the policy.
6. Show that

$$P + d \cdot {}_tV = v \cdot q_{x+t}(1 - {}_tV) + v \cdot p_{x+t}({}_{t+1}V - {}_tV),$$

and give a verbal interpretation of this equation.
7. Given that the net premium and first- and second-year terminal reserves, respectively, on a $1000 twenty-payment life policy issued at age 35 are $24.23, $22.50, and $45.61, find the first and second mean reserves for this policy.
8. A company which uses punched-card equipment finds it convenient to use the following formula to compute mean reserves:

$$_t(MV) = {}_tV \cdot F_{x+t} + G_{x+t},$$

where ${}_tV$ is the tth year terminal reserve for a given policy, and

$$F_{x+t} = \tfrac{1}{2}(1 + v \cdot p_{x+t-1}), \quad \text{and} \quad G_{x+t} = \tfrac{1}{2}v \cdot q_{x+t-1}.$$

Verify the formula.

4.11 NONFORFEITURE VALUES

For a century or more it has been customary for life insurance companies in the United States to grant so called *nonforfeiture values* to policyholders who elect to discontinue their policies. This practice is now a legal requirement in all states. The determination of the equitable amount to pay to a discontinuing policyholder is not a simple matter. If all of the assumptions underlying the computation of the net level premium reserves were to hold in actual fact, it might seem reasonable at first thought to give the policyholder a sum equal to the terminal reserve at the time of surrender. Upon reflection, however, it becomes clear that there are a number of reasons why the reserve might exceed the equitable amount due the policyholder. To illustrate, the withdrawal of a sizable number of policyholders at one time might cause considerable loss to the company because it might require the liquidation of investments at unfavorable prices. Furthermore, since the company would be staffed and otherwise equipped to serve a given number of policyholders, the withdrawal of any significant number might cause a sharp increase in the expense per remaining policyholder. In addition, the bulk of the expense of writing a policy is incurred in the first policy year and, in event of termination of the policy in the early years, these expenses might not have been fully recovered. For these and other important reasons, it would appear that withdrawing policyholders, at least those withdrawing during the earlier years, should be awarded nonforfeiture values which are somewhat less than full reserves.

For many years companies usually computed the nonforfeiture value by decreasing the terminal reserve by a more or less arbitrary amount, called the *surrender charge*. Most of the state laws at that time provided that this charge could not exceed $25 per $1000 of insurance. A few states restricted the surrender charge to 20 per cent of the reserve. Companies differed in their methods of determining the surrender charge; however, it was customary to employ a decreasing scale of charges and to make virtually no surrender charge after a period which varied from five to twenty years, depending upon the company and type of policy.

Because the term *surrender charge* erroneously implies an arbitrary penalty levied against the withdrawing policyholder, the legislatures of most states several years ago adopted a standard non-forfeiture law* prescribing a new minimum for nonforfeiture values which avoided the use of the term. Under this new standard law the mini-

---

*See *Reports and Statements on Nonforfeiture Benefits and Related Matters,* pp. 266–270. National Association of Insurance Commissioners, 1942.

mum amount of nonforfeiture value which may be awarded the discontinuing policyholder is defined as the present value of the
remaining benefits under the policy, valued on a prescribed table of
mortality and rate of interest, decreased by the present value of the
remaining *adjusted premiums*. For a policy providing a level amount
of insurance by means of level annual premiums, the adjusted premium is defined as a level amount such that the present value, at the
inception of the policy, of all adjusted premiums is equal to the sum
of (1) the then present value of all benefits provided by the policy;
(2) 2 per cent of the amount of insurance; (3) 40 per cent of the
smaller of (a) the adjusted premium for the first policy year or (b) 4
per cent of the amount of insurance; and (4) 25 per cent of the smallest of (a) adjusted premium for the first policy year, (b) the adjusted
premium for the first policy year of an ordinary life policy of the
same amount issued at the same age, or (c) 4 per cent of the amount
of insurance.

Reduced to a mathematical formula, the foregoing definition
means that

$$P^A \cdot \ddot{a}_{x:\overline{n}|} = A + .02 + .4 \left\{ \begin{array}{c} P^A \\ \overline{0.04} \end{array} \right\} + .25 \left\{ \begin{array}{c} ^{OL}P^A \\ P^A \\ \overline{0.04} \end{array} \right\} \quad (4.16)$$

where the symbols have the following meanings:

P^A = the adjusted annual premium for the given policy;
A = the value of the policy benefits at date of issue;
$^{OL}P^A$ = the value of the adjusted annual premium for an ordinary
   life policy issued at the same age;
n = the premium paying period, expressed in years.

Furthermore, in each case the smallest of the several quantities in-
side the brackets is to be used in the computation.

The first step in the computation of the adjusted premium for a
given policy is to compute the adjusted premium for an ordinary
life policy at the same age. In this case, assuming for the moment
that $^{OL}P^A$ is less than 0.04, we substitute $^{OL}P^A$ for P^A throughout
(4.16), finding

$$^{OL}P^A \cdot \ddot{a}_x = A_x + .02 + .65 \,^{OL}P^A, \quad (4.17)$$

and thus

$$^{OL}P^A = \frac{A_x + .02}{\ddot{a}_x - .65}. \quad (4.18)$$

For some of the higher ages at issue the value of $^{OL}P^A$ as first computed by (4.18) will exceed 0.04. In such event, 0.04 is used in place of $^{OL}P^A$ in the right member of (4.17) and a new value of $^{OL}P^A$ computed from this equation. In this case, we note that (4.18) becomes

$$_{OL}P^A = \frac{A_x + .02 + .026}{\ddot{a}_x} = \frac{A_x + .046}{\ddot{a}_x}. \tag{4.19}$$

Since the minimum nonforfeiture value is defined as the present value of the remaining benefits under the policy decreased by the present value of the remaining adjusted premiums, the minimum cash value for an ordinary life policy at the end of the tth policy year may now be written

$$_tCV = A_{x+t} - {}^{OL}P^A \cdot \ddot{a}_{x+t}. \tag{4.20}$$

We turn now to the task of determining the numerical value of adjusted premiums for plans of insurance other than ordinary life. Having previously computed the numerical value of $^{OL}P^A$ at the same age at issue from (4.18) or (4.19), as the case may be, it is possible to compare its value with 0.04 and eliminate one of the alternates from the last term of the right number of (4.16).

If we now assume for the moment that P^A is less than both $^{OL}P^A$ and 0.04, we can simplify (4.16) to

$$P^A \cdot \ddot{a}_{x:\overline{n}|} = A + .02 + .65\,P^A$$

or

$$P^A = \frac{A + .02}{\ddot{a}_{x:\overline{n}|} - .65}. \tag{4.21}$$

If the value of P^A computed by (4.21) is greater than the larger of $^{OL}P^A$ and 0.04, this result is discarded and P^A is recomputed using the alternate form of (4.16)

$$P^A \cdot \ddot{a}_{x:\overline{n}|} = A + .02 + .4(0.04) + .25\left\{\begin{array}{c} ^{OL}P^A \\ 0.04 \end{array}\right\},$$

or

$$P^A = \frac{A + .036 + .25\left\{\begin{array}{c} ^{OL}P^A \\ 0.04 \end{array}\right\}}{\ddot{a}_{x:\overline{n}|}}. \tag{4.22}$$

After having determined the value of the adjusted premium P^A, the minimum nonforfeiture value may now be computed in accordance with the definition by subtracting the present value of future

adjusted premiums from the present value of the future benefits to
be provided by the policy.

Exercises

1. Write out the six forms which equation (4.16) may take, depending upon
the relative sizes of P^A, $^{OL}P^A$ and 0.04, and solve each of the equations for
the adjusted premium P^A.
2. (a) Find the minimum nonforfeiture value under the standard nonforfeiture law for a $1000 ordinary life policy issued at age 30 and surrendered
at the end of the third policy year. (b) Compare this value with that obtained by using a surrender charge of $25.
Solution.   (a) The adjusted premium according to (4.18) is found to be

$$1000^{OL}P^A = \frac{1000A_{30} + 20}{\ddot{a}_{30} - 0.65}$$

$$= \frac{316.1858 + 20}{23.47762 - 0.65}$$

$$= 14.72715.$$

Hence, the minimum nonforfeiture value is

$$1,000A_{33} - 1000^{OL}P^A\ddot{a}_{33} = 340.9893 - 14.72715(22.62603)$$
$$= 7.77.$$

(b) At the end of the third year the terminal reserve for this policy is

$$1000_3V_{30} = 1000A_{33} - 1000P_{30} \cdot \ddot{a}_{33}$$
$$= 340.9893 - 13.46754(22.62603)$$
$$= 36.2722.$$

Hence, the amount to be provided after a surrender charge of $25 is
$36.27 − $25.00 = $11.27.
3. (a) Find the minimum nonforfeiture value under the standard nonforfeiture law for a $1000 twenty-payment life policy issued at age 30 and
surrendered at the end of the third policy year. (Note that use may be
made of the value of the ordinary life adjusted premium computed in
Exercise 2.) (b) Compare this value with that obtained by using a surrender charge of $15.
4. (a) Find the minimum nonforfeiture value under the standard nonforfeiture law for a $1000 twenty-year endowment insurance policy issued
at age 30 and surrendered at the end of the third policy year. (Note that
use may be made of the value of the ordinary life adjusted premium computed in Exercise 2.) (b) Compare this value with that obtained by using
a surrender charge of $10.
5. If a trial calculation of the value of $^{OL}P^A$ is made by using equation (4.17)

and found to exceed 0.04, a new value must be calculated using 0.04 in place of $^{OL}p^A$ in the right member of (4.17), leading to equation (4.19). Obviously, this new value for $^{OL}p^A$ will be less than that found in the first trial. Show algebraically that, under these circumstances, the new value found by using (4.19) cannot be less than 0.04.

4.12   NONFORFEITURE OPTIONS

There are usually three options available to the insured when he elects to discontinue premium payments:

1. *Cash value,* an amount payable immediately upon surrender.
2. *Paid-up insurance,* a fully paid policy upon the original plan of insurance for a portion of the original amount.
3. *Extended term insurance,* a fully paid policy for the original amount for a temporary period. In the event the cash value upon an endowment policy is sufficient to purchase extended insurance to the maturity date, the excess, if any, is used to purchase pure endowment payable at the maturity date.

The insurance laws of most of the states provide that these three options shall be actuarial equivalents, that is, they shall have the same value at the date of surrender and that such value shall be not less than the minimum nonforfeiture value defined by the standard nonforfeiture law. Mortality investigations have shown that the mortality experienced under the extended insurance option is higher than that experienced under policies remaining in full force or under the paid-up insurance option. For this reason the standard nonforfeiture law provides that the extended term insurance option may be computed upon a mortality table showing somewhat higher mortality, although many companies do not follow this practice. It is usual for the policy to provide that one of the options, (2) or (3), shall be automatically in effect in the event that the insured makes no choice.

Policies on which a policy loan is in effect, with the cash value serving as collateral for the loan, usually provide that the extended term option be computed on the face value of the policy less the amount of the loan, rather than upon the full face value of the policy. This provides a smaller amount of insurance for a longer period of time, equal in present value to the cash value less the indebtedness. The reason for the deduction is that otherwise the insured would be in a position to increase the risk which the company bears under the terms of the policy. If the insured were in very poor health, for example, he might borrow most of the cash value, and then permit the policy to be placed under the extended term option. Were it not for the restriction cited above, this procedure would result in insurance protection for the full face amount for a short period of time. In event of his death during this period, the company would be obligated to pay the face amount of the policy in addition to the loan proceeds previously paid.

Exercises

1. Determine (a) the amount of paid-up insurance and (b) the length of extended term insurance under the policy surrendered as described in Exercise 2(a) of Section 4.11.

Solution.   (a) The cash value at the end of the third policy year was found to be $7.77. The amount of paid-up insurance is such that its value is equal to the above cash value. Accordingly, if R represents the amount of paid-up insurance,

$$RA_{33} = 0.00777$$

so that

$$R = 0.00777/A_{33}$$

and, employing Table IV, we find

$$R = 22.79.$$

(b) The length of the period of extended term insurance may be found by interpolation in the M_x column of Table III or, alternatively, whenever the period is such that the value of the insurance falls between two tabular values not more than one year apart, by interpolation in Table XI. We will illustrate the former. Thus

$$7.77 = 1000A^1_{33:\overline{n}|} = 1000\frac{M_{33} - M_{33+n}}{D_{33}}.$$

Solving for M_{33+n}, we have

$$M_{33+n} = M_{33} - 0.00777D_{33} = 1,183,232.2.$$

Here, the value of $33 + n$ falls between 36 and 37. Linear interpolation results in a value for $33 + n$ of 36.418 years or 36 years and 153 days. Hence the length of the period of extended term insurance is three years and 153 days.

2. The fifth year cash value for a certain $1000 ten-year endowment insurance policy issued at age 45 is $452.00. Compute the equivalent paid-up and extended term options.

Solution.   (a) *Amount of paid-up endowment insurance at attained age 50, maturing in five years.* From Tables XI and VII, we find

$$1000A_{50:\overline{5}|} = 44.8406 + 820.1799 = 865.0205.$$

Hence the amount of paid-up endowment insurance which the cash value of $452.00 will purchase is

$$\frac{452.00}{0.8650205} = 522.53.$$

(b) *Extended insurance and pure endowment.* The cash value of $452.00 is more than sufficient to purchase extended term insurance for the five years remaining before the policy matures. The excess (using Table XI),

$$452.00 - 1000A^{1}_{50:\overline{5}|} = 452.00 - 44.84$$
$$= 407.16$$

is to be used to purchase pure endowment maturing at the end of five years. The amount of the pure endowment is

$$407.16(1/{}_{5}E_{50}) = (407.16)(1.219245)$$
$$= 496.43.$$

Hence, this second option provides for five years of extended term insurance for the face amount of $1000 together with a pure endowment of $496.43 payable at the end of five years if the insured be then living.

3. Compute the paid-up and extended term options for the third and sixth policy years on a $1000 ordinary life policy issued at age 20. Assume that the cash values are $14.87 and $46.94, respectively.

4. The fifth year cash value for a $1000 fifteen-year endowment insurance policy issued at age 40 is $275.00. Compute the paid-up and extended term options.

5. The tenth year cash value for a $1000 fifteen-year endowment insurance policy issued at age 40 is $610.00. Compute the paid-up and extended term options.

6. (a) Show that the amount of paid-up life insurance purchased by the tth terminal reserve for an ordinary life policy issued at age x is given by

$$1 - \frac{P_x}{P_{x+t}}.$$

(b) Show that the amount of paid-up endowment insurance purchased by the tth terminal reserve for an n year endowment policy issued at age x is given by

$$1 - \frac{P_{x:\overline{n}|}}{P_{x+t:\overline{n-t}|}}.$$

Review Exercises

1. Prove algebraically that the nth initial reserve for an n-year endowment policy, face amount $1, is v, and give a verbal interpretation.

2. Find the terminal reserve of the fifth year on a twenty-year endowment

insurance for $1000 issued at age 20, with premiums payable for ten years.

3. A man now aged 45 has a $1000 twenty-year endowment policy issued at age 30 and on which the terminal reserve is $688.10 at the end of the fifteenth policy year. What will be the terminal reserve at the end of the sixteenth policy year? The net annual premium is $37.7496.

4. Assuming that the cash value equals the policy reserve, show that the amount of paid-up insurance which may be given in event of the surrender, at the end of the tth policy year of an n-payment life policy issued at age x, is given by the expression

$$1 - \frac{{}_n P_x}{{}_{n-t} P_{x+t}}.$$

5. Prove that

$$P_{x+t}(1 - {}_tV_x) = P_x + d \cdot {}_tV_x,$$

and write down a similar relation which will hold for a twenty year endowment policy.

6. Given $P_{30} = 0.01828$; $P_{50} = 0.03636$; and $i = 3\%$, find the numerical value of ${}_{20}V_{30}$.

7. It is proposed that at the end of five years a twenty-payment life policy issued at age x be changed to an endowment policy maturing at age $x + 20$ with future premiums equal to $P_{x:\overline{20}|}$ and that the payment to effect the change be an amount equal to the difference in net premiums accumulated at the valuation rate of interest. Assuming that only net premiums and reserves need to be taken into consideration, discuss this proposal and determine whether it is equitable or inequitable and to what extent.

8. Show that the tth terminal reserve for a policy issued at age x for a face amount of $1, with an annual net premium of π, may be written in the form

$$A_{x+t} - \pi \ddot{a}_{x+t} + \frac{(\pi - P_x)N_x}{D_{x+t}},$$

if t years is less than or equal to the premium payment period.

9. A policy under which $2000 will be paid on death before age 60, and $1000 on death after age 60, is issued at age 30. The net annual premium is payable for twenty years. Find expressions in terms of commutation symbols for the thirty-fifth terminal reserve by both retrospective and prospective methods, and prove them equal.

10. By substituting commutation symbols for each term and simplifying, verify equation (4.10) for each of the following policies:
   (a) ordinary life;
   (b) twenty-year endowment.

CHAPTER 5

Modified
Reserve Systems

5.1 INTRODUCTION

The premiums received by a life insurance company from the policyholder are, as mentioned in a previous chapter, gross premiums
which are intended to provide for the contractual benefits and the
expenses, both direct and indirect, incurred in acquiring and maintaining the policy in force. The gross premium may be considered
as consisting of the net premium, an amount which is expected to
provide the policy benefits under the net premium assumptions, and
an additional charge for expenses, contingencies and profit, called
the *loading*. Under the net level premium reserve system, it is customary for the net premium to be a constant percentage of the gross
premium. The discussion in this chapter will be confined to policies
for which the gross premium is constant year after year and it follows that for such policies the net level premium will also be constant. This implies that the loading too will be constant throughout
the premium payment period.

In the calculation of net level premiums and reserves, two tacit
assumptions have been made: (a) that the whole of the net premium
in each policy year is available and required for the payment of death
claims and the maintenance of reserves, and (b) that the loading in
each policy year is adequate to meet all expenses as they become
payable. Under practical conditions, these assumptions are not
valid. The major expenses incurred by a life insurance company in
selling and issuing a policy must be met in the first policy year, while
the expenses incurred in the *renewal* years (the policy years following the first policy year) are comparatively small. In most cases the
expenses to be paid in the first year will exceed the loading avail-

able under the net level premium basis. As a result under the net level basis the insurance company is unable to pay the entire first year expense out of the first year loading but must draw on its surplus funds to make up the deficiency. This "loan" from the company's surplus is repaid gradually during the subsequent years when the expenses are smaller than the loading available. A new company, however, might conceivably write a sufficiently large amount of new business so as to deplete entirely its surplus account and thereby become technically insolvent. Thus, a requirement to maintain net level premium reserves might severely limit the amount of new business which a company could write and make it difficult for a new company to survive the first few years following organization. On the other hand, such a requirement would have little or no adverse effect on the older, established company with a large surplus in relation to the amount of new business written.

In order to solve these difficulties and for other reasons, the laws of the various states specify minimum legal standards for reserves which are less than the corresponding net level premium reserves during all or part of the premium payment period. This is accomplished by permitting the first year net premium to be less than the net level premium, the difference being adjusted for by providing in subsequent years for renewal net premiums which are greater than the net level premiums. Such a basis for reserves is called a *modified reserve system*. Some of the more important modified reserve systems will be considered in detail in this chapter.

5.2 MODIFIED NET PREMIUMS

It is convenient in the present discussion to consider an m-payment, n-year endowment insurance policy of \$1 issued at age x. By proper choice of the values of m and n this policy may be specialized to most of the common plans of permanent insurance* issued by life insurance companies. Thus, when m is 20 and n is extended to the end of the mortality table, the policy becomes a twenty-payment life policy; when both m and n are extended to the end of the table the policy becomes an ordinary life policy; when both m and n are chosen as 20, the policy becomes a twenty-year endowment insurance, and so forth. The standard notation used to denote the level premium for this m-payment n-year endowment insurance is $_mP_{x:\overline{n}|}$,

*This notation cannot, of course, be specialized to term policies, although similar formulas can be exhibited. It may be noted that modified reserves are seldom used for term policies, hence there will be little loss in generality through the use of the above approach.

but for convenience the subscripts will be dropped and the symbol P will generally be used to indicate the net level annual premium for whatever policy is under consideration.

The period during which the modified net premiums differ from the net level premiums will be designated by the symbol g. If g is less than m, the total number of premiums to be paid, the last m-g premiums will be net level premiums.

Let us assume that the life insurance company sets aside, for the purpose of paying claims and maintaining reserves, an *initial* net premium of α in the first policy year followed by a *renewal* net premium* of β in each succeeding policy year for the remaining portion of the modified period. Then, under the modified system, the sequence of net premiums

$$\alpha, \beta, \beta, \cdots, \beta, P, P, \cdots, P,$$

where there are $g - 1$ premiums of β and $m - g$ premiums of P, replaces the corresponding set of m level premiums

$$P, P, P, \cdots, P, P, P, \cdots, P.$$

It should be noted here that, since in many cases $g = m$, the first sequence above may consist merely of the two sizes of net premiums, an initial premium of α followed by renewal premiums of β.

Since the present value of all net premiums at the inception of the insurance contract equals the present value of all contractual benefits, it is apparent that one may equate the present value of the sequence of modified net premiums to the present value of the sequence of net level premiums, and obtain

$$\alpha + \beta \cdot a_{x:\overline{g-1}|} + P \cdot {}_{g|}\ddot{a}_{x:\overline{m-g}|} = P \cdot \ddot{a}_{x:\overline{m}|}. \tag{5.1}$$

The temporary annuity in the right member of the equation may be broken into two parts, $P\ddot{a}_{x:\overline{g}|} + P \cdot {}_{g|}\ddot{a}_{x:\overline{m-g}|}$, and upon subtracting $P \cdot {}_{g|}\ddot{a}_{x:\overline{m-g}|}$ from both members, we obtain the fundamental relationship connecting modified net premiums with net level premiums

$$\alpha + \beta \cdot a_{x:\overline{g-1}|} = P \cdot \ddot{a}_{x:\overline{g}|} \tag{5.2}$$

By adding and subtracting β, and rearranging terms, we have

$$\beta - P = \frac{\beta - \alpha}{\ddot{a}_{x:\overline{g}|}}, \tag{5.3}$$

another useful form.

*The general symbols, α and β, will be specialized in subsequent sections by the use of superscripts designating the particular modification method considered. Subscripts indicating plan and age at issue may also be used.

Equation (5.2) contains three parameters, α, β, and g. Only two additional conditions relating these parameters need be imposed in order to define a modified reserve method. In subsequent sections we will consider five of the methods which are in use at the present time in the United States or Canada. In each case the two additional conditions defining the method will be presented.

5.3   MODIFIED RESERVES

No new problem presents itself in finding the terminal reserves under a modified system. The basic principles of the retrospective and the prospective methods apply as well in such a case as for net level premium reserves, although the formulas may involve an extra term. Thus, the tth year modified reserve, $(t < g)$, determined retrospectively is

$$_tV' = \alpha \cdot \frac{1}{_tE_x} + \beta \cdot {_{t-1}u_{x+1}} - {_tk_x}. \tag{5.4}$$

Written prospectively, the reserve is

$$_tV' = A_{x+t:\overline{n-t}|} - \beta \cdot \ddot{a}_{x+t:\overline{g-t}|} - P \cdot {_{g-t}|\ddot{a}_{x+t:\overline{m-g}|}}. \tag{5.5}$$

This latter equation may be used to find an expression for the difference at the end of the tth policy year between the net level and modified reserves. Thus, the net level reserve may be expressed as

$$_tV = A_{x+t:\overline{n-t}|} - P \cdot \ddot{a}_{x+t:\overline{m-t}|} = A_{x+t:\overline{n-t}|} -$$

$$P \cdot \ddot{a}_{x+t:\overline{g-t}|} - P \cdot {_{g-t}|\ddot{a}_{x+t:\overline{m-g}|}}.$$

Subtracting (5.5) from the expression for the net level reserve gives us at once

$$_tV - {_tV'} = (\beta - P)\,\ddot{a}_{x+t:\overline{g-t}|}. \tag{5.6}$$

This result may be given a verbal interpretation. It states that at the end of any given year the reserve under the net level system exceeds the modified reserve by the present value of the difference between the net renewal premiums payable in the future under the modified system and the corresponding net level premiums. In other words, it is logical that the modified reserves be less than the net level reserves because under the modified system larger net premiums will be devoted to reserves in the future. The present value of this difference in net premiums is the measure of the difference in reserves.

It is apparent that the larger the difference $\beta - P$, the larger will be the difference between the corresponding terminal reserves. Furthermore, as t increases, the annuity value becomes smaller and, hence, the difference between the net level reserve and the corresponding modified reserve decreases progressively until, finally, at the end of the modified period, when $t = g$, the two reserves are equal.

5.4 LOADING

The diagram below, utilizing a g-year modified period with an m-year premium payment period, is helpful in illustrating the effect of modification upon loading (P' indicates the gross premium):

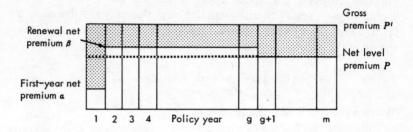

Under the modified system the loading, represented by the shaded area, is ($P' - \alpha$) for the first policy year, ($P' - \beta$) for each renewal year during the modified period, and ($P' - P$) from the end of the modified period to the end of the premium payment period, while under the net level system the loading is ($P' - P$) for every year. Subtracting both members of equation (5.1) from $P' \cdot \ddot{a}_{x:\overline{m}|}$, we find

$$(P' - \alpha) + (P' - \beta)a_{x:\overline{g-1}|} + (P' - P) \cdot {}_{g|}\ddot{a}_{x:\overline{m-g}|} = (P' - P)\ddot{a}_{x:\overline{m}|}.$$

A verbal interpretation of this equation shows that the present value of the loading under the two systems is precisely the same. Thus, in a sense, modification of net premiums means that a part of the loading available in the renewal years under the net level system is borrowed for additional expense in the first year, thereby reducing the loading available in renewal years. In the modified system, the excess of first year loading over renewal year loading is

$$(P' - \alpha) - (P' - \beta) = \beta - \alpha.$$

It should be noted that a modification of premiums and reserves is employed solely for the purpose of providing for relatively large preliminary expenses in the first policy year, and does not in any way affect the yearly amount of gross premium actually paid to the company by the policyholder. The modification is purely an internal transaction of the life insurance company, which releases a larger part of the gross premium for expenses in the first year and defers to a later date the setting up of a part of the reserve.

Exercises

1. From equations (5.3) and (5.6), show that the difference between net level and modified tth year terminal reserves may be written as

$$_tV - _tV' = (\beta - \alpha)\frac{\ddot{a}_{x+t:\overline{g-t}|}}{\ddot{a}_{x:\overline{g}|}}.$$

2. (a) For a $1000 twenty payment life policy issued at age 30, compute the value of β, if α has a value of $10.00 with a modification period of twenty years.

(b) For the policy in (a), what is the excess of the net level reserve over the modified reserve at the end of the tenth policy year?

Solution.   (a) Solving equation (5.2) for β, we obtain

$$\frac{1000\,_{20}P_{30} \cdot \ddot{a}_{30:\overline{20}|} - \alpha}{\ddot{a}_{30:\overline{20}|} - 1} = \frac{1000A_{30} - 10}{\ddot{a}_{30:\overline{20}|} - 1} = \frac{316.1858 - 10}{14.95309 - 1} = \$21.9439.$$

(b) From exercise 1 we obtain immediately

$$_{10}V - _{10}V' = (21.9439 - 10)\frac{\ddot{a}_{..:\overline{10}|}}{\ddot{a}_{30:\overline{20}|}} = \$6.89.$$

3. (a) For a $1000 twenty year endowment policy issued at age 30, compute the value of $(\beta - \alpha)$, if β is $1.25 more than the net level premium and g has a value of 20.

(b) For the policy in (a), what is the excess of the net level reserve over the modified reserve at the end of the tenth policy year?

4. For a $1000 fifteen year endowment policy issued at age 30, the difference between the renewal net premium and the first year net premium is $40.00. Compute the values of α and β and also the tenth modified reserve.

5. Prove that equations (5.4) and (5.5) give identical values for the reserves on an m payment n year endowment policy.

6. Show that if $g = n$, the tth year modified terminal reserve on an n-year endowment insurance policy may be written as

$$_tV' = 1 - (\beta + d)\ddot{a}_{x+t:\overline{n-t}|}.$$

5.5   LEGAL RESERVE STANDARDS

As has been mentioned previously, the laws of the various states and of the Dominion of Canada prescribe minimum reserve standards. The basic reason for this interest in reserve standards on the part of the various governments is to protect the solvency of the company. A secondary reason is to discourage the extravagance which could conceivably result if a company were free to devote as much of the early premiums as it wished for the purpose of paying acquisition expenses. Accordingly, valuation standards have been enacted into law which define the modified reserve methods which may be used for various classes of policies. Such standards usually provide that alternative methods may also be used if they result in higher reserves than the prescribed minimums.

Before discussing these valuation standards in detail, it is necessary to consider several special ways of modifying reserves which result from particular choices of the defining relationships mentioned in Section 5.2.

5.6 FULL PRELIMINARY TERM METHOD

The full preliminary term method (often abbreviated to FPT) was devised in the last century by the Swiss actuary Zillmer and is sometimes called by his name. The defining relationships are very simple:

$$\alpha^F = c_x \quad \text{and} \quad g = m.$$

The theory of the full preliminary term method is that the initial net premium is set as low as possible without producing a negative first year terminal reserve. Thus, if we set

$$_1V^F = 0,$$

we find from (5.4)

$$_1V^F = \alpha^F \cdot {_1u_x} - {_1k_x} = 0,$$

or

$$\alpha^F = \frac{k_x}{u_x} = \frac{C_x}{D_x} = c_x. \tag{5.7}$$

The modified period extends over the entire premium payment period. In the case of ordinary life policies, this means that the modified reserves are less than the corresponding net level reserves except at the end of the mortality table. Thus the sequence of net level premiums $P, P, P, P, \ldots$ is replaced by the sequence of modified premiums $c_x, \beta^F, \beta^F, \beta^F, \ldots$. Equating the present values of the sequences of modified and net level premiums, respectively, we obtain

$$c_x + \beta^F \cdot a_{x:\overline{m-1}|} = P \cdot \ddot{a}_{x:\overline{m}|},$$

which might also be obtained by specializing equation (5.2). Since the value of the net level premium P is determined by the equation

$$P \cdot \ddot{a}_{x:\overline{m}|} = A_{x:\overline{m}|},$$

it follows that

$$c_x + \beta^F \cdot a_{x:\overline{m-1}|} = A_{x:\overline{m}|},$$

or, solving for β^F we find

$$\beta^F = \frac{A_{x:\overline{n}|} - c_x}{a_{x:\overline{m-1}|}} = \frac{{}_1|A_{x:\overline{n-1}|}}{{}_1|\ddot{a}_{x:\overline{m-1}|}}$$

whence

$$\beta^F = {}_{m-1}P_{x+1:\overline{n-1}|}. \tag{5.8}$$

A verbal interpretation of equation (5.8) shows that the renewal net premium under the full preliminary term system for a given policy is equal to the net level premium for a similar policy issued one year later at an age one year higher, with premiums payable for a year less than the original premium payment period, and with the maturity of the policy at the same date as the original policy. This is reasonable since, under this modification, the initial net premium pays for the first year death claims only, leaving the continuing policyholder in the same position as if he had merely waited one year and had then taken out a new policy which required the usual net level premium for the attained age at that time.

Upon substituting the value of β^F, given in equation (5.8), into equation (5.5), we see that

$${}_tV^F = A_{x+t:\overline{n-t}|} - {}_{m-1}P_{x+1:\overline{n-1}|}\,\ddot{a}_{x+t:\overline{m-t}|},$$

or

$${}_tV^F = {}_{t-1}^{m-1}V_{x+1:\overline{n-1}|}, \quad \text{for } 1 \leq t \leq m. \tag{5.9}$$

Thus, under the full preliminary term system the terminal reserve on a given policy at the end of the first year is zero, and, in general, the tth terminal full preliminary term reserve is the $(t-1)$th net level reserve for a policy issued at an age one year higher, with premiums payable for a year less than the original premium payment period and with the maturity of the policy at the same date as the original policy.

Equation (5.9) can also be derived by setting $\alpha^F = c_x$ in equation (5.4). Doing so, we find

$$_tV^F = c_x\frac{1}{_tE_x} + \beta^F \cdot {_{t-1}}u_{x+1} - {_t}k_x,$$

which can be written in the form

$$_tV^F = \beta^F \cdot {_{t-1}}u_{x+1} - {_{t-1}}k_{x+1} = {_{t-1}^{m-1}}V_{x+1:\overline{n-1}|},$$

since

$$_tk_x = {_{t-1}}k_{x+1} + \frac{c_x}{_tE_x}; \qquad \beta^F = {_{m-1}}P_{x+1:\overline{n-1}|}.$$

It has been shown, by considering both net premiums and reserves, that the full preliminary term method implies that every policy is considered as a combination of two policies: (a) a one year term policy issued at the original age at issue x, for which the net premium is c_x and the first terminal reserve is zero, and (b), a level premium policy issued at an age one year higher, $x + 1$, providing for the balance of the benefits in the original policy, with premiums payable for the balance of the original premium payment period.

For the purpose of determining the net premiums and reserves, an ordinary life policy is considered under the full preliminary term system as a combination of a one-year term policy followed by a net level ordinary life policy issued at the next age; a twenty-year endowment policy is considered as a one-year term policy followed by a net level nineteen-year endowment policy at the next age; a twenty-payment life policy is considered as a one-year term policy followed by a net level nineteen-payment life policy; and a twenty-payment thirty-year-endowment policy is considered as a one-year term policy followed by a net level nineteen-payment twenty-nine-year-endowment.

It should be noted that after the expiration of the premium payment period the full preliminary term reserves are precisely those found by the net level premium system.

Exercises

1. Compute by the prospective method the terminal reserve at the end of the fifth policy year for each of the following $1000 policies issued at age 35, using the full preliminary term system: (a) ordinary life; (b) twenty payment life.
2. Same as problem (1) using the retrospective method.
3. Compute the net level premium, the first year and renewal FPT pre-

miums, and the fifth net level and fifth FPT terminal reserves for a $1000 ten year endowment policy issued at age 35.

4. Show that the tth terminal reserve for an ordinary life policy modified by the full preliminary term method may be expressed in the form

$$_tV^F = 1 - \frac{\ddot{a}_{x+t}}{\ddot{a}_{x+1}}, \qquad \text{for } t \geq 1.$$

5. (a) Show that the tth terminal reserve for an n-year endowment policy modified by the full preliminary term method may be expressed in the form

$$_tV^F = 1 - \frac{\ddot{a}_{x+t:\overline{n-t}|}}{\ddot{a}_{x+1:\overline{n-1}|}}, \qquad \text{for } 1 \leq t \leq n.$$

(b) Use the equation of (a) to compute all of the full preliminary term reserves for a $1000 five-year endowment policy issued at age 25.

6. A certain ten payment endowment insurance policy issued at age 30 provides for $2000 in event of death during the first twenty policy years and $1000 in cash if the insured survives the twenty years. Using the full preliminary term modification, compute
(a) the values of α^F and β^F,
(b) the fifth terminal reserve by both prospective and retrospective methods.

5.7   DISADVANTAGES OF THE FULL PRELIMINARY TERM SYSTEM

In the full preliminary term system it is assumed that the whole of the first year's gross premium is used in paying expenses and death claims, and that no reserve need be set up at the end of that year. For an ordinary life policy issued at all but the older ages the amount of loading released appears to be equitable, that is, it approximates the expense the life insurance company actually incurs in issuing the policy. Furthermore, the reduction in loading in the renewal years of the policy is not large and therefore does not materially reduce the expense allowance in the years following the first year.

However, further consideration of other plans of insurance and other ages at issue will show that the full preliminary term method of valuation is unsatisfactory in certain cases. For policies with relatively high premiums, such as short term endowment policies, the amount released for expense in the first year is far in excess of the amount actually required, and the application of the full preliminary term system to these policies might lead to extravagance on the part of the company. Furthermore, the increase in the net premium required for the renewal years of these policies is relatively large, and materially reduces the loading available for expense in these years.

These considerations have led, in many states, to the adoption of statutes permitting the use of the full preliminary term system for policies having relatively low premiums, while for higher premium plans other modifications are required. These are considered in subsequent sections.

5.8   NEW JERSEY METHOD

The New Jersey method resembles the full preliminary term method very closely, differing only in the requirement that the modified period be twenty years in all cases. It is obvious from this requirement that the method can be applied only to policies with premium payment periods of twenty years or more. Thus, the criteria are:

$$\alpha^J = c_x, \quad \text{and} \quad g = 20; \quad (m \geqq 20). \quad (5.10)$$

Substituting these values in equation (5.2), we have

$$c_x + \beta^J a_{x:\overline{19}|} = P \cdot \ddot{a}_{x:\overline{20}|}.$$

Solving this equation for β^J, we obtain

$$\beta^J = \frac{P \cdot \ddot{a}_{x:\overline{20}|} - c_x}{a_{x:\overline{19}|}},$$

and, since

$$\ddot{a}_{x:\overline{20}|} = 1 + a_{x:\overline{19}|},$$

it follows that

$$\beta^J = P + \frac{P - c_x}{a_{x:\overline{19}|}}. \quad (5.11)$$

It is clear that the first year terminal reserve is zero and that the terminal reserves for the twentieth and later years are identical with the net level reserves. Hence, it is of interest here only to consider the reserves for the second to the nineteenth year, inclusive. For the retrospective reserve we substitute in (5.4) and find

$$_tV^J = c_x \cdot \frac{1}{_tE_x} + \beta^J \cdot {}_{t-1}u_{x+1} - {}_tk_x, \quad (1 \leqq t \leqq 19). \quad (5.12)$$

Prospectively, we have

$$_tV^J = A_{x+t:\overline{n-t}|} - \beta^J \ddot{a}_{x+t:\overline{20-t}|} - P \cdot {}_{20-t|}\ddot{a}_{x+t:\overline{m-t}|}. \quad (5.13)$$

From equation (5.6), writing β_J for β and 20 for g, we have

$$_tV - {_tV}^{\,J} = (\beta^J - P)\ddot{a}_{x+t:\overline{20-t}|}.$$

Then, substituting the value of β^J obtained from equation (5.11), we have

$$_tV - {_tV}^{\,J} = (P - c_x)\frac{\ddot{a}_{x+t:\overline{20-t}|}}{a_{x:\overline{19}|}}.$$

Exercises

1. Find the initial and renewal net premiums under the New Jersey method for a $1000 ordinary life policy issued at age 28. Calculate the tenth terminal reserve both retrospectively and prospectively.

   Solution. From Table V we find $1000\,P_{28} = 12.52665$, $1000\,c_{28} = 1.97083 = \alpha^J$, and $1000\,(P_{28} - c_{28}) = 10.55582$. Substituting these values in equation (5.11) yields

   $$1000\,\beta^J = 12.52665 + \frac{10.55582}{13.990036} = 13.28117.$$

   The retrospective terminal reserve is

   $$1000\ {_{10}V}^{\,J} = 1.97083\,\frac{1}{{_{10}E_{28}}} + 13.28117\ {_9u_{29}} - 1000\ {_{10}k_{28}}$$
   $$= 2.71128 + 140.77824 - 26.90179 = 116.588.$$

   The prospective terminal reserve is

   $$1000\ {_{10}V}^{\,J} = 1000\,A_{38} - 13.28117\ddot{a}_{38:\overline{10}|} - 12.52665\ {_{10}|\ddot{a}_{38}}$$
   $$= 386.8264 - 114.83313 - 155.40537 = 116.588.$$

2. Find the net premiums and the fifth year terminal reserve for a $1000 thirty-year endowment policy issued at age 50 and modified under the New Jersey method.

3. A $1000 endowment insurance at age 60 is issued at age 20. Find the net premiums and the tenth terminal reserve under the New Jersey method.

4. A $1000 endowment at age 85 policy is issued at age 40. Find the net premiums and the fifth terminal reserve under the New Jersey method.

5. For a policy valued under the New Jersey method, show that

$$\beta^J = P + \frac{\beta^J - c_x}{\ddot{a}_{x:\overline{20}|}}.$$

6. Find the net premiums and the fifteenth and twenty-fifth terminal reserves under a $1000 endowment at age 65 policy issued at age 30 if the policy is valued under the New Jersey method.

7. Use Fackler's accumulation formula to compute the sixteenth to the

twentieth terminal reserves, inclusive, for a $1000 thirty-payment life policy issued at age 33 under (a) the New Jersey method; (b) the full net level method.

5.9   COMMISSIONERS METHOD

The Commissioners Reserve Valuation Method, often referred to simply by the initials CRVM, defines legal reserves required for new policies in most states. Strictly speaking, in spite of the use of the word *method* in the name, it is a reserve *standard* in that it not only defines a method for modifying reserves but also indicates the policy forms to which the method is to be applied. Thus, the CRVM prescribes the full preliminary term method for a policy whose renewal net premium under the FPT modification is less than or equal to the FPT renewal net premium for a twenty-payment life policy issued at the same age. For every other policy—that is for every policy whose FPT net renewal premium is greater than the FPT renewal net premium for a twenty-payment life policy issued at the same age, a different method, which we will refer to simply as the *Commissioners method,* is prescribed.

The Commissioners method is defined by the following relationships:

$$\beta^{\text{Com}} - \alpha^{\text{Com}} = {}_{19}P_{x+1} - c_x \qquad \text{and} \qquad g = m. \qquad (5.14)$$

It will be noted from the definition that, regardless of the plan of insurance under consideration, the difference $\beta^{\text{Com}} - \alpha^{\text{Com}}$ for any given policy and age at issue is equal to the difference between the net premium for a 19-payment life policy issued at an age one year greater and the one-year term net premium issued at the original age. For certain policies having relatively small net premiums, the application of this method would produce a value for α^{Com} which is less than the natural premium c_x. For such a policy, it is apparent that the Commissioners method is not suitable, and the legal description of the reserve standard prevents any attempt to use the Commissioners method in such a case by prescribing the use of full preliminary term.

The expression for the net renewal premium, β^{Com}, is obtained readily from equation (5.3) by substituting the specific net premiums, α^{Com} and β^{Com}, respectively, for α and β and making use of the defining relationships from equation (5.14). Thus, ${}_{19}P_{x+1} - c_x$ replaces $\beta^{\text{Com}} - \alpha^{\text{Com}}$ and m replaces g. After transposing P, we have the expression for β^{Com}

$$\beta^{\text{Com}} = P + \frac{{}_{19}P_{x+1} - c_x}{\ddot{a}_{x:\overline{m}|}}. \qquad (5.15)$$

It would be a simple algebraic exercise to determine an expression for α^{Com} from equations (5.14) and (5.15). However, in practice, the value of α^{Com} is found readily by subtracting the value of the quantity $(_{19}P_{x+1} - c_x)$ from the value of β^{Com} determined first from equation (5.15). Numerical values of the difference $(_{19}P_{x+1} - c_x)$ are given in Table V.

The numerical values of α^{Com} and β^{Com} and the values of the other functions may then be substituted in the equations for the retrospective and prospective terminal reserves, (5.4) and (5.5), given previously. When the reserves are to be computed sequentially, Fackler's accumulation formula may be applied directly.

Exercises

1. For a $1000 fifteen-year endowment policy issued at age 35 and modified on the Commissioners method, compute:
   - (a) the first year and renewal net premiums;
   - (b) the tenth terminal reserve by the prospective method;
   - (c) the tenth terminal reserve by the retrospective method.

   Solution. (a) The net level premium may be calculated by means of the identity

$$1000P_{35:\overline{15|}} = 1000\left(\frac{1}{\ddot{a}_{35:\overline{15|}}} - d\right) = \frac{1000}{12.02466} - 29.12621$$

$$= 54.03622. \qquad\qquad \text{(Table IX)}$$

   Substituting the value of

$$\beta^{\text{Com}} - \alpha^{\text{Com}} = 1000(_{19}P_{36} - c_{35}) = 23.36687$$

   obtained from Table V into equation (5.15), we obtain

$$\beta^{\text{Com}} = 54.03622 + \frac{23.36687}{12.02466} = 55.97947.$$

   The value of α^{Com} obtained from equation (5.14) is

$$\alpha^{\text{Com}} = 55.97947 - 23.36687 = 32.61260.$$

   (b) Applying the prospective formula (5.5), we have, by Tables XI, VII, and XIII.

$$_{10}V^{\text{Com}} = 1000A_{45:\overline{5|}} - \beta^{\text{Com}}\ddot{a}_{45:\overline{5|}}$$
$$= (28.87957 + 835.27936) - 55.97947(4.663877) = 603.078.$$

   (c) Similarly, the retrospective formula (5.4) yields, by Tables XII, VIII, and XIII,

$$_{10}V^{\text{Com}} = \alpha^{\text{Com}} \frac{1}{_{10}E_{35}} + \beta^{\text{Com}}\,_9u_{36} - 1000\,_{10}k_{35}$$
$$= 32.61260(1.3921554) + 55.97947(10.684165) - 40.41795$$
$$= 603.078.$$

2. Show that the net renewal premium for an m-payment n-year endowment policy modified on the Commissioners method may be expressed in the form

$$\beta^{\text{Com}} = \frac{A_{x:\overline{n}|} + (_{19}P_{x+1} - c_x)}{\ddot{a}_{x:\overline{m}|}}.$$

3. Compute the first year and renewal net premiums under the Commissioners method for each of the following $1000 policies issued at age 30: (a) ten-payment twenty-year endowment; (b) ten-payment life; (c) fifteen-payment life.

4. If $\ddot{a}'_{x:\overline{m}|}$ denotes the fraction

$$\frac{\ddot{a}_{x:\overline{m}|}}{1 + _{19}P_{x+1} - c_x},$$

show that for an n-year endowment policy modified on the Commissioners method,

(a)　　$\beta^{\text{Com}} = \dfrac{1}{\ddot{a}'_{x:\overline{m}|}} - d;$　　　(b)　　$_tV^{\text{Com}} = 1 - \dfrac{\ddot{a}_{x+t:\overline{n-t}|}}{\ddot{a}'_{x:\overline{n}|}}.$

5. Using the equations of Exercise 4, compute the modified reserves for the fifth to tenth years, inclusive, for a $1000 ten-year endowment policy issued at age 25.

6. Use Fackler's accumulation formula to compute all of the reserves on the Commissioners method for a $1000 ten-year endowment policy issued at age 25.

7. Find the initial and renewal net premiums and the fifteenth and twenty-fifth terminal reserves modified on the Commissioners method for a $1000 thirty-year endowment policy issued at age 25.

5.10　ILLINOIS METHOD

The Illinois method is identical with the Commissioners method except for policies with premiums payable for more than twenty years. The difference in the latter case arises because the Illinois method limits the modification period to twenty years. The defining relationships are

$$\beta^{\text{I}} - \alpha^{\text{I}} = _{19}P_{x+1} - c_x \quad \text{and} \quad g = m \text{ or } 20, \text{ whichever is smaller.}$$
$$(5.16)$$

Similar to the Commissioners method, the use of the Illinois method is restricted to policies for which the FPT renewal net premium exceeds the FPT renewal net premium for a twenty-payment life policy issued at the same age.

Because of the fact that the Commissioners and Illinois methods are identical for policies with twenty premiums or less, the following discussion will be confined to the case of policies with more than twenty premiums payable. Starting with equation (5.2), we substitute 20 for g and then proceed in the same manner as in the previous section when equation (5.15) was developed. The result is

$$\beta^{\mathrm{I}} = P + \frac{{}_{19}P_{x+1} - c_x}{\ddot{a}_{x:\overline{20}|}}, \qquad (m > 20). \qquad (5.17)$$

As in the case of the Commissioners method, we find the numerical value of α^{I} by the use of the first relationship of (5.16), that is, by subtracting the value of $({}_{19}P_{x+1} - c_x)$ from the value of β^{I} found from (5.17).

The numerical values of α^{I} and β^{I} and the values of the other given functions may then be substituted in the equations for the retrospective and prospective reserves, (5.4) and (5.5), given previously. When the reserves are to be computed sequentially, Fackler's accumulation formula may be applied directly.

It is interesting to compare the Illinois method with the Commissioners method in the area where the methods differ, that is, in the case of policies with premium payment periods of more than twenty years. By comparing expressions (5.17) and (5.15), it is apparent that for $m > 20$

$$\beta^{\mathrm{I}} > \beta^{\mathrm{Com}},$$

and hence

$$\alpha^{\mathrm{I}} > \alpha^{\mathrm{Com}}.$$

If we now write expressions for the two modified reserves in a manner similar to (5.4), we find for $t < 20$

$$_{t}V^{\mathrm{I}} = \alpha^{\mathrm{I}} \cdot \frac{1}{_{t}E_x} + \beta^{\mathrm{I}} \cdot {}_{t-1}u_{x+1} - {}_{t}k_x$$

$$_{t}V^{\mathrm{Com}} = \alpha^{\mathrm{Com}} \cdot \frac{1}{_{t}E_x} + \beta^{\mathrm{Com}} \cdot {}_{t-1}u_{x+1} - {}_{t}k_x,$$

and, upon subtracting, find

$$_tV^I - {}_tV^{Com} = (\alpha^I - \alpha^{Com})\frac{1}{{}_tE_x} + (\beta^I - \beta^{Com})\,{}_{t-1}u_{x+1}$$

from which it follows that for $t < 20$

$$_tV^I > {}_tV^{Com}.$$

For policy years beginning with the twentieth, the Illinois method reserves are identical with net level reserves, and hence exceed the corresponding Commissioners reserves at these durations also. Thus, for policies with premium payment periods of more than twenty years, reserves computed by the Illinois method exceed the corresponding Commissioners reserves throughout the premium payment period.

Exercises

1. For a $1000 twenty-five-year endowment policy issued at age 20 and modified on the Illinois method, compute:
   (a) the three net premiums α^I, β^I, and P;
   (b) the tenth terminal reserve by the retrospective method;
   (c) the twenty-third terminal reserve by the prospective method.
2. A twenty-payment policy issued at age 40 provides for $1000 of insurance for thirty years and an $800 pure endowment at the end of this period. Using the Illinois method, find:
   (a) the first year and renewal net premiums;
   (b) the tenth terminal reserve by both the retrospective and prospective methods.
3. Find the initial and renewal net premiums and the fifteenth and twenty-fifth terminal reserves for a $1000 thirty-year endowment insurance policy issued at age 25 under (a) the Illinois method; (b) the net level method. Compare with the answers for Exercise 7, Section 5.9.
4. Show that the net renewal premium for an m-payment n-year endowment policy $(20 < m \le n)$ under the Illinois method may be expressed as

$$\beta^I = \frac{A_{x:\overline{n}|} - {}_mP_{x:\overline{n}|} \cdot {}_{20|}\ddot{a}_{x:\overline{m-20}|} + (_{19}P_{x+1} - c_x)}{\ddot{a}_{x:\overline{20}|}}$$

5. Find the initial and renewal net premiums and the twentieth terminal reserve for a $1000 life paid up at 65 policy issued at age 46 and valued on the Illinois method.

6. Use Fackler's accumulation formula to compute the last five terminal reserves for a $1000 endowment at age 65 policy issued at age 43 under
   (a) the Illinois method; (b) the net level method.

5.11   CANADIAN METHOD

The Canadian method may be defined by equating the difference
between the net level premium and the initial modified premium to
the difference between the net level premium for an ordinary life
policy issued at the same age and the natural premium at that age.
The modified period extends over the entire premium payment period. Thus, the defining relationships are

$$P - \alpha^{\text{Can}} = P_x - c_x, \quad \text{and} \quad g = m. \tag{5.18}$$

The value of α^{Can} may be found at once by simple transposition,
and we have

$$\alpha^{\text{Can}} = P - (P_x - c_x). \tag{5.19}$$

To find the net renewal premium, we revert to the fundamental
equation (5.2) with the appropriate modification superscripts at-
tached to α and β and with g replacing m. Thus

$$\alpha^{\text{Can}} + \beta^{\text{Can}} \cdot a_{x:\overline{m-1}|} = P\ddot{a}_{x:\overline{m}|}.$$

Substituting the value of α^{Can} from equation (5.19), we have

$$\beta^{\text{Can}} = \frac{P\ddot{a}_{x:\overline{m}|} - \alpha^{\text{Can}}}{a_{x:\overline{m-1}|}}$$

$$= \frac{P\ddot{a}_{x:\overline{m}|} - P + (P_x - c_x)}{a_{x:\overline{m-1}|}},$$

and

$$\beta^{\text{Can}} = P + \frac{P_x - c_x}{a_{x:\overline{m-1}|}}. \tag{5.20}$$

As in the case of the other modified methods, the terminal
reserves may be found by substituting the numerical values of α^{Can}
and β^{Can} in the equations for the retrospective and prospective reserves, (5.4) and (5.5). When the reserves are to be computed
sequentially, Fackler's accumulation formula may be applied
directly.

Exercises

1. Find the initial and renewal net premiums under both the net level and the Canadian methods of valuation for the following policies issued at age 30: (a) ordinary life; (b) twenty-payment life; (c) thirty-payment life.
2. Find the fifth and twentieth year terminal reserves under the net level and Canadian methods for the policies described in Exercise 1.
3. Show that the difference between the tth year terminal reserves for an m payment n-year endowment policy under the net level and Canadian methods, ${}_{t}^{m}V_{x:\overline{n}|} - {}_{t}^{m}V_{x:\overline{n}|}^{Can}$, is given by the following expression:

$$\left(\frac{P_x - c_x}{a_{x:\overline{m-1}|}}\right) \ddot{a}_{x+t:\overline{m-t}|}.$$

4. Express in commutation symbols both the retrospective and prospective t^{th} year terminal reserves for an n-payment life policy on the Canadian method and prove that they are equal.
5. Find under the Canadian method the first year and renewal net premiums and the fifteenth and twenty-fifth year terminal reserves for the policy described in Exercise 7, Section 5.9 and Exercise 3, Section 5.10. Compare the results under all four of the methods employed in these three exercises.
6. Using the Canadian method, find the initial and renewal net premiums and the tenth terminal reserve for a twenty-payment policy issued at age 35 which provides for $1000 of insurance for 30 years and an $800 pure endowment at the end of this period.
7. Use Fackler's accumulation formula to compute the last five terminal reserves for a $1000 endowment at age 65 policy issued at age 43 under the Canadian method.

5.12   SUMMARY

For purposes of comparison, various characteristics of the five principal reserve modification methods are shown in tabular form on an adjacent page.

5.13   OTHER PROPERTIES OF MODIFIED SYSTEMS

It is readily apparent upon inspection of the table in Section 5.12 that in the case of the Commissioners, Illinois, and Canadian methods the difference between the net renewal premium β and the net level premium P for any given age is a function of the number of annual premiums in the modified period, but is completely independent of the policy plan, that is, of the type or duration of the

SUMMARY OF THE ESSENTIAL CHARACTERISTICS OF VARIOUS MODIFICATION METHODS

Modified Method (illustrations based on m-payment n-year endowment)	Defining Relationships		Modified Net Premiums		Additional First Year Expense Allowance Depends Upon[a]	Decrease in Renewal Expense Allowance Depends Upon[b]	Method Can Be Applied to Policies
	Modified period	Other relationship	Initial	Renewal			
Full preliminary term	Premium payment period	$\alpha^F = c_x$	c_x	$_{m-1}P_{x+1:\overline{n-1}|}$	Plan and age	Plan and age	Without restriction
New Jersey method	Twenty Years	$\alpha^J = c_x$	c_x	$P + \dfrac{P - c_x}{a_{x:\overline{19}|}}$	Plan and age	Plan and age	With more than twenty premiums
Commissioners method and Illinois method (for policies with less than 20 premiums)	Premium payment period	$\beta^{Com} - \alpha^{Com}$ $= \,_{19}P_{x+1} - c_x$	$\beta^{Com} -$ $(_{19}P_{x+1} - c_x)$	$P +$ $\dfrac{_{19}P_{x+1} - c_x}{\ddot{a}_{x:\overline{m}|}}$	Plan and age	Premium-payment period and age	With net premiums greater than corresponding twenty-payment life premiums (on FPT basis)
Illinois method (for policies with 20 or more premiums payable)	Twenty Years	$\beta^I - \alpha^I$ $= \,_{19}P_{x+1} - c_x$	$\beta^I -$ $(_{19}P_{x+1} - c_x)$	$P +$ $\dfrac{_{19}P_{x+1} - c_x}{\ddot{a}_{x:\overline{20}|}}$	Plan and age	Age only	Same as Commissioners
Canadian method	Premium payment period	$P - \alpha^{Can}$ $= P_x - c_x$	$P -$ $(P_x - c_x)$	$P +$ $\dfrac{P_x - c_x}{a_{x:\overline{m-1}|}}$	Age only	Premium-payment period and age	With net level premiums greater than corresponding ordinary life net premium

[a] The expression *Additional First Year Expense* is used to describe the difference between the net level premium and the first year modified net premium, that is, $P - \alpha$.

[b] The expression *Decrease in Renewal Expense Allowance* is used to describe the difference between the renewal modified net premium and the renewal net level premium, that is $\beta - P$.

benefits. For example, $\beta - P$ is the same for all twenty-payment policies issued at a given age x, whether the benefit provided is whole life or endowment insurance.

It follows from the above property that a similar one exists for the terminal reserves of policies valued on the Commissioners, Illinois, or Canadian methods. The difference between the net level and the modified reserves at a given duration t is a function of the age at issue x and the length of the modified period but is completely independent of the policy plan. Thus, for example, the difference is the same for the tenth year terminal reserves on a twenty-year endowment policy, a twenty-payment life policy, and a twenty-payment thirty-year endowment policy, if all policies are issued at the same age. Recognition of this property has obvious advantages in the computation of net premiums and reserves for an entire portfolio of policies.

The above statements may be demonstrated algebraically. Consider any policy with g modified premiums and issued at age x. The net level reserve (where $_tA$ represents the present value of the benefits at duration t when the insured has reached age $x + t$) is

$$_tV = {_tA} - P \cdot \ddot{a}_{x+t:\overline{g-t}|} - P \cdot {_{g-t}|}\ddot{a}_{x+t:\overline{m-g}|}$$

while the modified reserve is

$$_tV' = {_tA} - \beta \cdot \ddot{a}_{x+t:\overline{g-t}|} - P \cdot {_{g-t}|}\ddot{a}_{x+t:\overline{m-g}|}$$

Subtracting, we have

$$_tV - {_tV'} = (\beta - P)\ddot{a}_{x+t:\overline{g-t}|}.$$

The difference $\beta - P$ is independent of policy form for the three modifications under discussion here. Hence the difference in reserves is likewise independent of the type or duration of the benefits of the policy.

5.14 LEGAL RESERVE STANDARDS IN COMMON USE

As previously mentioned, legal standards for reserves divide policies into classes and prescribe the minimum reserves which may be held for each class by specifying the modified reserve method to be used. A company is permitted, of course, to use a reserve method which will produce higher reserves than the specified legal minimum.

A. *Commissioners Standard.* This legal reserve standard, in effect

in practically all states for policies issued since 1947, divides policies
into two classes:

1. Policies with net renewal premiums under the full preliminary term method which are equal to or less than the net level premium for a 19-payment whole life policy issued at the next age;

2. Policies with net renewal premiums under the full preliminary term method which are greater than the net level premium for
a 19-payment whole life policy issued at the next age.

The minimum reserve permitted for a policy in group (1) is that produced by the full preliminary term method, whereas the minimum
for a policy in group (2) is the reserve developed by the Commissioners method.

B. *Illinois Standard.*   The Illinois Standard, in effect in many
states for policies issued prior to 1948, divides policies into the same
two groups as the Commissioners Standard and prescribes the same
minimum for policies in group (1). For group (2), however, the minimum reserve is that produced by the use of the Illinois method. As
has been noted, Illinois method reserves are identical with Commissioners method reserves for policies with twenty or fewer premiums,
but are larger for policies with more than twenty premiums.

It is apparent that several plans of insurance commonly issued by
life insurance companies require, under the Illinois Standard, full
preliminary term reserves for some ages at issue and Illinois method
reserves for other ages. For example, if the 1958 CSO 3% table is
used, the thirty-year endowment policy is valued by the full preliminary term method for ages at issue 34 and above and by the Illinois
method for younger ages. For ages at issue in the vicinity of 34, a
tabulation of net premiums and twentieth terminal reserves for this
policy in accordance with the Illinois Standard shows:

THIRTY YEAR ENDOWMENT
1958 CSO 3%
$1,000—Illinois Standard

Age at Issue	Basis of Reserves	Net Premiums			Twentieth Reserve
		1st	*2-20*	*21-30*	
31	Ill. Method	3.41	24.41	23.00	564.07
32	Ill. Method	3.08	24.65	23.20	564.37
33	Ill. Method	2.76	24.92	23.43	564.66
34	FPT	2.33	24.87	24.87	555.12
35	FPT	2.44	25.17	25.17	555.32
36	FPT	2.56	25.50	25.50	555.51

The sharp break shown in the above table in the sequence of values for the twentieth reserve which occurs between ages 33 and 34 is due to the change in reserve methods at this point. The New Jersey Standard, defined below, is designed to eliminate this break* by requiring that reserves on this plan be brought up to net level by the end of the twentieth year for all ages at issue.

C. *New Jersey Standard.* The New Jersey Standard is identical with the Illinois Standard except in the case of a policy with a premium payment period of more than twenty years which has a premium† which is greater than 150 per cent of the FPT first year premium and less than the FPT renewal premium for a twenty-payment life policy issued at the same age. The minimum reserves specified for such policies are those produced by the New Jersey method.

It may be noted that this special class of policies prescribed for minimum valuation by the New Jersey method falls entirely within class (1) in the definitions of the Commissioners Standard and the Illinois Standard. The remainder of class (1) is composed solely of low premium term policies which are usually valued on a net level basis. The use of full preliminary term reserves is permitted for these term policies, but such usage seldom occurs because of the rather small effect of the modification upon the reserves for such policies.

It may be noted that under the New Jersey Standard no modified period is longer than twenty years. Thus, for all plans of insurance, reserves reach the net level basis on or before the end of the twentieth year. Many companies have adopted the New Jersey Standard for reserves because the foregoing property permits a more favorable comparison with companies using the net level basis.

D. *Canadian Standard.* The insurance act, applying to companies registered with the Dominion of Canada Insurance Department, provides a valuation basis which is commonly referred to as the Canadian Standard. Here policies are divided into two classes: (1) policies with net level premiums less than or equal to the corre-

---

*The student may note that this break does not occur under the Commissioners Standard, since every policy, irrespective of whether it falls in group (1) or group (2), has a modification period which coincides with the entire premium payment period of the policy.

†Both the New Jersey and Illinois statutes use the expression *premium charged* which might appear to mean gross premiums. However, the respective insurance departments have preferred the use of *net premiums* in the application of the criteria so as to have uniform application to all companies, irrespective of the level of gross premiums.

sponding net level ordinary life premiums and (2) policies with net level premiums greater than the corresponding net level ordinary life premiums. The act prescribes full preliminary term reserves as a minimum for group (1) and Canadian method reserves as a minimum for group (2).

5.15   PREMIUM DEFICIENCY RESERVES

Most states require an additional reserve in event that the gross premium for a policy is less than the net premium upon the valuation basis adopted by the company. In this event the total reserve required is the present value of future benefits less the present value of future *gross* premiums. The difference between the reserve found in this manner and the usual net premium reserve consists of the present value of the excess of the future net premiums over the gross premiums, or

$$(P - P') \cdot \ddot{a}_{x+t:\overline{m-t}|} ,$$

where P and P' are, respectively, the net and gross premiums for the given policy. This quantity is called the "premium deficiency reserve" and is maintained by the company in addition to the regular tabular net premium reserve.

As the policy grows older (as t increases) the premium deficiency reserve diminishes. It is relatively high at the shorter durations and younger ages; for example, if the gross premium on an ordinary life policy which is issued at age twenty is $1 less than the net premium, the premium deficiency reserve to be set up on the date of issue of the policy is $1 \cdot \ddot{a}_{20} = \$25.85$, on the 1958 CSO 3% Table. It has been usual for companies, in computing gross premiums, to arbitrarily make all gross premiums equal to or larger than the corresponding net premiums, thereby avoiding the necessity of maintaining large premium deficiency reserves.

The importance of the premium deficiency reserve problem has been considerably reduced with the adoption of the 1958 CSO table of mortality. Formerly, particularly when the old American Experience Table was the basis for net premiums and reserves, companies found it possible, for certain policies issued at the younger ages, to charge adequate gross premiums which were below the corresponding net premiums. This is unlikely to be the case when net premiums are based on the 1958 CSO table.

Review Exercises

1. Fill in the missing values in the following table assuming all policies to be issued at the same age and under the same assumptions regarding mortality and interest:

Policy	Net Level Premium	Fifth Net Level Reserve	α^{Com}	β^{Com}	Fifth Reserve Commissioners Method
10-payment life	$46.94	$235.19	$24.58	$49.80	$221.69
10-year endowment	89.05	464.90			
10-payment 15-yr. end.	79.34	411.94			
10-payment 20-yr. end.	71.11	367.00			

2. Fill in the missing values in the following table assuming all policies to be issued at the same age and under the same assumptions regarding mortality and interest:

Policy	Net Level Premium	Tenth Net Level Reserve	α^{I}	β^{I}	Tenth Reserve Illinois Method
20-payment life	$30.30	$291.43	$4.48	$32.14	$275.68
20-year endowment	41.98	430.71			
25-year endowment	33.10	324.75			
20-payment 30-yr. end.	35.27	350.69			

3. For an m-payment policy, show that

$$\beta^{\text{Can}} = \beta^F - \frac{P - P_x}{a_{x:\overline{m-1}|}}.$$

4. For an m-payment policy ($m > 20$), show that

$$\beta^{\text{I}} = \beta^{\text{Com}} + \left[\frac{1}{\ddot{a}_{x:\overline{20}|}} - \frac{1}{\ddot{a}_{x:\overline{m}|}}\right](_{19}P_{x+1} - c_x).$$

5. For a thirty-year endowment policy prove that the Commissioners method reserves will be greater than the corresponding full preliminary term reserves.

6. (a) Show that for an ordinary life policy the terminal reserves on the Canadian method are equal to the corresponding reserves on the full preliminary term method.

(b) Show that for a twenty-payment life policy the terminal reserves on the full preliminary term, Commissioners, and Illinois methods are equal.

7. For a policy valued under the New Jersey method, show that

$$\beta^J = {}_{19}P_{x+1} + \frac{P - {}_{20}P_x}{{}_{19}V_{x:\overline{20}|}},$$

where the symbol in the denominator denotes the nineteenth net level terminal reserve on a twenty-year endowment policy issued at the same age as the policy under consideration.

8. A certain life insurance company, which is using the 1958 CSO 3% table for net premiums and reserves, finds that it has in force 3,612 policies, valued on the Illinois method, for a total of $10,232,796 of insurance. Each of these policies was issued ten years ago at age 30 and provided for a premium-paying period of twenty years or more. The first year net premiums for all of the policies total $144,285.30. For the entire group of policies, find:

   (a) the total of the net renewal premiums;
   (b) the total of the net level premiums;
   (c) the total of the Illinois method terminal reserves;
   (d) the total amount of terminal reserve needed in addition to (c) to change from the Illinois method to the net level system.

9. Under the Canadian method the difference between the net renewal modified premium and the net level premium is $1.5177 for a certain $1000 policy issued at age 40. Find the length of the premium payment period.

10. For a certain twenty-payment $1000 policy issued at age 40 the first year net premium modified on the full preliminary term basis is $3.427 whereas the net level premium is $35.448. Find the net renewal full preliminary term premium.

11. For a certain $1000 25-payment policy issued at age 50 and modified on the New Jersey method the renewal net premium is $31.578. Find the net level premium.

CHAPTER 6

Gross Premiums

6.1 LIFE INSURANCE COMPANIES

Life insurance companies may be divided into two classes, stock companies and mutual companies. A stock company is one which is organized for the purpose of earning profits for the stockholders who provide the capital of the organization and take the risks of the business. The capital of such a company forms a guarantee fund which may be drawn upon to protect the interests of the policyholders. A mutual company is a cooperative association of policyholders established for the purpose of effecting insurance on their own lives. The policyholders are the owners of the company. There is no capital stock. In the case of both kinds of companies, the owners (stockholders in the one case and policyholders in the other) elect the board of directors who, in turn, elect the officers and delegate to them sufficient powers to carry out the details of management.

6.2 DISTRIBUTION OF SURPLUS

A life insurance company, whether stock or mutual, must have a surplus fund on hand to help tide over any unfavorable fluctuation in the business. At the start, this fund is commonly paid in by the organizers. Later on, if the business is successful, the surplus increases due to the earning and retention of profits. At the discretion of the board of directors, a portion of this increase in surplus will be distributed to the owners, usually on an annual basis. Thus, the stockholders may receive dividends on their stock and the policyholders may receive *policy dividends*. The dividends paid to the policyholder are determined, as accurately as is practicable, to be his equitable share of the profits—that is, the amount which his own policy has contributed to the surplus of the company during the previous year.

If a life insurance policy provides for the payment of policy dividends, it is called a *participating policy*. The life insurance policies issued by mutual companies are almost invariably participating. Stock companies, on the other hand, are permitted in many states to issue both kinds of policies, *participating* and *nonparticipating*. When a stock company issues participating insurance, the portion of earnings to be distributed to the stockholders is usually restricted voluntarily and the balance is paid to the policyholders as policy dividends. If the company issues both kinds of insurance, it is often organized in "divisions" according to the type of policy issued, and the expenses and earnings of the "par" and the "non–par" divisions carefully allocated.

6.3 GROSS PREMIUMS

The problem of determining the gross premiums for various ages and plans of insurance is more difficult for nonparticipating policies than for participating policies. The stock company issuing nonparticipating policies under the stress of competition is interested in obtaining a gross premium scale as low as possible consistent with safety and conservative business judgment.

The scale of premiums for participating policies, however, need not be so accurately determined. As long as the premiums are sufficiently high, any inequities in the rates can be adjusted in the distribution of dividends. Sometimes the net premiums are loaded rather crudely to obtain the gross premiums for participating policies although many companies carry out as careful a computation for participating policies as for nonparticipating. The desired dividend scale is often taken into account in computing these rates. Of course, no projection into the future can be completely accurate and the actual dividends paid may not coincide with those used in the gross premium computation but, unless conditions change drastically, it is likely that they will be fairly close to the predicted scale.

6.4 MORTALITY, INTEREST, AND EXPENSE

The nonparticipating gross premiums charged by most companies usually bear little relationship to the valuation net premiums used in computing the statutory terminal reserves. Gross premiums are computed upon a set of assumptions which the actuary feels to be realistic, whereas net premiums are computed upon the somewhat artificial assumptions prescribed by statute and defined in the policy contract. Thus, in practice, the word *loading* implies merely the difference between two independently computed quantities, the gross premium and the valuation net premium.

The first step in the preparation of a scale of nonparticipating gross premiums is the adoption of a table of mortality which seems likely to reflect the rate of mortality to be experienced by the company in the future. It seems fundamental, since insurance is issued only to *select* lives, that the entering policyholder should be given the benefit of the reduction in mortality due to the select class to which he belongs. The mortality table used in the formation of the gross premium scale should be a select table, showing the rate of mortality to be expected in each policy year following the date of issue. It has been argued that, in the computation of gross premiums, a company should use an ultimate rate of mortality, reflecting the mortality rate to be experienced after the effect of the selection has disappeared. The savings in mortality effected during the early policy years could then be used as an offset against the expense of selling the policy. The actual expense of selling a policy, however, bears no relation to the mortality savings resulting from the use of an ultimate table, and should properly be considered separately.

Recent mortality investigations have shown that there has been a continuous improvement in mortality at the younger ages, and the table adopted should reflect this improvement. Endowment and limited payment life policies have shown lower rates of mortality than whole life and term policies. While it may seem advisable to take account of this fluctuation in mortality reflected by the various plans of insurance, too great a refinement should be avoided because of the resulting inconvenience in computation.

The interest assumption to be used in computing the gross premium should be a conservative rate which may be expected to be earned on invested funds for many years in the future. Insurance is essentially a long-time investment and the proper choice of an interest rate is an important factor. If the rate of interest chosen is close to the rate which has been earned on similar investments in the past, it may be considered advisable to assume a reduction in the rate after a period of ten or twenty years. It is usual, however, to allow a fair margin between the assumed rate and the rate actually being earned. This margin will prove to be a source of profit and can be used to build up a substantial fund available in contingencies.

It is obvious that in the aggregate the premium income of a non-participating company should contain a sufficient allowance to pay expenses. The major problem in computing gross premiums consists in properly distributing the total expense of a company among the policies in force at various ages on the several plans of insurance. Not only do expenses vary in different companies, but different methods are used in allocating these expenses. Some of the expenses, such as agents' commissions and premium taxes, are computed directly as percentages of the gross premium. Other expenses, such as medical fees, inspection fees, collection expense, and certain clerical expenses, vary according to the number of policies considered.

In spite of the fact that a number of initial expense items and some of the continuing administrative expense items do not vary much, if at all, with the size of the policy, until recently there were legal prohibitions against varying the premium rate per unit with the size of the policy. Thus, the charge for a $10,000 policy was required to be ten times the charge for a $1000 policy of exactly the same kind. In recent years, however, premium rates per $1000 have been permitted to vary with the size of the policy provided that the insurer can demonstrate that such a variation is justified. Such justification is not at all difficult and at present most companies do vary their premium rates slightly with policy size. This practice will not be taken into consideration in the subsequent sections of this chapter.

The expense factors considered in the illustrations to follow are not in any sense to be considered as applicable to any particular company or group of companies. They are offered only for the purpose of illustrating the method of computation.

6.5   COMPUTATION OF NONPARTICIPATING GROSS PREMIUMS

As was indicated above, expense items may be expressed as a percentage of the gross premium, a percentage of the amount of insurance, or a flat amount per policy. These latter expenses may be translated into an amount per $1000 of insurance by the assumption of an average amount of insurance per policy. This average amount is usually based upon a study of the policies in force in the company and is usually computed separately for each plan of insurance and occasionally for each age at issue.

After the expenses are established as percentages of the premium or the amount of insurance, the premium formula can be derived from the principle that the present value of the gross premiums must equal the present value of all policy benefits plus the present value of all expenses, contingency items, and anticipated profit margins. For simplicity in the illustrations and exercises, allowances for contingencies, anticipated profit margins, and similar items will be considered as having been included in the stated allowances for expenses.

As an illustration of the method of computing nonparticipating gross premiums, consider the following hypothetical example: A life insurance company estimates that the following expenses will be needed for a $1000 thirty-year endowment insurance policy issued at age 35:

1. agent's commission, 55% of the first premium, 10% of the second premium, 5% of the third through the tenth premiums, followed by a "service fee" of 2% on all premiums collected thereafter;
2. premium taxes, 3% of each gross premium;
3. administrative expenses, $12 in the first year and $5 in each subsequent year;
4. cost of settlement at the time of death claim or maturity, $5.

It is customary for life insurance companies to pay the face amount of insurance immediately upon receipt of proof of death of the insured. All of the formulas derived in the previous chapters have been based upon the assumption that death claims are payable at the end of the year in which the insured dies. Since it is reasonable to assume that, on the average, the date of death will fall in the middle of the policy year, it is necessary to add a half-year's interest to the face amount of insurance when these formulas are used for the purpose of computing gross premiums.

Let us assume that the life insurance company issuing the above policy adopts the X_{18} Mortality Table with Anderson's select modification (see p. 15) with interest at $3\frac{3}{4}\%$ as a basis for its gross premium computations. If one denotes by P' the minimum gross premium for the thirty-year endowment policy in question, then P' is determined by equating the present value of the gross premiums to the present value of the benefits plus the present value of the estimated expenses. Hence, we write the equation

$$
\begin{aligned}
P'\ddot{a}_{[35]:\overline{30|}} = {}& 1005\,(1.0375)^{\frac{1}{2}}\,A^{1}_{[35]:\overline{30|}} + 1005A_{[35]:\frac{1}{30|}} \\
& + .55\,P' + .10\,P'\,(\ddot{a}_{[35]:\overline{2|}} - \ddot{a}_{[35]:\overline{1|}}) \\
& + .05P'(\ddot{a}_{[35]:\overline{10|}} - \ddot{a}_{[35]:\overline{2|}}) + .02P'(\ddot{a}_{[35]:\overline{30|}} - \ddot{a}_{[35]:\overline{10|}}) \\
& + .03P'\ddot{a}_{[35]:\overline{30|}} + 12 + 5a_{[35]:\overline{29|}},
\end{aligned} \tag{6.1}
$$

where the bracket enclosing the age [35] is used to indicate that the life under discussion is a select life at age 35. In using select tables it should be noted that the value of a given symbol depends not only upon the attained age of the insured, but also upon the age at which the policy was issued. In general, the symbol $[x] + t$ indicates a life, now aged $x + t$, which was accepted for insurance t years ago at age x. After the select period expires, all lives of the same attained age are considered to be subject to the same ultimate rate of mortality and the bracket enclosing the age at issue is dropped. Thus in the present instance the bracket is omitted after the insured reaches age 40, inasmuch as Anderson's select modification of the X_{18} table extends for only five years.

Solving equation (6.1) for the gross premium, P', we may write

$$P' = \frac{1005\,(1.0375)^{\frac{1}{2}}\,A_{[35]:\overline{30}|}^{\frac{1}{2}} + 1005A_{[35]:\overline{30}|}^{\frac{1}{2}} + 12 + 5a_{[35]:\overline{29}|}}{.95\ddot{a}_{[35]:\overline{30}|} - .03\ddot{a}_{[35]:\overline{10}|} - .05\ddot{a}_{[35]:\overline{2}|} + .10\ddot{a}_{[35]:\overline{1}|} - .55}$$

Upon inserting commutation symbols and simplifying, we have

$$P' = \frac{1005\,(1.0375)^{\frac{1}{2}}\,(M_{[35]} - M_{65}) + 1005D_{65} + 12D_{[35]} + 5N_{[35]+1} - 5N_{65}}{.97N_{[35]} - .10N_{[35]+1} + .05N_{[35]+2} + .03N_{45} - .95N_{65} - .55D_{[35]}},$$
$$(6.2)$$

where the symbol $[35] + 1$ indicates a life aged 36 which was a select life one year previously at age 35. Equation (6.2) gives

$$P' = 28.968$$

after a computation which makes use of the table of values appearing below.

The following table shows the values of some of the symbols based upon Anderson's select modification of the X_{18} table with interest at $3\frac{3}{4}\%$. These are sufficient for the solution of equation (6.1) and the exercises in Section 6.5 and certain exercises in Section 6.6.

Commutation Values			Accumulation Factors		
			t	$u_{[35]+t}$	$1000k_{[35]+t}$
$D_{[35]}$	2,664,436.6				
D_{55}	1,168,179.5				
D_{65}	678,876.4		0	1.038 455	0.920 844
$N_{[35]}$	54,239,841		1	1.038 643	1.101 206
$N_{[35]+1}$	51,575,404		2	1.038 882	1.331 770
$N_{[35]+2}$	49,009,636		3	1.039 173	1.612 595
N_{45}	31,686,673		4	1.039 528	1.953 808
N_{55}	16,655,482				
N_{65}	7,273,873		5	1.039 954	2.365 629
$M_{[35]}$	703,959.31		6	1.040 246	2.646 966
M_{45}	658,785.49		7	1.040 570	2.958 725
M_{55}	566,174.11		8	1.040 914	3.290 778
M_{65}	415,965.35		9	1.041 280	3.643 277
$(1.0375)^{\frac{1}{2}}$	1.018 5774				

Exercises

1. It is estimated that the following expenses are required for a $1000 ten-year term policy issued at age 35:

   (a) commission, 40% of gross premium in the first year and 5% thereafter;

   (b) premium taxes, 2% of each gross premium;

   (c) administrative expense, $4.50 the first year and $2.00 in each succeeding year;

   (d) cost of settlement, $2.00.

Using the commutation symbols of Section 6.5, compute the minimum gross premium for this policy.

2. A life insurance company estimates that the following expenses are required for a $1000 twenty-year endowment policy issued at age 35:

   (a) commission, 35% of the first year gross premium and 5% thereafter for the next nine years;

   (b) premium taxes, 3% of each gross premium;

   (c) administrative expense, $5.50 in the first year and $1.50 in each succeeding year;

   (d) cost of settlement, $2.50.

Using the commutation symbols of Section 6.5, compute the minimum gross premium for this policy.

3. It is estimated that the following expenses will be incurred on a $1000 twenty-payment life policy issued at age 35:

   (a) commission, 60% of the first year gross premium and 5% thereafter;

   (b) premium tax, 2.5% of each gross premium;

   (c) administrative expense, $5.50 in the first year and $2.00 in each succeeding year until the death of the policyholder;

   (d) cost of settlement, $3.00.

Using the commutation symbols of Section 6.5, compute the minimum gross premium for this policy.

4. An insurance company actuary estimates that the following expenses will be incurred on a $1000 ordinary life policy issued at age 35:

   (a) commission, 65% of the first year gross premium, 15% of the second year gross premium, 5% of the next eight gross premiums, and 2% of all gross premiums thereafter;

   (b) premium tax, 2% of each gross premium;

   (c) administrative expense, $7.50 in the first year and $1.50 thereafter until the death of the policyholder;

   (d) cost of settlement, $3.50.

Using the commutation symbols of Section 6.5, compute the minimum gross premium for this policy.

6.6 ASSET SHARES

In Section 6.5 the minimum gross premium P' for a $1000 thirty-year endowment insurance policy issued at age 35 was found to be $28.968

under certain assumptions regarding mortality, interest, and expense. Let us assume that the company maintains legal reserves based upon the Commissioners Method and the 1958 CSO Table at 3%. Since the gross premium is not based upon the same mortality table and interest rate as the net premium and terminal reserves, an additional investigation is required to disclose whether this minimum gross premium is sufficient to meet the legal requirements for surrender values.

The expenses to be paid by the company in the first year of the thirty-year endowment policy in the illustration amount to $12 plus 58% of the gross premium, a total of $28.801. The deduction of this amount from the gross premium leaves a balance of $0.167. This is called the *effective premium,* and is sometimes negative for the first year. When the effective premium is accumulated with benefit of interest and survivorship to the end of the year and the accumulated cost of insurance is deducted, one obtains (using the values shown in Section 6.5)

$$0.167 u_{[35]} - (1.0375)^{1/2} 1005 k_{[35]} = 0.167(1.038455) - (1.0375)^{1/2}(1.005)(0.920844)$$
$$= 0.173 - 0.943 = -0.770.$$

This amount, $-\$0.770$, which represents the accumulated excess (or deficiency in this instance) of the gross premium over expenses and the cost of insurance, is called the *asset share* at the end of the first policy year. It may be thought of as the equitable share of the policyholder in the assets of the company, that is, the sum which this particular policy has contributed to the assets during the first policy year.

The expenses to be paid by the company in the second policy year amount to $5 plus 13% of the gross premium, a total of $8.766. The effective premium for this second year is $20.202, and the second year asset share is

$$(-0.770 + 20.202)(1.038643) - (1.0375)^{1/2}(1.005)(1.101206) = 20.183 - 1.127$$
$$= 19.056$$

This procedure is repeated until all of the thirty asset shares for the policy have been computed. A comparison of the asset shares with the corresponding Commissioners Method 1958 CSO 3% reserves, and the minimum nonforfeiture values computed according to the adjusted premium method is shown below for the first ten years:

COMPARISON OF ASSET SHARES, RESERVES, AND MINIMUM NONFORFEITURE VALUES—I

Thirty-Year Endowment   Gross Premium $28.968   Age at Issue 35

End of Year	Asset Share Anderson's X_{18} Select $3\frac{3}{4}\%$	Terminal Reserve, CRVM, 1958 CSO 3%	Difference	Minimum Nonforfeiture Value, 1958 CSO 3%	Difference
1	-0.77	0	-0.77	(-11.51)	10.74
2	19.06	23.35	-4.29	11.58	7.48
3	40.93	47.31	-6.38	35.34	5.59
4	63.38	71.86	-8.48	59.77	3.61
5	86.39	97.01	-10.62	84.88	1.51
6	109.94	122.76	-12.82	110.67	-0.73
7	134.17	149.10	-14.93	137.12	-2.95
8	159.12	176.06	-16.94	164.25	-5.13
9	184.80	203.67	-18.87	192.06	-7.26
10	211.24	231.92	-20.68	220.55	-9.31

The above table shows that the terminal reserve exceeds the asset share in every year and the difference is increasing. Furthermore, the required nonforfeiture value exceeds the asset share for the last five years shown and the indication is that this difference will continue to increase. Of course, in an actual case these comparisons would be extended for the entire life of the policy. Nevertheless, merely from the trend of the ten-year figures shown, it is fairly obvious that the minimum gross premium of $28.968 is unsatisfactory.

It is interesting to note the effect of an increase of only $2.50 in the gross premium, bringing it to $31.468. The new asset share comparisons are shown in the following table:

COMPARISON OF ASSET SHARES, RESERVES, AND MINIMUM NONFORFEITURE VALUES—II

Thirty-Year Endowment   Gross Premium $31.468   Age at Issue 35

End of Year	Asset Share Anderson's X_{18} Select $3\frac{3}{4}\%$	Terminal Reserve, CRVM, 1958 CSO 3%	Difference	Minimum Nonforfeiture Value, 1958 CSO 3%	Difference
1	0.32	0	0.32	(-11.51)	11.83
2	22.45	23.35	-0.90	11.58	10.87
3	46.84	47.31	-0.47	35.34	11.50
4	71.91	71.86	0.05	59.77	12.14
5	97.65	97.01	0.64	84.88	12.77
6	124.04	122.76	1.28	110.67	13.37
7	151.24	149.10	2.14	137.12	14.12
8	179.27	176.06	3.21	164.25	15.02
9	208.16	203.67	4.49	192.06	16.10
10	237.96	231.92	6.04	220.55	17.41

The foregoing table shows that the addition of only $2.50 to the gross premium results in asset shares which are very close to the Commissioners terminal reserves and which exceed the required nonforfeiture values over the entire period shown. If the comparison over the final twenty years of the policy proved to be equally favorable, the increased gross premium of $31.468 might be considered satisfactory. Perhaps an additional specific allowance for contingencies or profit might be added. However, competition seriously restricts the size of such allowances.

In Chapter 4 it was stated that the minimum surrender values, based upon the standard nonforfeiture law and computed by the adjusted premium method, are usually quite close to the older values computed by subtracting a *surrender charge* from the legal terminal reserve. This surrender charge in most states was not permitted to exceed 2.5% of the amount of insurance, that is, $25 per $1000. An examination of the above table shows that in this particular instance the minimum nonforfeiture value is well within $25 of the corresponding terminal reserve computed under the Commissioners method. It should be noted that the law specifies only minimum values. The insurance company may at its discretion provide higher surrender values, taking care that the values are reasonable and equitable as between the various classes of policyholders and are not out of line with asset share computations.

Exercises

1. A certain life insurance company charges a gross premium of $15.59 for a $1000 ordinary life policy issued at age 35. The expenses incurred by this policy amount to $17.95 the first year, $4.15 the second year, and $2.59 in each subsequent renewal year. (a) On the basis of Anderson's select modification of Table X_{18} at $3\frac{3}{4}\%$, compute the first five asset shares. (b) Compare the third asset share with the minimum nonforfeiture value of $13.78 and the Commissioners Method terminal reserve of $30.04.

2. A life insurance company charges a gross premium of $42.00 for a $1000 twenty-year endowment policy issued at age 35. The expenses incurred by this policy amount to $21.46 in the first year and $4.86 in each renewal year. On the basis of Anderson's select modification of Table X_{18}, compute the first five asset shares.

3. A life insurance company charges a gross premium of $26.63 for a $1000 twenty-payment life policy issued at age 35. The expenses incurred by this policy amount to $22.14 the first year and $4.00 in each renewal year during the premium paying period. Compute the first five asset shares, using Anderson's select modification of Table X_{18}.

6.7   GROSS PREMIUMS FOR PARTICIPATING POLICIES

Some actuaries contend that it is unnecessary to compute with great accuracy the gross premium for a participating policy, since it is expected that a part of the premium will be refunded to the policyholder in the form of dividends. It is only necessary that the gross premium scale be sufficient to care for all fluctuations in mortality, interest, and expense that might occur. Minor inequities in the scale of gross premiums can be adjusted in the distribution of dividends. The method of determining participating gross premiums varies with different companies. Many life insurance companies compute the gross premium for a given policy by adding a constant to the net level premium and multiplying the sum by a percentage factor. Thus, if P' denotes the gross premium, this method implies that

$$P' = (P + c)(1 + k), \tag{6.3}$$

where c and k are constants and P denotes the net level premium for the policy under consideration. It is customary, in applying equation (6.3), to vary the values of c and k with the plan of insurance.

On the other hand, it is not uncommon for participating gross premiums to be calculated upon realistic assumptions regarding mortality, interest, commissions, administrative expenses, taxes, and so forth, as in the case of nonparticipating gross premiums. In addition, the actuary may include the policy dividends which he thinks it would be desirable to pay. Even though actual future experience might differ enough from the gross premium assumptions so that the future policy dividends actually paid would differ from those used in the premium computations, it is probable that these dividends would be more satisfactory than those based upon a purely arbitrary set of gross premiums.

Exercises

1. A single premium whole life policy is sold at age 25 with the provision that the gross premium without interest will be returned, together with the face amount $1000, at the death of the insured. Assuming the gross premium is obtained by the method of equation (6.3), with $c = \$5$ for a $1000 policy and $k = .1$, compute the net and gross premiums for this policy.

   Solution. Denote the net premium by W and the gross premium by W'. Since the net premium W must be sufficient to provide whole life insurance of $(1000 + W')$, we have immediately

   $$W = (1000 + W')A_{25}.$$

Equation (6.3) implies that

$$W' = (W + 5)(1.1).$$

Solving these two equations simultaneously for W, we get, by Table IV,

$$W = \frac{1005.5 A_{25}}{1 - 1.1 A_{25}} = \frac{(1005.5)(0.27913564)}{1 - (1.1)(0.27913564)} = \$405.04,$$

and hence

$$W' = (W + 5)(1.1) = \$451.04.$$

2. An ordinary life policy is issued at age 30 with the provision that the gross premiums paid by the insured will be returned without interest, together with the face amount $1000, at the death of the insured. Assuming that the gross premium is obtained by the method of equation (6.3), with $c = \$4$ for a $1000 policy and $k = 0.07$, compute the net and gross premiums for the policy.

3. A formula, used in England, for loading the net level annual premium for an ordinary life policy is

$$P'_x = 1.075\left[P_x + \frac{0.01}{\ddot{a}_x} + 0.00125\right].$$

Show that this method is equivalent to that of equation (6.3) and find the values of c and k corresponding to an interest rate of 3%.

4. A twenty-payment life policy is issued at age 30 with the provision that the gross premiums paid by the insured will be returned without interest, together with the face amount $1000, at the death of the insured. Assuming that the gross premium is obtained by the method of equation (6.3), with $c = 0.005$ and $k = 0.09$, show that
   (a) the net premium for this policy is

$$\frac{1000 M_{30} + 5.45(R_{30} - R_{50})}{N_{30} - N_{50} - 1.09(R_{30} - R_{50})};$$

   (b) the gross premium for this policy is

$$1.09 \frac{1000 M_{30} + 5(N_{30} - N_{50})}{N_{30} - N_{50} - 1.09(R_{30} - R_{50})}.$$

Tables

1958 CSO 3%

Table I—Compound Interest Functions—3% Interest

n	$(1 + i)^n$	$v^n = (1 + i)^{-n}$	$s_{\overline{n}\rvert}$	$a_{\overline{n}\rvert}$	n
1	1.030 000	.970 873 79	1.000 000	.970 8738	1
2	1.060 900	.942 595 91	2.030 000	1.913 4697	2
3	1.092 727	.915 141 66	3.090 900	2.828 6114	3
4	1.125 509	.888 487 05	4.183 627	3.717 0984	4
5	1.159 274	.862 608 78	5.309 136	4.579 7072	5
6	1.194 052	.837 484 26	6.468 410	5.417 1914	6
7	1.229 874	.813 091 51	7.662 462	6.230 2830	7
8	1.266 770	.789 409 23	8.892 336	7.019 6922	8
9	1.304 773	.766 416 73	10.159 106	7.786 1089	9
10	1.343 916	.744 093 91	11.463 879	8.530 2028	10
11	1.384 234	.722 421 28	12.807 796	9.252 6241	11
12	1.425 761	.701 379 88	14.192 030	9.954 0040	12
13	1.468 534	.680 951 34	15.617 790	10.634 9553	13
14	1.512 590	.661 117 81	17.086 324	11.296 0731	14
15	1.557 967	.641 861 95	18.598 914	11.937 9351	15
16	1.604 706	.623 166 94	20.156 881	12.561 1020	16
17	1.652 848	.605 016 45	21.761 588	13.166 1185	17
18	1.702 433	.587 394 61	23.414 435	13.753 5131	18
19	1.753 506	.570 286 03	25.116 868	14.323 7991	19
20	1.806 111	.553 675 75	26.870 374	14.877 4749	20
21	1.860 295	.537 549 28	28.676 486	15.415 0241	21
22	1.916 103	.521 892 50	30.536 780	15.936 9166	22
23	1.973 587	.506 691 75	32.452 884	16.443 6084	23
24	2.032 794	.491 933 74	34.426 470	16.935 5421	24
25	2.093 778	.477 605 57	36.459 264	17.413 1477	25
26	2.156 591	.463 694 73	38.553 042	17.876 8424	26
27	2.221 289	.450 189 06	40.709 633	18.327 0315	27
28	2.287 928	.437 076 75	42.930 922	18.764 1082	28
29	2.356 566	.424 346 36	45.218 850	19.188 4546	29
30	2.427 262	.411 986 76	47.575 416	19.600 4414	30
31	2.500 080	.399 987 15	50.002 678	20.000 4285	31
32	2.575 083	.388 337 03	52.502 758	20.388 7655	32
33	2.652 335	.377 026 25	55.077 841	20.765 7918	33
34	2.731 905	.366 044 90	57.730 176	21.131 8367	34
35	2.813 862	.355 383 40	60.462 082	21.487 2201	35
36	2.898 278	.345 032 43	63.275 944	21.832 2525	36
37	2.985 227	.334 982 94	66.174 222	22.167 2355	37
38	3.074 784	.325 226 15	69.159 449	22.492 4616	38
39	3.167 027	.315 753 55	72.234 233	22.808 2152	39
40	3.262 038	.306 556 84	75.401 260	23.114 7720	40
41	3.359 899	.297 628 00	78.663 297	23.412 4000	41
42	3.460 696	.288 959 22	82.023 196	23.701 3592	42
43	3.564 517	.280 542 94	85.483 892	23.981 9022	43
44	3.671 452	.272 371 78	89.048 409	24.254 2739	44
45	3.781 596	.264 438 62	92.719 861	24.518 7126	45
46	3.895 044	.256 736 53	96.501 457	24.775 4491	46
47	4.011 895	.249 258 76	100.396 501	25.024 7079	47
48	4.132 252	.241 998 80	104.408 396	25.266 7067	48
49	4.256 219	.234 950 29	108.540 648	25.501 6569	49
50	4.383 906	.228 107 08	112.796 867	25.729 7640	50

Table I (*Continued*)—Compound Interest Functions—3% Interest

n	$(1 + i)^n$	$v^n = (1 + i)^{-n}$	$s_{\overline{n}\rvert}$	$a_{\overline{n}\rvert}$	n
51	4.515 423	.221 463 18	117.180 773	25.951 2272	51
52	4.650 886	.215 012 80	121.696 197	26.166 2400	52
53	4.790 413	.208 750 29	126.347 083	26.374 9903	53
54	4.934 125	.202 670 19	131.137 495	26.577 6605	54
55	5.082 149	.196 767 17	136.071 620	26.774 4277	55
56	5.234 613	.191 036 09	141.153 768	26.965 4637	56
57	5.391 651	.185 471 93	146.388 381	27.150 9357	57
58	5.553 401	.180 069 84	151.780 033	27.331 0055	58
59	5.720 003	.174 825 08	157.333 434	27.505 8306	59
60	5.891 603	.169 733 09	163.053 437	27.675 5637	60
61	6.068 351	.164 789 41	168.945 040	27.840 3531	61
62	6.250 402	.159 989 72	175.013 391	28.000 3428	62
63	6.437 914	.155 329 82	181.263 793	28.155 6726	63
64	6.631 051	.150 805 65	187.701 706	28.306 4783	64
65	6.829 983	.146 413 25	194.332 758	28.452 8915	65
66	7.034 882	.142 148 79	201.162 741	28.595 0403	66
67	7.245 929	.138 008 53	208.197 623	28.733 0489	67
68	7.463 306	.133 988 87	215.443 552	28.867 0377	68
69	7.687 206	.130 086 28	222.906 858	28.997 1240	69
70	7.917 822	.126 297 36	230.594 064	29.123 4214	70
71	8.155 356	.122 618 80	238.511 886	29.246 0402	71
72	8.400 018	.119 047 37	246.667 242	29.365 0875	72
73	8.652 017	.115 579 98	255.067 260	29.480 6675	73
74	8.911 578	.112 213 57	263.719 277	29.592 8811	74
75	9.178 926	.108 945 21	272.630 855	29.701 8263	75
76	9.454 293	.105 772 05	281.809 781	29.807 5983	76
77	9.737 922	.102 691 31	291.264 075	29.910 2897	77
78	10.030 060	.099 700 30	301.001 997	30.009 9900	78
79	10.330 962	.096 796 41	311.032 057	30.106 7864	79
80	10.640 890	.093 977 10	321.363 019	30.200 7635	80
81	10.960 117	.091 239 90	332.003 909	30.292 0034	81
82	11.288 920	.088 582 43	342.964 026	30.380 5858	82
83	11.627 588	.086 002 36	354.252 946	30.466 5882	83
84	11.976 417	.083 497 43	365.880 534	30.550 0856	84
85	12.335 708	.081 065 47	377.856 951	30.631 1511	85
86	12.705 780	.078 704 34	390.192 659	30.709 8554	86
87	13.086 953	.076 411 98	402.898 439	30.786 2674	87
88	13.479 561	.074 186 39	415.985 392	30.860 4538	88
89	13.883 949	.072 025 62	429.464 953	30.932 4794	89
90	14.300 466	.069 927 79	443.348 902	31.002 4072	90
91	14.729 482	.067 891 05	457.649 368	31.070 2982	91
92	15.171 367	.065 913 64	472.378 850	31.136 2119	92
93	15.626 506	.063 993 83	487.550 217	31.200 2057	93
94	16.095 302	.062 129 93	503.176 723	31.262 3356	94
95	16.578 161	.060 320 32	519.272 026	31.322 6559	95
96	17.075 505	.058 563 42	535.850 187	31.381 2194	96
97	17.587 770	.056 857 69	552.925 692	31.438 0771	97
98	18.115 404	.055 201 64	570.513 463	31.493 2787	98
99	18.658 864	.053 593 83	588.628 867	31.546 8725	99
100	19.218 632	.052 032 84	607.287 731	31.598 9054	100

Table II—1958 CSO Mortality Table—Males

x	l_x	d_x	q_x	$\mathring{e}_x$	x
0	10 000 000	70 800	.007 08	68.30	0
1	9 929 200	17 475	.001 76	67.78	1
2	9 911 725	15 066	.001 52	66.90	2
3	9 896 659	14 449	.001 46	66.00	3
4	9 882 210	13 835	.001 40	65.10	4
5	9 868 375	13 322	.001 35	64.19	5
6	9 855 053	12 812	.001 30	63.27	6
7	9 842 241	12 401	.001 26	62.35	7
8	9 829 840	12 091	.001 23	61.43	8
9	9 817 749	11 879	.001 21	60.51	9
10	9 805 870	11 865	.001 21	59.58	10
11	9 794 005	12 047	.001 23	58.65	11
12	9 781 958	12 325	.001 26	57.72	12
13	9 769 633	12 896	.001 32	56.80	13
14	9 756 737	13 562	.001 39	55.87	14
15	9 743 175	14 225	.001 46	54.95	15
16	9 728 950	14 983	.001 54	54.03	16
17	9 713 967	15 737	.001 62	53.11	17
18	9 698 230	16 390	.001 69	52.19	18
19	9 681 840	16 846	.001 74	51.28	19
20	9 664 994	17 300	.001 79	50.37	20
21	9 647 694	17 655	.001 83	49.46	21
22	9 630 039	17 912	.001 86	48.55	22
23	9 612 127	18 167	.001 89	47.64	23
24	9 593 960	18 324	.001 91	46.73	24
25	9 575 636	18 481	.001 93	45.82	25
26	9 557 155	18 732	.001 96	44.90	26
27	9 538 423	18 981	.001 99	43.99	27
28	9 519 442	19 324	.002 03	43.08	28
29	9 500 118	19 760	.002 08	42.16	29
30	9 480 358	20 193	.002 13	41.25	30
31	9 460 165	20 718	.002 19	40.34	31
32	9 439 447	21 239	.002 25	39.43	32
33	9 418 208	21 850	.002 32	38.51	33
34	9 396 358	22 551	.002 40	37.60	34
35	9 373 807	23 528	.002 51	36.69	35
36	9 350 279	24 685	.002 64	35.78	36
37	9 325 594	26 112	.002 80	34.88	37
38	9 299 482	27 991	.003 01	33.97	38
39	9 271 491	30 132	.003 25	33.07	39
40	9 241 359	32 622	.003 53	32.18	40
41	9 208 737	35 362	.003 84	31.29	41
42	9 173 375	38 253	.004 17	30.41	42
43	9 135 122	41 382	.004 53	29.54	43
44	9 093 740	44 741	.004 92	28.67	44
45	9 048 999	48 412	.005 35	27.81	45
46	9 000 587	52 473	.005 83	26.95	46
47	8 948 114	56 910	.006 36	26.11	47
48	8 891 204	61 794	.006 95	25.27	48
49	8 829 410	67 104	.007 60	24.45	49

Table II (*Continued*)—1958 CSO Mortality Table—Males

x	l_x	d_x	q_x	$\mathring{e}_x$	x
50	8 762 306	72 902	.008 32	23.63	50
51	8 689 404	79 160	.009 11	22.82	51
52	8 610 244	85 758	.009 96	22.03	52
53	8 524 486	92 832	.010 89	21.25	53
54	8 431 654	100 337	.011 90	20.47	54
55	8 331 317	108 307	.013 00	19.71	55
56	8 223 010	116 849	.014 21	18.97	56
57	8 106 161	125 970	.015 54	18.23	57
58	7 980 191	135 663	.017 00	17.51	58
59	7 844 528	145 830	.018 59	16.81	59
60	7 698 698	156 592	.020 34	16.12	60
61	7 542 106	167 736	.022 24	15.44	61
62	7 374 370	179 271	.024 31	14.78	62
63	7 195 099	191 174	.026 57	14.14	63
64	7 003 925	203 394	.029 04	13.51	64
65	6 800 531	215 917	.031 75	12.90	65
66	6 584 614	228 749	.034 74	12.31	66
67	6 355 865	241 777	.038 04	11.73	67
68	6 114 088	254 835	.041 68	11.17	68
69	5 859 253	267 241	.045 61	10.64	69
70	5 592 012	278 426	.049 79	10.12	70
71	5 313 586	287 731	.054 15	9.63	71
72	5 025 855	294 766	.058 65	9.15	72
73	4 731 089	299 289	.063 26	8.69	73
74	4 431 800	301 894	.068 12	8.24	74
75	4 129 906	303 011	.073 37	7.81	75
76	3 826 895	303 014	.079 18	7.39	76
77	3 523 881	301 997	.085 70	6.98	77
78	3 221 884	299 829	.093 06	6.59	78
79	2 922 055	295 683	.101 19	6.21	79
80	2 626 372	288 848	.109 98	5.85	80
81	2 337 524	278 983	.119 35	5.51	81
82	2 058 541	265 902	.129 17	5.19	82
83	1 792 639	249 858	.139 38	4.89	83
84	1 542 781	231 433	.150 01	4.60	84
85	1 311 348	211 311	.161 14	4.32	85
86	1 100 037	190 108	.172 82	4.06	86
87	909 929	168 455	.185 13	3.80	87
88	741 474	146 997	.198 25	3.55	88
89	594 477	126 303	.212 46	3.31	89
90	468 174	106 809	.228 14	3.06	90
91	361 365	88 813	.245 77	2.82	91
92	272 552	72 480	.265 93	2.58	92
93	200 072	57 881	.289 30	2.33	93
94	142 191	45 026	.316 66	2.07	94
95	97 165	34 128	.351 24	1.80	95
96	63 037	25 250	.400 56	1.51	96
97	37 787	18 456	.488 42	1.18	97
98	19 331	12 916	.668 15	.83	98
99	6 415	6 415	1.000 00	.50	99

Table III—Commutation Columns—1958 CSO—3%

x	D_x	N_x	S_x	10,000,000/D_x	x
0	10 000 000.0	288 963 016.7	6 979 643 888.8	1.000 0000	0
1	9 640 000.0	278 963 016.7	6 690 680 872.1	1.037 3444	1
2	9 342 751.4	269 323 016.7	6 411 717 855.4	1.070 3485	2
3	9 056 844.9	259 980 265.3	6 142 394 838.7	1.104 1373	3
4	8 780 215.6	250 923 420.4	5 882 414 573.4	1.138 9242	4
5	8 512 546.9	242 143 204.8	5 631 491 153.0	1.174 7366	5
6	8 253 451.8	233 630 657.9	5 389 347 948.2	1.211 6143	6
7	8 002 642.6	225 377 206.1	5 155 717 290.3	1.249 5872	7
8	7 759 766.4	217 374 563.5	4 930 340 084.2	1.288 6986	8
9	7 524 487.1	209 614 797.1	4 712 965 520.7	1.328 9942	9
10	7 296 488.1	202 090 310.0	4 503 350 723.6	1.370 5223	10
11	7 075 397.6	194 793 821.9	4 301 260 413.6	1.413 3481	11
12	6 860 868.5	187 718 424.3	4 106 466 591.7	1.457 5414	12
13	6 652 644.7	180 857 555.8	3 918 748 167.4	1.503 1616	13
14	6 450 352.6	174 204 911.1	3 737 890 611.6	1.550 3028	14
15	6 253 773.3	167 754 558.5	3 563 685 700.5	1.599 0346	15
16	6 062 760.0	161 500 785.2	3 395 931 142.0	1.649 4138	16
17	5 877 109.8	155 438 025.2	3 234 430 356.8	1.701 5166	17
18	5 696 688.0	149 560 915.4	3 078 992 331.6	1.755 4059	18
19	5 521 418.1	143 864 227.4	2 929 431 416.2	1.811 1289	19
20	5 351 272.8	138 342 809.3	2 785 567 188.8	1.868 7143	20
21	5 186 111.0	132 991 536.5	2 647 224 379.5	1.928 2271	21
22	5 025 845.1	127 805 425.5	2 514 232 843.0	1.989 7151	22
23	4 870 385.5	122 779 580.4	2 386 427 417.5	2.053 2256	23
24	4 719 592.6	117 909 194.9	2 263 647 837.1	2.118 8270	24
25	4 573 377.1	113 189 602.3	2 145 738 642.2	2.186 5680	25
26	4 431 602.4	108 616 225.2	2 032 549 039.9	2.256 5201	26
27	4 294 093.7	104 184 622.8	1 923 932 814.7	2.328 7801	27
28	4 160 726.8	99 890 529.1	1 819 748 191.9	2.403 4262	28
29	4 031 340.5	95 729 802.3	1 719 857 662.8	2.480 5645	29
30	3 905 782.0	91 698 461.8	1 624 127 860.5	2.560 3067	30
31	3 783 944.4	87 792 679.8	1 532 429 398.7	2.642 7450	31
32	3 665 686.8	84 008 735.4	1 444 636 718.9	2.728 0017	32
33	3 550 911.6	80 343 048.6	1 360 627 983.5	2.816 1782	33
34	3 439 488.9	76 792 137.0	1 280 284 934.9	2.907 4087	34
35	3 331 295.4	73 352 648.1	1 203 492 797.9	3.001 8353	35
36	3 226 149.5	70 021 352.7	1 130 140 149.8	3.099 6704	36
37	3 123 914.9	66 795 203.2	1 060 118 797.1	3.201 1115	37
38	3 024 434.7	63 671 288.3	993 323 593.9	3.306 4030	38
39	2 927 506.2	60 646 853.6	929 652 305.6	3.415 8766	39
40	2 833 001.8	57 719 347.4	869 005 452.0	3.529 8248	40
41	2 740 778.0	54 886 345.6	811 286 104.6	3.648 5990	41
42	2 650 731.3	52 145 567.6	756 399 759.0	3.772 5438	42
43	2 562 794.0	49 494 836.3	704 254 191.4	3.901 9913	43
44	2 476 878.2	46 932 042.3	654 759 355.1	4.037 3402	44
45	2 392 904.8	44 455 164.1	607 827 312.8	4.179 0212	45
46	2 310 779.5	42 062 259.3	563 372 148.7	4.327 5440	46
47	2 230 395.8	39 751 479.8	521 309 889.4	4.483 5092	47
48	2 151 660.7	37 521 084.0	481 558 409.6	4.647 5729	48
49	2 074 472.4	35 369 423.3	444 037 325.6	4.820 5028	49

Table III (*Continued*)—Commutation Columns—1958 CSO—3%

x	D_x	N_x	S_x	$10{,}000{,}000/D_x$	x
50	1 998 744.0	33 294 950.9	408 667 902.3	5.003 1420	50
51	1 924 383.0	31 296 206.9	375 372 951.4	5.196 4708	51
52	1 851 312.7	29 371 823.9	344 076 744.5	5.401 5726	52
53	1 779 488.9	27 520 511.2	314 704 920.6	5.619 5911	53
54	1 708 844.9	25 741 022.3	287 184 409.4	5.851 9062	54
55	1 639 329.7	24 032 177.4	261 443 387.1	6.100 0542	55
56	1 570 891.7	22 392 847.7	237 411 209.7	6.365 8112	56
57	1 503 465.3	20 821 956.0	215 018 362.0	6.651 3008	57
58	1 436 991.7	19 318 490.7	194 196 406.0	6.958 9824	58
59	1 371 420.2	17 881 499.0	174 877 915.3	7.291 7112	59
60	1 306 723.8	16 510 078.8	156 996 416.3	7.652 7266	60
61	1 242 859.2	15 203 355.0	140 486 337.5	8.045 9637	61
62	1 179 823.4	13 960 495.8	125 282 982.5	8.475 8448	62
63	1 117 613.4	12 780 672.4	111 322 486.7	8.947 6379	63
64	1 056 231.5	11 663 059.0	98 541 814.3	9.467 6214	64
65	995 687.8	10 606 827.5	86 878 755.3	10.043 3088	65
66	935 994.9	9 611 139.7	76 271 927.8	10.683 8189	66
67	877 163.6	8 675 144.8	66 660 788.1	11.400 3819	67
68	819 219.7	7 797 981.2	57 985 643.3	12.206 7377	68
69	762 208.4	6 978 761.5	50 187 662.1	13.119 7714	69
70	706 256.4	6 216 553.1	43 208 900.6	14.159 1637	70
71	651 545.5	5 510 296.7	36 992 347.5	15.348 1223	71
72	598 314.8	4 858 751.2	31 482 050.8	16.713 6096	72
73	546 819.2	4 260 436.4	26 623 299.6	18.287 5802	73
74	497 308.1	3 713 617.2	22 362 863.2	20.108 2588	74
75	449 933.5	3 216 309.1	18 649 246.0	22.225 5067	75
76	404 778.5	2 766 375.6	15 432 936.9	24.704 8695	76
77	361 872.0	2 361 597.1	12 666 561.3	27.634 0806	77
78	321 222.8	1 999 725.1	10 304 964.2	31.131 0405	78
79	282 844.4	1 678 502.3	8 305 239.1	35.355 1281	79
80	246 818.8	1 395 657.9	6 626 736.8	40.515 5523	80
81	213 275.5	1 148 839.1	5 231 078.9	46.887 7110	81
82	182 350.6	935 563.6	4 082 239.8	54.839 4137	82
83	154 171.2	753 213.0	3 146 676.2	64.862 9575	83
84	128 818.2	599 041.8	2 393 463.2	77.628 7823	84
85	106 305.0	470 223.6	1 794 421.4	94.068 9525	85
86	86 577.7	363 918.6	1 324 197.8		86
87	69 529.5	277 340.9	960 279.2		87
88	55 007.3	207 811.4	682 938.3		88
89	42 817.6	152 804.1	475 126.9		89
90	32 738.4	109 986.5	322 322.8		90
91	24 533.4	77 248.1	212 336.3		91
92	17 964.9	52 714.7	135 088.2		92
93	12 803.4	34 749.8	82 373.5		93
94	8 834.3	21 946.4	47 623.7		94
95	5 861.0	13 112.1	25 677.3		95
96	3 691.7	7 251.1	12 565.2		96
97	2 148.5	3 559.4	5 314.1		97
98	1 067.1	1 410.9	1 754.7		98
99	343.8	343.8	343.8		99

Table III (*Continued*)—Commutation Columns—1958 CSO—3%

x	C_x	M_x	R_x	$D_x - M_x$	x
0	68 737.864	1 583 601.456	85 672 418.432	8 416 398.5	0
1	16 471.864	1 514 863.592	84 088 816.976	8 125 136.4	1
2	13 787.524	1 498 391.728	82 573 953.384	7 844 359.7	2
3	12 837.749	1 484 604.204	81 075 561.656	7 572 240.7	3
4	11 934.192	1 471 766.455	79 590 957.452	7 308 449.1	4
5	11 156.965	1 459 832.263	78 119 190.997	7 052 714.6	5
6	10 417.328	1 448 675.298	76 659 358.734	6 804 776.5	6
7	9 789.464	1 438 257.970	75 210 683.436	6 564 384.6	7
8	9 266.745	1 428 468.506	73 772 425.466	6 331 297.9	8
9	8 839.092	1 419 201.761	72 343 956.960	6 105 285.3	9
10	8 571.528	1 410 362.669	70 924 755.199	5 886 125.4	10
11	8 449.523	1 401 791.141	69 514 392.530	5 673 606.5	11
12	8 392.725	1 393 341.618	68 112 601.389	5 467 526.9	12
13	8 525.775	1 384 948.893	66 719 259.771	5 267 695.8	13
14	8 704.932	1 376 423.118	65 334 310.878	5 073 929.5	14
15	8 864.550	1 367 718.186	63 957 887.760	4 886 055.1	15
16	9 064.961	1 358 853.636	62 590 169.574	4 703 906.4	16
17	9 243.829	1 349 788.675	61 231 315.938	4 527 321.1	17
18	9 346.988	1 340 544.846	59 881 527.263	4 356 143.2	18
19	9 327.222	1 331 197.858	58 540 982.417	4 190 220.2	19
20	9 299.603	1 321 870.636	57 209 784.559	4 029 402.2	20
21	9 214.012	1 312 571.033	55 887 913.923	3 873 540.0	21
22	9 075.863	1 303 357.021	54 575 342.890	3 722 488.1	22
23	8 936.960	1 294 281.158	53 271 985.869	3 576 104.3	23
24	8 751.644	1 285 344.198	51 977 704.711	3 434 248.4	24
25	8 569.542	1 276 592.554	50 692 360.513	3 296 784.5	25
26	8 432.941	1 268 023.012	49 415 767.959	3 163 579.4	26
27	8 296.154	1 259 590.071	48 147 744.947	3 034 503.6	27
28	8 200.069	1 251 293.917	46 888 154.876	2 909 432.9	28
29	8 140.858	1 243 093.848	45 636 860.959	2 788 246.7	29
30	8 076.941	1 234 952.990	44 393 767.111	2 670 829.0	30
31	8 045.567	1 226 876.049	43 158 814.121	2 557 068.4	31
32	8 007.661	1 218 830.482	41 931 938.072	2 446 856.3	32
33	7 998.081	1 210 822.821	40 713 107.590	2 340 088.8	33
34	8 014.251	1 202 824.740	39 502 284.769	2 236 664.2	34
35	8 117.923	1 194 810.489	38 299 460.029	2 136 484.9	35
36	8 269.054	1 186 692.566	37 104 649.540	2 039 456.9	36
37	8 492.305	1 178 423.512	35 917 956.974	1 945 491.4	37
38	8 838.258	1 169 931.207	34 739 533.462	1 854 503.5	38
39	9 237.171	1 161 092.949	33 569 602.255	1 766 413.3	39
40	9 709.221	1 151 855.778	32 408 509.306	1 681 146.0	40
41	10 218.176	1 142 146.557	31 256 653.528	1 598 631.4	41
42	10 731.609	1 131 928.381	30 114 506.971	1 518 802.9	42
43	11 271.289	1 121 196.772	28 982 578.590	1 441 597.2	43
44	11 831.248	1 109 925.483	27 861 381.818	1 366 952.7	44
45	12 429.129	1 098 094.235	26 751 456.335	1 294 810.6	45
46	13 079.355	1 085 665.106	25 653 362.100	1 225 114.4	46
47	13 772.152	1 072 585.751	24 567 696.994	1 157 810.0	47
48	14 518.518	1 058 813.599	23 495 111.243	1 092 847.1	48
49	15 306.897	1 044 295.081	22 436 297.644	1 030 177.3	49

Table III (*Continued*)—Commutation Columns—1958 CSO—3%

x	C_x	M_x	R_x	$D_x - M_x$	x
50	16 145.109	1 028 988.184	21 392 002.563	969 755.8	50
51	17 020.413	1 012 843.075	20 363 014.379	911 539.9	51
52	17 902.007	995 822.662	19 350 171.304	855 490.0	52
53	18 814.279	977 920.655	18 354 348.642	801 568.2	53
54	19 743.028	959 106.376	17 376 427.987	749 738.5	54
55	20 690.546	939 363.348	16 417 321.611	699 966.4	55
56	21 672.210	918 672.802	15 477 958.263	652 218.9	56
57	22 683.398	897 000.592	14 559 285.461	606 464.7	57
58	23 717.295	874 317.194	13 662 284.869	562 674.5	58
59	24 752.177	850 599.899	12 787 967.675	520 820.3	59
60	25 804.703	825 847.722	11 937 367.776	480 876.1	60
61	26 836.036	800 043.019	11 111 520.054	442 816.2	61
62	27 846.132	773 206.983	10 311 477.035	406 616.4	62
63	28 830.119	745 360.851	9 538 270.052	372 252.5	63
64	29 779.577	716 530.732	8 792 909.201	339 700.8	64
65	30 692.340	686 751.155	8 076 378.469	308 936.6	65
66	31 569.313	656 058.815	7 389 627.314	279 936.1	66
67	32 395.427	624 489.502	6 733 568.499	252 674.1	67
68	33 150.537	592 094.075	6 109 078.997	227 125.6	68
69	33 751.833	558 943.538	5 516 984.922	203 264.9	69
70	34 140.262	525 191.705	4 958 041.384	181 064.7	70
71	34 253.619	491 051.443	4 432 849.679	160 494.1	71
72	34 069.048	456 797.824	3 941 798.236	141 517.0	72
73	33 584.287	422 728.776	3 485 000.412	124 090.4	73
74	32 889.905	389 144.489	3 062 271.636	108 163.6	74
75	32 050.095	356 254.584	2 673 127.147	93 678.9	75
76	31 116.905	324 204.489	2 316 872.563	80 574.0	76
77	30 109.191	293 087.584	1 992 668.074	68 784.4	77
78	29 022.371	262 978.393	1 699 580.490	58 244.4	78
79	27 787.431	233 956.022	1 436 602.097	48 888.4	79
80	26 354.463	206 168.591	1 202 646.075	40 650.2	80
81	24 712.992	179 814.128	996 477.484	33 461.4	81
82	22 868.200	155 101.136	816 663.356	27 249.5	82
83	20 862.501	132 232.936	661 562.220	21 938.3	83
84	18 761.225	111 370.435	529 329.284	17 447.8	84
85	16 631.093	92 609.210	417 958.849	13 695.8	85
86	14 526.529	75 978.117	325 349.639	10 599.6	86
87	12 497.068	61 451.588	249 371.522	8 077.9	87
88	10 587.550	48 954.520	187 919.934	6 052.8	88
89	8 832.090	38 366.970	138 965.414	4 450.6	89
90	7 251.375	29 534.880	100 598.444	3 203.5	90
91	5 853.988	22 283.505	71 063.564	2 249.9	91
92	4 638.273	16 429.517	48 780.059	1 535.4	92
93	3 596.142	11 791.244	32 350.542	1 012.2	93
94	2 715.983	8 195.102	20 559.298	639.2	94
95	1 998.652	5 479.119	12 364.196	381.9	95
96	1 435.657	3 480.467	6 885.077	211.2	96
97	1 018.801	2 044.810	3 404.610	103.7	97
98	692.218	1 026.009	1 359.800	41.1	98
99	333.791	333.791	333.791	10.0	99

Table IV—Life Annuity Due, Single Premium Insurance,
and Reciprocals

x	$\ddot{a}_x$	$1000/\ddot{a}_x$	$1000A_x$	$1/A_x$	x
0	28.896 30	34.606 50	158.3601	6.314 720	0
1	28.938 07	34.556 55	157.1435	6.363 609	1
2	28.826 95	34.689 76	160.3801	6.235 186	2
3	28.705 39	34.836 66	163.9207	6.100 511	3
4	28.578 28	34.991 61	167.6230	5.965 767	4
5	28.445 45	35.155 01	171.4918	5.831 182	5
6	28.307 02	35.326 92	175.5236	5.697 241	6
7	28.162 85	35.507 77	179.7229	5.564 122	7
8	28.013 03	35.697 67	184.0865	5.432 228	8
9	27.857 69	35.896 74	188.6111	5.301 915	9
10	27.696 93	36.105 09	193.2934	5.173 484	10
11	27.531 15	36.322 49	198.1219	5.047 398	11
12	27.360 74	36.548 72	203.0853	4.924 039	12
13	27.185 81	36.783 89	208.1802	4.803 531	13
14	27.007 04	37.027 39	213.3873	4.686 315	14
15	26.824 53	37.279 30	218.7029	4.572 414	15
16	26.638 16	37.540 13	224.1312	4.461 673	16
17	26.448 04	37.809 99	229.6688	4.354 096	17
18	26.254 01	38.089 42	235.3200	4.249 532	18
19	26.055 67	38.379 37	241.0971	4.147 707	19
20	25.852 32	38.681 25	247.0199	4.048 258	20
21	25.643 79	38.995 80	253.0935	3.951 109	21
22	25.429 64	39.324 19	259.3309	3.856 077	22
23	25.209 42	39.667 72	265.7451	3.763 004	23
24	24.982 92	40.027 35	272.3422	3.671 851	24
25	24.749 68	40.404 57	279.1356	3.582 488	25
26	24.509 47	40.800 56	286.1319	3.494 891	26
27	24.262 31	41.216 19	293.3308	3.409 120	27
28	24.007 95	41.652 87	300.7393	3.325 139	28
29	23.746 39	42.111 66	308.3574	3.242 990	29
30	23.477 62	42.593 76	316.1858	3.162 697	30
31	23.201 37	43.100 91	324.2320	3.084 211	31
32	22.917 60	43.634 59	332.4972	3.007 544	32
33	22.626 03	44.196 87	340.9893	2.932 643	33
34	22.326 61	44.789 60	349.7103	2.859 510	34
35	22.019 26	45.414 79	358.6624	2.788 137	35
36	21.704 31	46.073 80	367.8356	2.718 606	36
37	21.381 89	46.768 55	377.2265	2.650 927	37
38	21.052 29	47.500 76	386.8264	2.585 139	38
39	20.716 22	48.271 36	396.6150	2.521 337	39
40	20.373 92	49.082 36	406.5849	2.459 511	40
41	20.025 83	49.935 52	416.7235	2.399 673	41
42	19.672 14	50.833 30	427.0249	2.341 784	42
43	19.312 84	51.779 02	437.4900	2.285 766	43
44	18.948 06	52.775 85	448.1147	2.231 572	44
45	18.577 91	53.827 38	458.8959	2.179 143	45
46	18.202 63	54.937 12	469.8264	2.128 446	46
47	17.822 61	56.108 50	480.8948	2.079 457	47
48	17.438 20	57.345 38	492.0913	2.032 143	48
49	17.049 84	58.651 58	503.4027	1.986 481	49

Table IV (*Continued*)—Life Annuity Due, Single Premium
Insurance, and Reciprocals

x	$\ddot{a}_x$	$1000/\ddot{a}_x$	$1000A_x$	$1/A_x$	x
50	16.657 94	60.031 44	514.8174	1.942 436	50
51	16.262 98	61.489 34	526.3209	1.899 981	51
52	15.865 40	63.030 23	537.9008	1.859 079	52
53	15.465 40	64.660 46	549.5514	1.819 666	53
54	15.063 40	66.386 05	561.2600	1.781 705	54
55	14.659 76	68.213 95	573.0167	1.745 150	55
56	14.254 86	70.151 49	584.8098	1.709 958	56
57	13.849 31	72.205 77	596.6221	1.676 103	57
58	13.443 70	74.384 26	608.4358	1.643 559	58
59	13.038 67	76.694 92	620.2329	1.612 298	59
60	12.634 71	79.147 04	631.9987	1.582 282	60
61	12.232 56	81.749 01	643.7117	1.553 490	61
62	11.832 70	84.511 57	655.3582	1.525 883	62
63	11.435 68	87.445 59	666.9219	1.499 426	63
64	11.042 14	90.562 13	678.3842	1.474 091	64
65	10.652 76	93.872 35	689.7254	1.449 852	65
66	10.268 37	97.386 46	700.9214	1.426 694	66
67	9.890 00	101.112 27	711.9419	1.404 609	67
68	9.518 79	105.055 36	722.7537	1.383 597	68
69	9.155 98	109.218 29	733.3211	1.363 659	69
70	8.802 12	113.609 00	743.6275	1.344 759	70
71	8.457 27	118.241 46	753.6718	1.326 838	71
72	8.120 73	123.141 68	763.4740	1.309 802	72
73	7.791 31	128.348 17	773.0686	1.293 546	73
74	7.467 44	133.914 74	782.5018	1.277 952	74
75	7.148 41	139.891 25	791.7939	1.262 955	75
76	6.834 29	146.320 88	800.9430	1.248 528	76
77	6.526 06	153.231 90	809.9206	1.234 689	77
78	6.225 35	160.633 48	818.6791	1.221 480	78
79	5.934 37	168.509 99	827.1545	1.208 964	79
80	5.654 59	176.847 64	835.3034	1.197 170	80
81	5.386 64	185.644 36	843.1073	1.186 089	81
82	5.130 58	194.909 89	850.5655	1.175 688	82
83	4.885 56	204.684 73	857.7019	1.165 906	83
84	4.650 29	215.040 42	864.5551	1.156 664	84
85	4.423 34	226.073 30	871.1651	1.147 888	85
86	4.203 38	237.904 03	877.5714	1.139 508	86
87	3.988 82	250.700 49	883.8204	1.131 452	87
88	3.777 89	264.698 18	889.9641	1.123 641	88
89	3.568 72	280.212 38	896.0561	1.116 002	89
90	3.359 56	297.658 35	902.1479	1.108 466	90
91	3.148 69	317.592 28	908.2926	1.100 967	91
92	2.934 32	340.794 88	914.5343	1.093 453	92
93	2.714 11	368.445 29	920.9463	1.085 840	93
94	2.484 23	402.539 82	927.6459	1.077 998	94
95	2.237 18	446.991 71	934.8437	1.069 698	95
96	1.964 16	509.122 75	942.7816	1.060 691	96
97	1.656 69	603.612 97	951.7384	1.050 709	97
98	1.322 18	756.325 75	961.4928	1.040 049	98
99	1.000 00	1 000.000 00	970.8871	1.029 986	99

Table V—Annual Premiums and Difference Between First Year and Renewal Premiums

x	$1000c_x$	$1000P_x$	$1000\,_{20}P_x$	$1000\,_{19}P_x$	$1000\,(_{19}P_{x+1} - c_x)$	x
20	1.737 83	9.555 04	16.395 61	17.013 38	15.699 83	20
21	1.776 67	9.869 58	16.805 17	17.437 66	16.097 35	21
22	1.805 84	10.197 98	17.226 53	17.874 02	16.517 93	22
23	1.834 96	10.541 50	17.660 99	18.323 77	16.952 68	23
24	1.854 32	10.901 14	18.109 27	18.787 64	17.412 80	24
25	1.873 79	11.278 36	18.572 82	19.267 12	17.889 34	25
26	1.902 91	11.674 34	19.052 55	19.763 12	18.373 04	26
27	1.931 99	12.089 98	19.548 79	20.275 95	18.874 69	27
28	1.970 83	12.526 65	20.062 61	20.806 68	19.384 98	28
29	2.019 39	12.985 44	20.594 53	21.355 80	19.904 52	29
30	2.067 94	13.467 54	21.145 18	21.923 91	20.444 48	30
31	2.126 24	13.974 70	21.715 98	22.512 43	20.995 98	31
32	2.184 49	14.508 38	22.307 82	23.122 22	21.570 54	32
33	2.252 40	15.070 66	22.922 47	23.755 03	22.159 72	33
34	2.330 07	15.663 38	23.561 18	24.412 12	22.764 86	34
35	2.436 87	16.288 58	24.225 45	25.094 93	23.366 87	35
36	2.563 13	16.947 58	24.915 60	25.803 74	23.976 53	36
37	2.718 48	17.642 34	25.632 81	26.539 66	24.584 89	37
38	2.922 28	18.374 55	26.377 84	27.303 37	25.172 05	38
39	3.155 30	19.145 15	27.150 32	28.094 34	25.758 30	39
40	3.427 18	19.956 15	27.951 38	28.913 60	26.334 61	40
41	3.728 20	20.809 30	28.781 77	29.761 79	26.912 31	41
42	4.048 55	21.707 09	29.643 22	30.640 51	27.503 94	42
43	4.398 05	22.652 80	30.538 53	31.552 49	28.102 13	43
44	4.776 68	23.649 63	31.470 30	32.500 17	28.709 87	44
45	5.194 16	24.701 16	32.441 60	33.486 54	29.320 23	45
46	5.660 15	25.810 91	33.455 40	34.514 39	29.926 24	46
47	6.174 76	26.982 28	34.514 55	35.586 38	30.531 05	47
48	6.747 59	28.219 16	35.622 58	36.705 81	31.128 38	48
49	7.378 69	29.525 36	36.783 05	37.875 97	31.722 26	49
50	8.077 63	30.905 23	38.000 33	39.100 96	32.307 42	50
51	8.844 61	32.363 13	39.278 93	40.385 05	32.888 79	51
52	9.669 90	33.904 01	40.624 15	41.733 40	33.483 00	52
53	10.572 86	35.534 25	42.042 89	43.152 90	34.077 06	53
54	11.553 43	37.259 84	43.541 51	44.649 92	34.678 35	54
55	12.621 35	39.087 73	45.127 27	46.231 79	35.284 74	55
56	13.796 12	41.025 28	46.807 84	47.906 08	35.883 84	56
57	15.087 41	43.079 55	48.590 64	49.679 96	36.473 75	57
58	16.504 82	45.258 05	50.483 81	51.561 16	37.053 42	58
59	18.048 57	47.568 71	52.496 46	53.558 24	37.633 15	59
60	19.747 63	50.020 82	54.639 72	55.681 72	38.194 18	60
61	21.592 18	52.622 79	56.924 27	57.941 81	38.759 66	61
62	23.601 95	55.385 35	59.363 61	60.351 83	39.323 67	62
63	25.796 15	58.319 38	61.971 60	62.925 62	39.881 29	63
64	28.194 18	61.435 92	64.762 26	65.677 44	40.427 51	64
65	30.825 26	64.746 14	67.749 63	68.621 69	40.946 40	65

Table VI—Valuation Factors

x	u_x	$1000\,k_x$	x	u_x	$1000\,k_x$
0	1.037 344	7.130 48	50	1.038 641	8.389 76
1	1.031 816	1.763 06	51	1.039 469	9.193 70
2	1.031 568	1.522 33	52	1.040 362	10.060 20
3	1.031 506	1.462 12	53	1.041 340	11.009 94
4	1.031 444	1.401 95	54	1.042 405	12.043 35
5	1.031 392	1.351 79	55	1.043 566	13.171 21
6	1.031 341	1.301 74	56	1.044 847	14.414 84
7	1.031 299	1.261 57	57	1.046 259	15.785 34
8	1.031 268	1.231 55	58	1.047 813	17.293 97
9	1.031 248	1.211 42	59	1.049 510	18.942 16
10	1.031 248	1.211 46	60	1.051 385	20.762 37
11	1.031 269	1.231 55	61	1.053 428	22.745 81
12	1.031 299	1.261 56	62	1.055 663	24.915 71
13	1.031 361	1.321 75	63	1.058 114	27.295 27
14	1.031 434	1.391 95	64	1.060 806	29.908 55
15	1.031 506	1.462 13	65	1.063 775	32.791 14
16	1.031 589	1.542 42	66	1.067 070	35.990 22
17	1.031 671	1.622 67	67	1.070 731	39.544 25
18	1.031 744	1.692 86	68	1.074 798	43.492 75
19	1.031 795	1.742 99	69	1.079 223	47.789 77
20	1.031 847	1.793 17	70	1.083 971	52.398 89
21	1.031 888	1.833 33	71	1.088 968	57.250 16
22	1.031 919	1.863 48	72	1.094 173	62.304 04
23	1.031 950	1.893 59	73	1.099 558	67.532 15
24	1.031 971	1.913 61	74	1.105 292	73.099 48
25	1.031 992	1.933 73	75	1.111 555	79.179 34
26	1.032 023	1.963 85	76	1.118 568	85.988 71
27	1.032 054	1.993 92	77	1.126 545	93.733 04
28	1.032 095	2.034 08	78	1.135 687	102.608 96
29	1.032 147	2.084 31	79	1.145 960	112.582 31
30	1.032 199	2.134 53	80	1.157 277	123.570 04
31	1.032 261	2.194 83	81	1.169 590	135.524 60
32	1.032 323	2.255 10	82	1.182 780	148.329 91
33	1.032 395	2.325 37	83	1.196 812	161.953 05
34	1.032 478	2.405 75	84	1.211 779	176.484 88
35	1.032 592	2.516 29	85	1.227 857	192.094 42
36	1.032 726	2.647 02	86	1.245 194	208.926 12
37	1.032 892	2.807 90	87	1.264 005	227.189 26
38	1.033 110	3.019 04	88	1.284 689	247.270 98
39	1.033 358	3.260 56	89	1.307 871	269.777 69
40	1.033 649	3.542 51	90	1.334 442	295.571 55
41	1.033 971	3.854 85	91	1.365 630	325.856 98
42	1.034 313	4.187 46	92	1.403 135	362.268 85
43	1.034 687	4.550 60	93	1.449 283	407.065 87
44	1.035 093	4.944 30	94	1.507 303	463.399 25
45	1.035 540	5.378 76	95	1.587 615	541.390 69
46	1.036 040	5.864 14	96	1.718 269	668.213 64
47	1.036 593	6.400 71	97	2.013 401	954.738 08
48	1.037 209	6.998 66	98	3.103 839	
49	1.037 888	7.658 26	99		

Table VII—Single Premium Pure Endowment $1000\ _nE_x = 1000\ D_{x+n}/D_x$

x	n = 1	n = 2	n = 3
20	969.1360	939.1869	910.1359
21	969.0971	939.1210	910.0447
22	969.0680	939.0645	909.9718
23	969.0388	939.0175	909.9079
24	969.0195	938.9799	909.8441
25	969.0000	938.9328	909.7712
26	968.9709	938.8764	909.6801
27	968.9418	938.8106	909.5707
28	968.9030	938.7259	909.4431
29	968.8544	938.6318	909.2972
30	968.8058	938.5283	909.1423
31	968.7475	938.4154	908.9692
32	968.6893	938.2932	908.7780
33	968.6214	938.1522	908.5412
34	968.5437	937.9735	908.2497
35	968.4369	937.7478	907.8855
36	968.3106	937.4751	907.4304
37	968.1553	937.1274	906.8755
38	967.9515	936.7046	906.2117
39	967.7185	936.2160	905.4571
40	967.4466	935.6617	904.6214
41	967.1456	935.0608	903.7135
42	966.8253	934.4132	902.7338
43	966.4757	933.7094	901.6642
44	966.0971	932.9403	900.4867
45	965.6797	932.0871	899.1836
46	965.2136	931.1406	897.7371
47	964.6990	930.0916	896.1387
48	964.1262	928.9308	894.3710
49	963.4951	927.6494	892.4258
50	962.7961	926.2380	890.3036
51	962.0292	924.7062	887.9963
52	961.2039	923.0450	885.4958
53	960.3010	921.2363	882.7769
54	959.3204	919.2711	879.8138
55	958.2524	917.1220	876.5727
56	957.0776	914.7618	873.0202
57	955.7864	912.1728	869.1413
58	954.3689	909.3468	864.9035
59	952.8253	906.2570	860.2931
60	951.1262	902.8866	855.2790
61	949.2816	899.2277	849.8400
62	947.2718	895.2454	843.9295
63	945.0777	890.9054	837.4943
64	942.6795	886.1645	830.4653
65	940.0486	880.9625	822.7676

Table VII (*Continued*)—Single Premium Pure Endowment $1000 \, _nE_x = 1000 \, D_{x+n}/D_x$

x	n = 4	n = 5	n = 10
20	881.9570	854.6335	729.8791
21	881.8510	854.5136	729.6304
22	881.7626	854.4023	729.3672
23	881.6743	854.2911	729.0822
24	881.5860	854.1713	728.7582
25	881.4800	854.0258	728.4104
26	881.3476	853.8547	727.9871
27	881.1974	853.6579	727.4911
28	881.0208	853.4354	726.9006
29	880.8265	853.1874	726.1868
30	880.6147	852.9138	725.3354
31	880.3764	852.5890	724.3177
32	880.0941	852.2045	723.1200
33	879.7501	851.7347	721.7285
34	879.3268	851.1457	720.1297
35	878.7891	850.4205	718.3106
36	878.1372	849.5508	716.2655
37	877.3536	848.5287	713.9746
38	876.4386	847.3630	711.4257
39	875.4188	846.0710	708.6142
40	874.2946	844.6535	705.5216
41	873.0750	843.1108	702.1302
42	871.7517	841.4266	698.4158
43	870.2985	839.5761	694.3550
44	868.6986	837.5351	689.9188
45	866.9264	835.2794	685.0794
46	864.9653	832.7852	679.8103
47	862.7989	830.0377	674.0800
48	860.4111	827.0304	667.8524
49	857.8031	823.7492	661.0935
50	854.9594	820.1799	653.7725
51	851.8729	816.3093	645.8481
52	848.5286	812.1077	637.2902
53	844.8860	807.5306	628.0530
54	840.9141	802.5422	618.0968
55	836.5738	797.1086	607.3750
56	831.8357	791.1807	595.8367
57	826.6630	784.7360	583.4279
58	821.0370	777.7452	570.0936
59	814.9314	770.1735	555.7804
60	808.3051	761.9727	540.4787
61	801.1268	753.0981	524.2311
62	793.3347	743.4703	507.1223
63	784.8542	733.0081	489.2740
64	775.6062	721.6301	470.8325
65	765.5094	709.3151	451.8821

Table VII (*Continued*)—Single Premium Pure Endowment $1000 \, _nE_x = 1000 \, D_{x+n}/D_x$

x	n = 15	n = 20	n = 25
20	622.5239	529.4071	447.1655
21	622.0749	528.4843	445.5708
22	621.5701	527.4200	443.7852
23	620.9847	526.1994	441.7845
24	620.2879	524.8076	439.5448
25	619.4551	523.2249	437.0390
26	618.4621	521.4320	434.2409
27	617.2970	519.4101	431.1300
28	615.9486	517.1358	427.6870
29	614.4056	514.5863	423.8900
30	612.6570	511.7398	419.7187
31	610.6801	508.5653	415.1466
32	608.4524	505.0384	410.1456
33	605.9460	501.1358	404.6825
34	603.1339	496.8311	398.7279
35	599.9900	492.0998	392.2570
36	596.4953	486.9246	385.2454
37	592.6258	481.2760	377.6746
38	588.3707	475.1274	369.5280
39	583.7203	468.4602	360.7956
40	578.6547	461.2506	351.4603
41	573.1554	453.4695	341.5070
42	567.1889	445.0935	330.9138
43	560.7129	436.0918	319.6588
44	553.6890	426.4366	307.7295
45	546.0827	416.1000	295.1461
46	537.8528	405.0559	281.9592
47	528.9749	393.2771	268.2550
48	519.4190	380.7383	254.1382
49	509.1567	367.4228	239.7275
50	498.1567	353.3501	225.1081
51	486.3870	338.5737	210.3420
52	473.8063	323.1841	195.4678
53	460.3680	307.2900	180.5141
54	446.0372	291.0200	165.5179
55	430.8202	274.4619	150.5608
56	414.7616	257.6744	135.7672
57	397.9572	240.6920	121.2869
58	380.5305	223.5384	107.2875
59	362.6227	206.2420	93.9305
60	344.3218	188.8837	81.3523
61	325.6833	171.6007	69.6601
62	306.7171	154.5575	58.9321
63	287.4185	137.9468	49.2185
64	267.7864	121.9602	40.5381
65	247.8877	106.7654	32.8802

Table VII (*Continued*)—Single Premium Pure Endowment $1000 \, _nE_x = 1000 \, D_{x+n}/D_x$

x	n = 30	n = 60 − x	n = 65 − x
20	373.5081	244.1893	186.0656
21	371.0648	251.9660	191.9912
22	368.3585	260.0008	198.1135
23	365.3692	268.2999	204.4372
24	362.0747	276.8722	210.9690
25	358.4506	285.7240	217.7139
26	354.4749	294.8649	224.6790
27	350.1240	304.3072	231.8738
28	345.3704	314.0614	239.3062
29	340.1896	324.1413	246.9868
30	334.5614	334.5614	254.9266
31	328.4560	345.3338	263.1349
32	321.8560	356.4745	271.6238
33	314.7399	367.9967	280.4034
34	307.0897	379.9180	289.4871
35	298.8891	392.2570	298.8891
36	290.1276	405.0413	308.6304
37	280.7899	418.2969	318.7308
38	270.8670	432.0556	329.2145
39	260.3610	446.3607	340.1147
40	249.2961	461.2506	351.4603
41	237.7228	476.7711	363.2866
42	225.7169	492.9673	375.6276
43	213.3684	509.8825	388.5165
44	200.7802	527.5689	401.9930
45	188.0282	546.0827	416.1000
46	175.1697	565.4905	430.8883
47	162.2456	585.8708	446.4175
48	149.2906	607.3094	462.7532
49	136.3452	629.9066	479.9716
50	123.4869	653.7725	498.1567
51	110.8280	679.0352	517.4063
52	98.4980	705.8364	537.8280
53	86.6379	734.3253	559.5358
54	75.3832	764.6825	582.6672
55	64.8466	797.1086	607.3750
56	55.1137	831.8357	633.8361
57	46.2462	869.1413	662.2619
58	38.2795	909.3468	692.8974
59	31.2214	952.8253	726.0268
60	25.0538	1 000.0000	761.9727
61	19.7395		801.1268
62	15.2268		843.9295
63	11.4560		890.9054
64	8.3640		942.6795
65	5.8864		1 000.0000

Table VIII—Accumulated Pure Endowment $\quad 1/{}_nE_x = D_x/D_{x+n}$

x	n = 1	n = 2	n = 3
20	1.031 847	1.064 751	1.098 737
21	1.031 888	1.064 826	1.098 847
22	1.031 919	1.064 890	1.098 935
23	1.031 950	1.064 943	1.099 012
24	1.031 971	1.064 986	1.099 089
25	1.031 992	1.065 039	1.099 177
26	1.032 023	1.065 103	1.099 288
27	1.032 054	1.065 178	1.099 420
28	1.032 095	1.065 274	1.099 574
29	1.032 147	1.065 380	1.099 750
30	1.032 199	1.065 498	1.099 938
31	1.032 261	1.065 626	1.100 147
32	1.032 323	1.065 765	1.100 379
33	1.032 395	1.065 925	1.100 666
34	1.032 478	1.066 128	1.101 019
35	1.032 592	1.066 385	1.101 461
36	1.032 726	1.066 695	1.102 013
37	1.032 892	1.067 091	1.102 687
38	1.033 110	1.067 572	1.103 495
39	1.033 358	1.068 130	1.104 415
40	1.033 649	1.068 762	1.105 435
41	1.033 971	1.069 449	1.106 545
42	1.034 313	1.070 190	1.107 746
43	1.034 687	1.070 997	1.109 060
44	1.035 093	1.071 880	1.110 511
45	1.035 540	1.072 861	1.112 120
46	1.036 040	1.073 952	1.113 912
47	1.036 593	1.075 163	1.115 899
48	1.037 209	1.076 506	1.118 104
49	1.037 888	1.077 994	1.120 541
50	1.038 641	1.079 636	1.123 212
51	1.039 469	1.081 425	1.126 131
52	1.040 362	1.083 371	1.129 311
53	1.041 340	1.085 498	1.132 789
54	1.042 405	1.087 818	1.136 604
55	1.043 566	1.090 367	1.140 807
56	1.044 847	1.093 181	1.145 449
57	1.046 259	1.096 283	1.150 561
58	1.047 813	1.099 690	1.156 198
59	1.049 510	1.103 440	1.162 394
60	1.051 385	1.107 559	1.169 209
61	1.053 428	1.112 065	1.176 692
62	1.055 663	1.117 012	1.184 933
63	1.058 114	1.122 454	1.194 038
64	1.060 806	1.128 459	1.204 144
65	1.063 775	1.135 122	1.215 410

Table VIII (*Continued*)—Accumulated Pure Endowment $1/_nE_x = D_x/D_{x+n}$

x	n = 4	n = 5	n = 10
20	1.133 842	1.170 092	1.370 090
21	1.133 978	1.170 256	1.370 557
22	1.134 092	1.170 409	1.371 051
23	1.134 206	1.170 561	1.371 587
24	1.134 319	1.170 725	1.372 178
25	1.134 456	1.170 925	1.372 852
26	1.134 626	1.171 159	1.373 651
27	1.134 819	1.171 430	1.374 587
28	1.135 047	1.171 735	1.375 704
29	1.135 297	1.172 075	1.377 056
30	1.135 570	1.172 451	1.378 673
31	1.135 878	1.172 898	1.380 610
32	1.136 242	1.173 427	1.382 896
33	1.136 686	1.174 074	1.385 563
34	1.137 234	1.174 887	1.388 639
35	1.137 929	1.175 889	1.392 155
36	1.138 774	1.177 093	1.396 130
37	1.139 791	1.178 511	1.400 610
38	1.140 981	1.180 132	1.405 628
39	1.142 310	1.181 934	1.411 205
40	1.143 779	1.183 917	1.417 391
41	1.145 377	1.186 084	1.424 237
42	1.147 116	1.188 458	1.431 812
43	1.149 031	1.191 077	1.440 185
44	1.151 147	1.193 980	1.449 446
45	1.153 500	1.197 204	1.459 685
46	1.156 116	1.200 790	1.470 999
47	1.159 019	1.204 764	1.483 503
48	1.162 235	1.209 145	1.497 337
49	1.165 769	1.213 962	1.512 645
50	1.169 646	1.219 245	1.529 584
51	1.173 884	1.225 026	1.548 352
52	1.178 511	1.231 364	1.569 144
53	1.183 592	1.238 343	1.592 222
54	1.189 182	1.246 040	1.617 870
55	1.195 352	1.254 534	1.646 429
56	1.202 160	1.263 934	1.678 312
57	1.209 683	1.274 314	1.714 008
58	1.217 972	1.285 768	1.754 098
59	1.227 097	1.298 409	1.799 272
60	1.237 157	1.312 383	1.850 212
61	1.248 242	1.327 848	1.907 555
62	1.250 502	1.345 044	1.971 911
63	1.274 122	1.364 241	2.043 844
64	1.289 314	1.385 752	2.123 898
65	1.306 320	1.409 811	2.212 967

Table VIII (*Continued*)—Accumulated Pure Endowment $1/_nE_x = D_x/D_{x+n}$

x	n = 15	n = 20	n = 25
20	1.606 364	1.888 906	2.236 308
21	1.607 523	1.892 204	2.244 312
22	1.608 829	1.896 022	2.253 342
23	1.610 346	1.900 420	2.263 547
24	1.612 155	1.905 460	2.275 081
25	1.614 322	1.911 224	2.288 125
26	1.616 914	1.917 795	2.302 869
27	1.619 966	1.925 261	2.319 486
28	1.623 512	1.933 728	2.338 158
29	1.627 589	1.943 309	2.359 103
30	1.632 235	1.954 118	2.382 548
31	1.637 519	1.966 316	2.408 788
32	1.643 514	1.980 047	2.438 159
33	1.650 312	1.995 467	2.471 073
34	1.658 007	2.012 757	2.507 976
35	1.666 694	2.032 108	2.549 349
36	1.676 459	2.053 706	2.595 748
37	1.687 405	2.077 810	2.647 782
38	1.699 609	2.104 699	2.706 155
39	1.713 149	2.134 653	2.771 652
40	1.728 146	2.168 019	2.845 271
41	1.744 728	2.205 220	2.928 198
42	1.763 081	2.246 719	3.021 935
43	1.783 444	2.293 095	3.128 335
44	1.806 068	2.345 015	3.249 608
45	1.831 225	2.403 268	3.388 153
46	1.859 245	2.468 795	3.546 613
47	1.890 449	2.542 736	3.727 796
48	1.925 228	2.626 476	3.934 867
49	1.964 032	2.721 660	4.171 403
50	2.007 400	2.830 054	4.442 310
51	2.055 976	2.953 567	4.754 163
52	2.110 567	3.094 212	5.115 932
53	2.172 175	3.254 255	5.539 734
54	2.241 965	3.436 190	6.041 643
55	2.321 154	3.643 493	6.641 835
56	2.411 024	3.880 867	7.365 552
57	2.512 833	4.154 688	8.244 916
58	2.627 910	4.473 505	9.320 753
59	2.757 687	4.848 674	10.646 168
60	2.904 260	5.294 264	12.292 214
61	3.070 467	5.827 482	14.355 419
62	3.260 333	6.470 082	16.968 674
63	3.479 247	7.249 171	20.317 547
64	3.734 320	8.199 397	24.668 162
65	4.034 084	9.366 331	30.413 453

Table VIII (*Continued*)—Accumulated Pure Endowment $1/_nE_x = D_x/D_{x+n}$

x	n = 30	n = 60 − x	n = 65 − x
20	2.677 318	4.095 183	5.374 448
21	2.694 947	3.968 789	5.208 571
22	2.714 747	3.846 142	5.047 611
23	2.736 958	3.727 173	4.891 479
24	2.761 861	3.611 775	4.740 033
25	2.789 785	3.499 880	4.593 184
26	2.821 074	3.391 384	4.450 795
27	2.856 131	3.286 153	4.312 691
28	2.895 442	3.184 090	4.178 746
29	2.939 537	3.085 075	4.048 800
30	2.988 988	2.988 988	3.922 697
31	3.044 548	2.895 749	3.800 332
32	3.106 979	2.805 250	3.681 562
33	3.177 227	2.717 416	3.566 290
34	3.256 378	2.632 147	3.454 385
35	3.345 723	2.549 349	3.345 723
36	3.446 760	2.468 884	3.240 122
37	3.561 382	2.390 647	3.137 444
38	3.691 848	2.314 517	3.037 533
39	3.840 821	2.240 340	2.940 185
40	4.011 294	2.168 019	2.845 271
41	4.206 580	2.097 442	2.752 648
42	4.430 329	2.028 532	2.662 211
43	4.686 730	1.961 236	2.573 893
44	4.980 571	1.895 487	2.487 605
45	5.318 352	1.831 225	2.403 268
46	5.708 751	1.768 376	2.320 787
47	6.163 494	1.706 861	2.240 055
48	6.698 344	1.646 607	2.160 979
49	7.334 324	1.587 537	2.083 457
50	8.098 022	1.529 584	2.007 400
51	9.022 991	1.472 678	1.932 717
52	10.152 490	1.416 759	1.859 331
53	11.542 291	1.361 794	1.787 196
54	13.265 555	1.307 732	1.716 246
55	15.421 003	1.254 534	1.646 429
56	18.144 299	1.202 160	1.577 695
57	21.623 416	1.150 561	1.509 977
58	26.123 654	1.099 690	1.443 215
59	32.029 357	1.049 510	1.377 360
60	39.914 101	1.000 000	1.312 383
61	50.659 884		1.248 242
62	65.673 808		1.184 933
63	87.290 360		1.122 454
64	119.560 293		1.060 806
65	169.883 603		1.000 000

Table IX—Temporary Life Annuity Due $\ddot{a}_{x:\overline{n}|} = (N_x - N_{x+n})/D_x$

x	n = 1	n = 2	n = 3
20	1.000 00	1.969 14	2.908 32
21	1.000 00	1.969 10	2.908 22
22	1.000 00	1.969 07	2.908 13
23	1.000 00	1.969 04	2.908 06
24	1.000 00	1.969 02	2.908 00
25	1.000 00	1.969 00	2.907 93
26	1.000 00	1.968 97	2.907 85
27	1.000 00	1.968 94	2.907 75
28	1.000 00	1.968 90	2.907 63
29	1.000 00	1.968 85	2.907 49
30	1.000 00	1.968 81	2.907 33
31	1.000 00	1.968 75	2.907 16
32	1.000 00	1.968 69	2.906 98
33	1.000 00	1.968 62	2.906 77
34	1.000 00	1.968 54	2.906 52
35	1.000 00	1.968 44	2.906 18
36	1.000 00	1.968 31	2.905 79
37	1.000 00	1.968 16	2.905 28
38	1.000 00	1.967 95	2.904 66
39	1.000 00	1.967 72	2.903 93
40	1.000 00	1.967 45	2.903 11
41	1.000 00	1.967 15	2.902 21
42	1.000 00	1.966 83	2.901 24
43	1.000 00	1.966 48	2.900 19
44	1.000 00	1.966 10	2.899 04
45	1.000 00	1.965 68	2.897 77
46	1.000 00	1.965 21	2.896 35
47	1.000 00	1.964 70	2.894 79
48	1.000 00	1.964 13	2.893 06
49	1.000 00	1.963 50	2.891 14
50	1.000 00	1.962 80	2.889 03
51	1.000 00	1.962 03	2.886 74
52	1.000 00	1.961 20	2.884 25
53	1.000 00	1.960 30	2.881 54
54	1.000 00	1.959 32	2.878 59
55	1.000 00	1.958 25	2.875 37
56	1.000 00	1.957 08	2.871 84
57	1.000 00	1.955 79	2.867 96
58	1.000 00	1.954 37	2.863 72
59	1.000 00	1.952 83	2.859 08
60	1.000 00	1.951 13	2.854 01
61	1.000 00	1.949 28	2.848 51
62	1.000 00	1.947 27	2.842 52
63	1.000 00	1.945 08	2.835 98
64	1.000 00	1.942 68	2.828 84
65	1.000 00	1.940 05	2.821 01

Table IX (*Continued*)—Temporary Life Annuity Due $\ddot{a}_{x:\overline{n}|} = (N_x - N_{x+n})/D_x$

x	n = 4	n = 5	n = 10
20	3.818 46	4.700 42	8.716 50
21	3.818 26	4.700 11	8.715 37
22	3.818 10	4.699 87	8.714 29
23	3.817 96	4.699 64	8.713 18
24	3.817 84	4.699 43	8.711 99
25	3.817 70	4.699 18	8.710 62
26	3.817 53	4.698 87	8.709 01
27	3.817 32	4.698 52	8.707 17
28	3.817 07	4.698 09	8.705 03
29	3.816 78	4.697 61	8.702 55
30	3.816 48	4.697 09	8.699 70
31	3.816 13	4.696 51	8.696 30
32	3.815 76	4.695 85	8.692 28
33	3.815 31	4.695 06	8.687 41
34	3.814 77	4.694 09	8.681 55
35	3.814 07	4.692 86	8.674 55
36	3.813 22	4.691 35	8.666 40
37	3.812 16	4.689 51	8.657 00
38	3.810 87	4.687 31	8.646 31
39	3.809 39	4.684 81	8.634 46
40	3.807 73	4.682 02	8.621 38
41	3.805 92	4.678 99	8.607 10
42	3.803 97	4.675 72	8.591 49
43	3.801 85	4.672 15	8.574 36
44	3.799 52	4.668 22	8.555 54
45	3.796 95	4.663 88	8.534 81
46	3.794 09	4.659 06	8.512 02
47	3.790 93	4.653 73	8.487 07
48	3.787 43	4.647 84	8.459 79
49	3.783 57	4.641 37	8.430 06
50	3.779 34	4.634 30	8.397 71
51	3.774 73	4.626 60	8.362 60
52	3.769 74	4.618 27	8.324 54
53	3.764 31	4.609 20	8.283 19
54	3.758 41	4.599 32	8.238 29
55	3.751 95	4.588 52	8.189 54
56	3.744 86	4.576 70	8.136 59
57	3.737 10	4.563 76	8.079 21
58	3.728 62	4.549 66	8.017 10
59	3.719 38	4.534 31	7.949 96
60	3.709 29	4.517 60	7.877 35
61	3.698 35	4.499 48	7.799 00
62	3.686 45	4.479 78	7.714 50
63	3.673 48	4.458 33	7.623 60
64	3.659 31	4.434 92	7.526 23
65	3.643 78	4.409 29	7.422 53

Table IX (*Continued*)—Temporary Life Annuity Due $\ddot{a}_{x:\overline{n}|} = (N_x - N_{x+n})/D_x$

x	n = 15	n = 20	n = 25
20	12.144 80	15.066 22	17.544 92
21	12.142 08	15.060 45	17.533 23
22	12.139 30	15.054 16	17.520 23
23	12.136 27	15.047 01	17.505 49
24	12.132 90	15.038 83	17.488 75
25	12.128 95	15.029 25	17.469 51
26	12.124 26	15.018 04	17.447 42
27	12.118 75	15.005 06	17.422 26
28	12.112 23	14.990 04	17.393 60
29	12.104 60	14.972 78	17.361 17
30	12.095 73	14.953 09	17.324 64
31	12.085 38	14.930 58	17.283 51
32	12.073 39	14.904 96	17.237 36
33	12.059 43	14.875 77	17.185 60
34	12.043 28	14.842 65	17.127 73
35	12.024 66	14.805 19	17.063 20
36	12.003 52	14.763 27	16.991 77
37	11.979 64	14.716 55	16.912 98
38	11.952 90	14.664 82	16.826 49
39	11.923 40	14.608 12	16.732 26
40	11.890 98	14.546 15	16.629 89
41	11.855 57	14.478 73	16.519 11
42	11.816 97	14.405 49	16.399 41
43	11.774 78	14.325 83	16.270 08
44	11.728 69	14.239 29	16.130 50
45	11.678 31	14.145 29	15.980 00
46	11.623 31	14.043 36	15.818 02
47	11.563 41	13.933 10	15.644 19
48	11.498 29	13.814 03	15.458 13
49	11.427 66	13.685 73	15.259 69
50	11.351 19	13.547 71	15.048 77
51	11.268 58	13.399 57	14.825 44
52	11.179 46	13.240 91	14.589 77
53	11.083 26	13.071 21	14.341 64
54	10.979 50	12.890 23	14.081 16
55	10.867 63	12.697 79	13.808 40
56	10.747 11	12.493 84	13.523 53
57	10.617 61	12.278 54	13.227 04
58	10.478 87	12.052 10	12.919 54
59	10.330 81	11.814 76	12.601 87
60	10.173 36	11.566 65	12.274 86
61	10.006 75	11.308 21	11.939 76
62	9.831 05	11.039 73	11.597 63
63	9.646 40	10.761 74	11.249 74
64	9.453 00	10.474 99	10.897 47
65	9.251 06	10.180 50	10.542 30

Table IX (*Continued*)—Temporary Life Annuity Due $\ddot{a}_{x:\overline{n}|} = (N_x - N_{x+n})/D_x$

x	$n = 30$	$n = 60 - x$	$n = 65 - x$
20	19.630 44	22.767 06	23.870 21
21	19.609 17	22.460 27	23.598 55
22	19.585 48	22.144 60	23.319 18
23	19.558 84	21.819 53	23.031 60
24	19.528 84	21.484 72	22.735 51
25	19.494 88	21.139 64	22.430 42
26	19.456 48	20.783 94	22.116 02
27	19.413 33	20.417 47	21.792 21
28	19.364 90	20.039 88	21.458 68
29	19.310 77	19.650 96	21.115 30
30	19.250 53	19.250 53	20.761 95
31	19.183 51	18.838 17	20.398 25
32	19.109 17	18.413 65	20.024 05
33	19.026 77	17.976 50	19.638 96
34	18.935 68	17.526 46	19.242 77
35	18.835 26	17.063 20	18.835 26
36	18.725 17	16.586 73	18.416 54
37	18.604 88	16.096 83	17.986 53
38	18.473 97	15.593 40	17.545 25
39	18.332 36	15.076 58	17.093 06
40	18.179 58	14.546 15	16.629 89
41	18.015 34	14.001 96	16.155 82
42	17.839 16	13.443 64	15.670 67
43	17.650 42	12.870 62	15.174 07
44	17.448 75	12.282 38	14.665 73
45	17.233 81	11.678 31	14.145 29
46	17.005 47	11.057 82	13.612 48
47	16.763 79	10.420 30	13.067 03
48	16.508 81	9.765 02	12.508 60
49	16.240 72	9.091 15	11.936 82
50	15.959 67	8.397 71	11.351 19
51	15.665 99	7.683 57	10.751 18
52	15.360 05	6.947 37	10.136 05
53	15.042 13	6.187 41	9.504 80
54	14.712 85	5.401 86	8.856 39
55	14.372 92	4.588 52	8.189 54
56	14.023 20	3.744 86	7.502 76
57	13.664 84	2.867 96	6.794 39
58	13.299 09	1.954 37	6.062 43
59	12.927 25	1.000 00	5.304 48
60	12.550 54		4.517 60
61	12.170 41		3.698 35
62	11.788 02		2.842 52
63	11.404 59		1.945 08
64	11.021 36		1.000 00
65	10.639 60		

Table X—Reciprocal of Temporary Life Annuity Due

$$1000/\ddot{a}_{x:\overline{n}|} = 1000\ D_x/(N_x - N_{x+n})$$

x	$n = 1$	$n = 2$	$n = 3$
20	1 000.000 00	507.836 95	343.840 78
21	1 000.000 00	507.846 97	343.853 17
22	1 000.000 00	507.854 49	343.863 29
23	1 000.000 00	507.862 00	343.872 30
24	1 000.000 00	507.867 00	343.879 03
25	1 000.000 00	507.872 02	343.886 90
26	1 000.000 00	507.879 53	343.897 02
27	1 000.000 00	507.887 03	343.908 24
28	1 000.000 00	507.897 05	343.922 85
29	1 000.000 00	507.909 57	343.939 72
30	1 000.000 00	507.922 10	343.957 72
31	1 000.000 00	507.937 14	343.977 97
32	1 000.000 00	507.952 17	343.999 32
33	1 000.000 00	507.969 69	344.024 05
34	1 000.000 00	507.989 73	344.054 38
35	1 000.000 00	508.017 29	344.093 75
36	1 000.000 00	508.049 89	344.141 00
37	1 000.000 00	508.089 99	344.200 59
38	1 000.000 00	508.142 60	344.274 84
39	1 000.000 00	508.202 78	344.360 39
40	1 000.000 00	508.273 00	344.458 38
41	1 000.000 00	508.350 79	344.565 44
42	1 000.000 00	508.433 57	344.680 39
43	1 000.000 00	508.523 95	344.805 58
44	1 000.000 00	508.621 88	344.942 08
45	1 000.000 00	508.729 89	345.093 33
46	1 000.000 00	508.850 54	345.261 63
47	1 000.000 00	508.983 81	345.448 12
48	1 000.000 00	509.132 26	345.655 13
49	1 000.000 00	509.295 90	345.883 79
50	1 000.000 00	509.477 26	346.136 44
51	1 000.000 00	509.676 40	346.412 07
52	1 000.000 00	509.890 90	346.710 72
53	1 000.000 00	510.125 75	347.036 99
54	1 000.000 00	510.381 06	347.392 13
55	1 000.000 00	510.659 39	347.780 79
56	1 000.000 00	510.965 94	348.208 88
57	1 000.000 00	511.303 28	348.679 99
58	1 000.000 00	511.674 12	349.196 67
59	1 000.000 00	512.078 59	349.762 58
60	1 000.000 00	512.524 52	350.383 86
61	1 000.000 00	513.009 50	351.060 82
62	1 000.000 00	513.539 00	351.800 86
63	1 000.000 00	514.118 28	352.611 41
64	1 000.000 00	514.752 94	353.501 28
65	1 000.000 00	515.451 01	354.482 84

Table X (*Continued*)—Reciprocal of Temporary Life Annuity Due

$$1000/\ddot{a}_{x:\overline{n}|} = 1000\ D_x/(N_x - N_{x+n})$$

x	n = 4	n = 5	n = 10
20	261.885 77	212.747 14	114.725 0C
21	261.899 21	212.760 81	114.739 87
22	261.91J 09	212.771 99	114.753 99
23	261.919 69	212.782 32	114.768 7C
24	261.927 97	212.791 79	114.784 30
25	261.937 54	212.8J2 90	114.802 38
26	261.949 66	212.816 9J	114.823 61
27	261.963 68	212.832 95	114.847 83
28	261.980 91	212.852 33	114.876 15
29	262.00J 72	212.874 21	114.908 83
3C	262.J21 8J	212.897 72	114.946 55
31	262.J45 44	212.924 13	114.991 37
32	262.J70 96	212.953 78	115.J44 64
33	262.1C1 57	212.989 60	115.1J9 15
34	262.139 21	213.033 67	115.186 80
35	262.187 1C	213.089 7J	115.279 77
36	262.245 82	213.158 11	115.388 2J
37	262.318 60	213.241 82	115.513 49
38	262.40/ 43	213.342 15	11J.65b 2o
39	262.5J9 12	213.455 81	115.815 J2
4C	262.623 68	213.582 83	115.990 66
41	262.748 57	213.721 11	116.183 21
42	262.883 10	213.870 62	116.394 18
43	263.J29 89	214.J34 33	116.626 74
44	263.190 86	214.214 29	116.883 39
45	263.369 26	214.413 9J	117.167 23
46	263.567 72	214.635 73	117.48J 87
47	263.787 56	214.881 48	117.826 30
48	264.J31 42	215.153 75	118.206 27
49	264.3JJ 63	215.453 47	118.623 13
5J	264.596 62	215.782 45	119.J80 J9
51	264.919 49	216.141 23	119.579 99
52	265.269 95	216.531 15	120.126 75
53	265.652 64	216.957 38	120.726 48
54	266.J70 30	217.423 48	121.384 38
55	266.528 27	217.935 15	122.107 04
56	267.J32 71	218.498 27	122.901 55
57	267.587 13	219.117 40	123.774 48
58	268.195 79	219.796 82	124.733 35
59	268.862 34	220.54J 88	125.786 78
60	269.593 25	221.356 63	126.946 18
61	270.390 9J	222.248 10	128.221 57
62	271.263 92	223.225 17	129.626 J7
63	272.221 63	224.299 15	131.171 65
64	273.275 61	225.483 44	132.868 64
65	274.440 38	226.793 98	134.725 03

Table X (*Continued*)—Reciprocal of Temporary Life Annuity Due

$$1000/\ddot{a}_{x:\overline{n}|} = 1000\, D_x/(N_x - N_{x+n})$$

x	$n = 15$	$n = 20$	$n = 25$
20	82.339 74	66.373 64	56.996 56
21	82.358 20	66.399 06	57.034 56
22	82.377 10	66.426 84	57.076 89
23	82.397 67	66.458 38	57.124 93
24	82.420 53	66.494 53	57.179 62
25	82.447 38	66.536 91	57.242 59
26	82.479 29	66.586 60	57.315 07
27	82.516 75	66.644 18	57.397 85
28	82.561 16	66.710 98	57.492 41
29	82.613 23	66.787 86	57.599 81
30	82.673 78	66.875 81	57.721 24
31	82.744 58	66.976 65	57.858 63
32	82.826 80	67.091 76	58.013 51
33	82.922 67	67.223 42	58.188 24
34	83.033 89	67.373 43	58.384 85
35	83.162 43	67.543 87	58.605 64
36	83.308 91	67.735 69	58.852 01
37	83.474 95	67.950 71	59.126 19
38	83.661 68	68.190 39	59.430 11
39	83.868 69	68.455 09	59.764 79
40	84.097 35	68.746 71	60.132 67
41	84.348 51	69.066 82	60.535 96
42	84.624 06	69.418 00	60.977 81
43	84.927 25	69.803 96	61.462 53
44	85.260 99	70.228 23	61.994 36
45	85.628 82	70.694 90	62.578 24
46	86.034 02	71.208 01	63.219 03
47	86.479 67	71.771 52	63.921 51
48	86.969 48	72.390 18	64.690 88
49	87.506 98	73.068 83	65.532 13
50	88.096 49	73.813 23	66.450 61
51	88.742 31	74.629 24	67.451 61
52	89.449 75	75.523 49	68.541 18
53	90.226 20	76.504 01	69.727 04
54	91.078 84	77.578 13	71.016 87
55	92.016 40	78.753 85	72.419 69
56	93.048 24	80.039 43	73.945 16
57	94.183 17	81.442 91	75.602 72
58	95.430 10	82.973 10	77.402 11
59	96.797 83	84.639 91	79.353 31
60	98.295 96	86.455 43	81.467 31
61	99.932 56	88.431 31	83.753 80
62	101.718 57	90.581 92	86.224 52
63	103.665 60	92.921 82	88.890 94
64	105.786 52	95.465 46	91.764 39
65	108.095 70	98.226 96	94.855 95

Table X (*Continued*)—Reciprocal of Temporary Life Annuity Due

$$1000/\ddot{a}_{x:\overline{n}|} = 1000\ D_x/(N_x - N_{x+n})$$

x	n = 30	n = 60 − x	n = 65 − x
20	50.941 28	43.923 11	41.893 23
21	50.996 55	44.523 06	42.375 48
22	51.058 23	45.157 73	42.883 15
23	51.127 79	45.830 51	43.418 61
24	51.206 32	46.544 71	43.984 05
25	51.295 53	47.304 51	44.582 31
26	51.396 76	48.114 08	45.216 10
27	51.510 99	48.977 66	45.887 96
28	51.639 84	49.900 51	46.601 19
29	51.784 56	50.888 09	47.359 02
30	51.946 62	51.946 62	48.165 04
31	52.128 11	53.083 70	49.023 81
32	52.330 89	54.307 55	49.939 94
33	52.557 53	55.628 17	50.919 19
34	52.810 34	57.056 59	51.967 56
35	53.091 91	58.605 64	53.091 91
36	53.404 04	60.289 16	54.299 00
37	53.749 34	62.124 04	55.597 17
38	54.130 23	64.129 71	56.995 49
39	54.548 36	66.328 05	58.503 29
40	55.006 76	68.746 71	60.132 67
41	55.508 25	71.418 57	61.897 20
42	56.056 46	74.384 59	63.813 47
43	56.655 86	77.696 31	65.901 91
44	57.310 70	81.417 43	68.186 20
45	58.025 49	85.628 82	70.694 90
46	58.804 62	90.433 75	73.462 02
47	59.652 39	95.966 50	76.528 48
48	60.573 72	102.406 37	79.945 02
49	61.573 63	109.997 06	83.774 43
50	62.657 94	119.080 09	88.096 49
51	63.832 54	130.147 86	93.013 08
52	65.103 94	143.939 46	98.657 77
53	66.479 96	161.618 44	105.210 01
54	67.967 79	185.121 37	112.912 84
55	69.575 29	217.935 15	122.107 04
56	71.310 40	267.032 71	133.284 32
57	73.180 50	348.679 99	147.180 26
58	75.193 13	511.674 12	164.950 33
59	77.355 96	1 000.000 00	188.519 88
60	79.677 83		221.356 63
61	82.166 50		270.390 90
62	84.831 89		351.800 86
63	87.683 99		514.118 28
64	90.732 87		1 000.000 00
65	93.988 54		

Table XI—Single Premium Term Insurance $1000 \, A^{1}_{x:\overline{n}|} = 1000 \, (M_x - M_{x+n})/D_x$

x	n = 1	n = 2	n = 3
20	1.7378	3.4597	5.1557
21	1.7767	3.5267	5.2500
22	1.8058	3.5840	5.3254
23	1.8350	3.6319	5.3914
24	1.8543	3.6701	5.4569
25	1.8738	3.7177	5.5317
26	1.9029	3.7750	5.6253
27	1.9320	3.8416	5.7374
28	1.9708	3.9274	5.8687
29	2.0194	4.0229	6.0187
30	2.0679	4.1279	6.1781
31	2.1262	4.2425	6.3561
32	2.1845	4.3664	6.5527
33	2.2524	4.5094	6.7955
34	2.3301	4.6903	7.0944
35	2.4369	4.9191	7.4684
36	2.5631	5.1955	7.9350
37	2.7185	5.5477	8.5046
38	2.9223	5.9765	9.1867
39	3.1553	6.4719	9.9623
40	3.4272	7.0340	10.8221
41	3.7282	7.6437	11.7562
42	4.0485	8.3007	12.7641
43	4.3980	9.0146	13.8644
44	4.7767	9.7947	15.0753
45	5.1942	10.6600	16.4155
46	5.6601	11.6201	17.9031
47	6.1748	12.6841	19.5470
48	6.7476	13.8616	21.3651
49	7.3787	15.1614	23.3661
50	8.0776	16.5932	25.5498
51	8.8446	18.1473	27.9241
52	9.6699	19.8326	30.4969
53	10.5729	21.6676	33.2949
54	11.5534	23.6613	36.3437
55	12.6213	25.8415	39.6785
56	13.7961	28.2359	43.3339
57	15.0874	30.8625	47.3259
58	16.5048	33.7298	51.6873
59	18.0486	36.8646	56.4327
60	19.7476	40.2845	61.5944
61	21.5922	43.9971	67.1937
62	23.6019	48.0379	73.2786
63	25.7961	52.4418	79.9042
64	28.1942	57.2525	87.1412
65	30.8253	62.5313	95.0670

Table XI (*Continued*)—Single Premium Term Insurance

$$1000\, A_{x:\overline{n}|}^{1} = 1000\, (M_x - M_{x+n})/D_x$$

x	n = 4	n = 5	n = 10
20	6.8257	8.4612	16.2424
21	6.9375	8.5899	16.5239
22	7.0305	8.7084	16.8184
23	7.1229	8.8263	17.1359
24	7.2147	8.9521	17.4844
25	7.3247	9.1048	17.8822
26	7.4623	9.2849	18.3524
27	7.6184	9.4920	18.9019
28	7.8023	9.7269	19.5549
29	8.0050	9.9890	20.3409
30	8.2258	10.2777	21.2754
31	8.4741	10.6195	22.3918
32	8.7672	11.0230	23.7069
33	9.1242	11.5158	25.2403
34	9.5635	12.1331	27.0096
35	10.1215	12.8943	29.0326
36	10.7983	13.8078	31.3152
37	11.6127	14.8036	33.0798
38	12.5653	16.1136	36.7400
39	13.6280	17.4782	39.8967
40	14.8007	18.9769	43.3701
41	16.0729	20.6078	47.1777
42	17.4530	22.3873	51.3465
43	18.9680	24.3419	55.9062
44	20.6356	26.4972	60.8908
45	22.4828	28.8796	66.3340
46	24.5272	31.5141	72.2667
47	26.7857	34.4168	78.7238
48	29.2755	37.5956	85.7460
49	31.9958	41.0652	93.3708
50	34.9629	44.8406	101.6341
51	38.1835	48.9353	110.5809
52	41.6731	53.3795	120.2475
53	45.4738	58.2209	130.6891
54	49.6178	63.4970	141.9530
55	54.1462	69.2451	154.0948
56	59.0907	75.5175	167.1751
57	64.4894	82.3389	181.2553
58	70.3624	89.7405	196.3986
59	76.7373	97.7594	212.6674
60	83.6573	106.4468	230.0838
61	91.1542	115.8492	248.6135
62	99.2930	126.0506	268.1835
63	108.1513	137.1376	288.6795
64	117.8119	149.1976	309.9569
65	128.3611	162.2591	331.9279

Table XI (*Continued*)—Single Premium Term Insurance

$$1000 \, A \, \tfrac{1}{x:\overline{n}|} = 1000 \, (M_x - M_{x+n})/D_x$$

x	n = 15	n = 20	n = 25
20	23.7439	31.7709	41.8174
21	24.2722	32.8617	43.7526
22	24.8582	34.1094	45.9169
23	25.5318	35.5381	48.3468
24	26.3267	37.1682	51.0741
25	27.2745	39.0299	54.1404
26	28.4043	41.1494	57.5819
27	29.7296	43.5492	61.4256
28	31.2679	46.2612	65.7032
29	33.0333	49.3133	70.4449
30	35.0400	52.7333	75.6800
31	37.3185	56.5635	81.4503
32	39.8956	60.8366	87.7953
33	42.8085	65.5894	94.7660
34	46.0911	70.8589	102.4062
35	49.7771	76.6810	110.7565
36	53.8876	83.0773	119.8486
37	58.4526	90.0866	129.7143
38	63.4864	97.7419	140.3801
39	68.9961	106.0606	151.8570
40	75.0061	115.0751	164.1738
41	81.5366	124.8199	177.3539
42	88.6275	135.3292	191.4335
43	96.3322	146.6509	206.4554
44	104.6986	158.8268	222.4502
45	113.7724	171.9011	239.4172
46	123.6042	185.9140	257.3217
47	134.2267	200.9044	276.0891
48	145.6795	216.9113	295.6251
49	157.9989	233.9638	315.8155
50	171.2260	252.0565	336.5782
51	185.4019	271.1475	357.8490
52	200.5783	291.1582	379.5875
53	216.8188	311.9951	401.7683
54	234.1715	333.5363	424.3512
55	252.6469	355.6995	447.2528
56	272.2157	378.4273	470.3435
57	292.7921	401.6807	493.4596
58	314.2596	425.4296	516.4151
59	336.4800	449.6389	539.0248
60	359.3668	474.2235	561.1274
61	382.8580	499.0339	582.5800
62	406.9417	523.8969	603.2728
63	431.6184	548.6047	623.1192
64	456.8835	572.9429	642.0598
65	482.6639	596.7151	660.0626

Table XI (*Continued*)—Single Premium Term Insurance

$$1000 \, A_{\overline{x:n}}^{1} = 1000 \, (M_x - M_{x+n})/D_x$$

x	n = 30	n = 60 − x	n = 65 − x
20	54.7314	92.6925	118.6857
21	57.7944	93.8513	120.6723
22	61.1906	95.0107	122.6870
23	64.9559	96.1800	124.7396
24	69.1241	97.3594	126.8315
25	73.7375	98.5584	128.9728
26	78.8316	99.7777	131.1652
27	84.4391	101.0091	133.4016
28	90.6036	102.2529	135.6837
29	97.3607	103.5006	138.0044
30	104.7435	104.7435	140.3565
31	112.8011	105.9816	142.7412
32	121.5662	107.2058	145.1513
33	131.0824	108.4158	147.5879
34	141.3855	109.6026	150.0437
35	152.5110	110.7565	152.5110
36	164.4790	111.8500	154.9654
37	177.3205	112.8634	157.3898
38	191.0562	113.7679	159.7588
39	205.6868	114.5156	162.0293
40	221.2014	115.0751	164.1738
41	237.5585	115.4048	166.1555
42	254.6960	115.4703	167.9451
43	272.5416	115.2449	169.5203
44	291.0038	114.6919	170.8499
45	310.0164	113.7724	171.9011
46	329.5254	112.4371	172.6318
47	349.4887	110.6252	172.9893
48	369.8702	108.2726	172.9187
49	390.6242	105.3026	172.3541
50	411.6683	101.6341	171.2260
51	432.8811	97.1716	169.4527
52	454.1218	91.8132	166.9472
53	475.2419	85.4588	163.6254
54	496.0871	77.9817	159.3797
55	516.5246	69.2451	154.0948
56	536.4435	59.0907	147.6369
57	555.7488	47.3259	139.8432
58	574.3684	33.7298	130.5269
59	592.2568	18.0486	119.4738
60	609.3964		106.4468
61	625.7825		91.1542
62	641.4328		73.2786
63	656.3715		52.4418
64	670.6254		28.1942
65	684.2225		

Table XII—Forborne Life Annuity Due $\ddot{s}_{x:\overline{n}|} = {}_n u_x = (N_x - N_{x+n})/D_{x+n}$

x	$n = 1$	$n = 2$	$n = 3$
20	1.031 85	2.096 64	3.195 48
21	1.031 89	2.096 74	3.195 69
22	1.031 92	2.096 84	3.195 85
23	1.031 95	2.096 91	3.195 99
24	1.031 97	2.096 98	3.196 15
25	1.031 99	2.097 06	3.196 33
26	1.032 02	2.097 16	3.196 56
27	1.032 05	2.097 27	3.196 84
28	1.032 10	2.097 42	3.197 15
29	1.032 15	2.097 58	3.197 51
30	1.032 20	2.097 76	3.197 89
31	1.032 26	2.097 95	3.198 31
32	1.032 32	2.098 16	3.198 78
33	1.032 40	2.098 40	3.199 39
34	1.032 48	2.098 72	3.200 13
35	1.032 59	2.099 11	3.201 05
36	1.032 73	2.099 59	3.202 21
37	1.032 89	2.100 20	3.203 62
38	1.033 11	2.100 93	3.205 27
39	1.033 36	2.101 78	3.207 15
40	1.033 65	2.102 73	3.209 20
41	1.033 97	2.103 76	3.211 42
42	1.034 31	2.104 88	3.213 84
43	1.034 69	2.106 09	3.216 48
44	1.035 09	2.107 42	3.219 41
45	1.035 54	2.108 90	3.222 66
46	1.036 04	2.110 54	3.226 28
47	1.036 59	2.112 37	3.230 29
48	1.037 21	2.114 39	3.234 74
49	1.037 89	2.116 63	3.239 65
50	1.038 64	2.119 11	3.245 00
51	1.039 47	2.121 79	3.250 84
52	1.040 36	2.124 71	3.257 21
53	1.041 34	2.127 90	3.264 17
54	1.042 40	2.131 38	3.271 82
55	1.043 57	2.135 21	3.280 25
56	1.044 85	2.139 44	3.289 55
57	1.046 26	2.144 10	3.299 76
58	1.047 81	2.149 20	3.311 02
59	1.049 51	2.154 82	3.323 38
60	1.051 39	2.160 99	3.336 94
61	1.053 43	2.167 73	3.351 82
62	1.055 66	2.175 13	3.368 19
63	1.058 11	2.183 26	3.386 27
64	1.060 81	2.192 23	3.406 34
65	1.063 77	2.202 19	3.428 69

Table XII (*Continued*)—Forborne Life Annuity Due $\ddot{s}_{x:\overline{n}|} = {}_nu_x = (N_x - N_{x+n})/D_{x+n}$

x	n = 4	n = 5	n = 10
20	4.329 53	5.499 92	11.942 38
21	4.329 83	5.500 34	11.944 91
22	4.330 08	5.500 77	11.947 74
23	4.330 36	5.501 21	11.950 88
24	4.330 65	5.501 74	11.954 41
25	4.331 02	5.502 39	11.958 40
26	4.331 47	5.503 13	11.963 14
27	4.331 97	5.503 99	11.968 77
28	4.332 56	5.504 92	11.975 54
29	4.333 18	5.505 95	11.983 90
30	4.333 88	5.507 11	11.994 03
31	4.334 66	5.508 53	12.006 20
32	4.335 63	5.510 24	12.020 52
33	4.336 82	5.512 36	12.036 95
34	4.338 28	5.515 03	12.055 54
35	4.340 14	5.518 28	12.076 32
36	4.342 39	5.522 16	12.099 42
37	4.345 06	5.526 64	12.125 08
38	4.348 13	5.531 64	12.153 50
39	4.351 51	5.537 14	12.184 99
40	4.355 20	5.543 13	12.219 87
41	4.359 21	5.549 68	12.258 55
42	4.363 60	5.556 90	12.301 40
43	4.368 44	5.564 89	12.348 67
44	4.373 81	5.573 76	12.400 79
45	4.379 78	5.583 61	12.458 13
46	4.386 41	5.594 55	12.521 18
47	4.393 76	5.606 65	12.590 60
48	4.401 88	5.619 91	12.667 15
49	4.410 77	5.634 45	12.751 69
50	4.420 49	5.650 34	12.845 00
51	4.431 10	5.667 71	12.948 25
52	4.442 68	5.686 77	13.062 40
53	4.455 41	5.707 77	13.188 67
54	4.469 43	5.730 94	13.328 48
55	4.484 90	5.756 46	13.483 49
56	4.501 92	5.784 64	13.655 75
57	4.520 71	5.815 67	13.847 83
58	4.541 35	5.849 80	14.062 78
59	4.564 03	5.887 38	14.304 14
60	4.588 97	5.928 82	14.574 77
61	4.616 43	5.974 62	14.877 02
62	4.646 77	6.025 50	15.212 30
63	4.680 46	6.082 24	15.581 45
64	4.718 00	6.145 69	15.984 94
65	4.759 94	6.216 26	16.425 80

Table XII (*Continued*)—Forborne Life Annuity Due $\ddot{s}_{x:\overline{n}|} = {}_n u_x = (N_x - N_{x+n})/D_{x+n}$

x	n = 15	n = 20	n = 25
20	19.508 98	28.458 67	39.235 85
21	19.518 68	28.497 45	39.350 04
22	19.530 05	28.543 01	39.479 07
23	19.543 58	28.595 64	39.624 51
24	19.560 11	28.655 89	39.788 32
25	19.580 03	28.724 27	39.972 43
26	19.603 88	28.801 52	40.179 12
27	19.631 96	28.888 66	40.410 68
28	19.664 36	28.986 65	40.668 99
29	19.701 32	29.096 74	40.956 78
30	19.743 07	29.220 11	41.276 80
31	19.790 04	29.358 23	41.632 30
32	19.842 78	29.512 52	42.027 43
33	19.901 82	29.684 11	42.466 88
34	19.967 83	29.874 63	42.955 94
35	20.041 43	30.085 75	43.500 06
36	20.123 41	30.319 41	44.106 36
37	20.214 51	30.578 19	44.781 88
38	20.315 26	30.865 03	45.535 08
39	20.426 56	31.183 26	46.376 00
40	20.549 36	31.536 33	47.316 56
41	20.684 75	31.928 79	48.371 21
42	20.834 28	32.365 07	49.557 94
43	20.999 67	32.850 50	50.898 26
44	21.182 82	33.391 34	52.417 79
45	21.385 61	33.994 93	54.142 68
46	21.610 58	34.670 19	56.100 40
47	21.860 04	35.428 21	58.318 34
48	22.136 82	36.282 21	60.825 68
49	22.444 29	37.247 90	63.654 31
50	22.786 38	38.340 75	66.851 31
51	23.167 93	39.576 53	70.482 58
52	23.595 00	40.970 19	74.640 28
53	24.074 78	42.537 05	79.448 86
54	24.615 66	44.293 28	85.073 35
55	25.225 43	46.264 32	91.713 11
56	25.911 55	48.486 94	99.608 29
57	26.680 28	51.013 50	109.055 81
58	27.537 54	53.915 12	120.419 88
59	28.489 14	57.285 90	134.161 61
60	29.546 08	61.236 91	150.885 24
61	30.725 40	65.898 41	171.400 22
62	32.052 49	71.427 96	196.796 39
63	33.562 21	78.013 66	228.567 14
64	35.300 53	85.888 62	268.820 65
65	37.319 56	95.353 97	320.627 79

Table XII (*Continued*)—Forborne Life Annuity Due $\ddot{s}_{x:\overline{n}|} = {}_nu_x = (N_x - N_{x+n})/D_{x+n}$

x	n = 30	n = 60 − x	n = 65 − x
20	52.556 93	93.235 26	128.289 19
21	52.845 68	89.140 08	122.914 74
22	53.169 62	85.171 29	117.706 17
23	53.531 70	81.325 14	112.658 56
24	53.935 95	77.597 97	107.767 08
25	54.386 51	73.986 20	103.027 05
26	54.888 17	70.486 32	98.433 86
27	55.447 02	67.094 93	93.983 07
28	56.069 94	63.808 78	89.670 38
29	56.764 73	60.624 69	85.491 63
30	57.539 61	57.539 61	81.442 83
31	58.405 11	54.550 63	77.520 13
32	59.371 80	51.654 88	73.719 80
33	60.452 37	48.849 63	70.038 24
34	61.661 75	46.132 21	66.471 95
35	63.017 56	43.500 06	63.017 56
36	64.541 18	40.950 71	59.671 84
37	66.259 09	38.481 83	56.431 72
38	68.203 08	36.091 18	53.294 28
39	70.411 31	33.776 67	50.256 74
40	72.923 65	31.536 33	47.316 56
41	75.782 96	29.368 31	44.471 29
42	79.033 34	27.270 87	41.718 64
43	82.722 77	25.242 33	39.056 43
44	86.904 73	23.281 10	36.482 53
45	91.655 44	21.385 61	33.994 93
46	97.079 97	19.554 39	31.591 66
47	103.323 50	17.786 01	29.270 87
48	110.581 69	16.079 15	27.030 82
49	119.114 68	14.432 54	24.869 84
50	129.241 75	12.845 00	22.786 38
51	141.354 11	11.315 42	20.778 98
52	155.942 78	9.842 74	18.846 27
53	173.620 61	8.425 98	16.986 93
54	195.174 13	7.064 19	15.199 74
55	221.644 83	5.756 46	13.483 49
56	254.441 14	4.501 92	11.837 06
57	295.480 55	3.299 76	10.259 37
58	347.420 78	2.149 20	8.749 39
59	414.051 58	1.049 51	7.306 18
60	500.943 61		5.928 82
61	616.551 59		4.616 43
62	774.164 13		3.368 19
63	995.510 77		2.183 26
64	1 317.717 60		1.060 81
65	1 807.492 82		

Table XIII—Accumulated Cost of Insurance $1000\ _nk_x = 1000\ (M_x - M_{x+n})/D_{x+n}$

x	n = 1	n = 2	n = 3
20	1.7932	3.6837	5.6647
21	1.8333	3.7553	5.7689
22	1.8635	3.8166	5.8522
23	1.8936	3.8677	5.9252
24	1.9136	3.9086	5.9976
25	1.9337	3.9595	6.0803
26	1.9638	4.0207	6.1838
27	1.9939	4.0920	6.3078
28	2.0341	4.1838	6.4530
29	2.0843	4.2860	6.6191
30	2.1345	4.3982	6.7955
31	2.1948	4.5209	6.9927
32	2.2551	4.6535	7.2104
33	2.3254	4.8066	7.4796
34	2.4057	5.0004	7.8111
35	2.5163	5.2457	8.2261
36	2.6470	5.5420	8.7445
37	2.8079	5.9199	9.3779
38	3.0190	6.3803	10.1375
39	3.2606	6.9128	11.0025
40	3.5425	7.5177	11.9631
41	3.8549	8.1746	13.0087
42	4.1875	8.8833	14.1394
43	4.5506	9.6546	15.3765
44	4.9443	10.4988	16.7413
45	5.3788	11.4368	18.2560
46	5.8641	12.4794	19.9424
47	6.4007	13.6375	21.8125
48	6.9987	14.9221	23.8884
49	7.6583	16.3439	26.1827
50	8.3898	17.9146	28.6979
51	9.1937	19.6250	31.4462
52	10.0602	21.4860	34.4405
53	11.0099	23.5202	37.7161
54	12.0434	25.7392	41.3084
55	13.1712	28.1767	45.2655
56	14.4148	30.8670	49.6368
57	15.7853	33.8340	54.4513
58	17.2940	37.0924	59.7607
59	18.9422	40.6779	65.5970
60	20.7624	44.6175	72.0167
61	22.7458	48.9276	79.0663
62	24.9157	53.6589	86.8303
63	27.2953	58.8635	95.4087
64	29.9085	64.6071	104.9305
65	32.7911	70.9807	115.5454

Table XIII (*Continued*)—Accumulated Cost of Insurance

$$1000 \, _nk_x = 1000 \, (M_x - M_{x+n})/D_{x+n}$$

x	n = 4	n = 5	n = 10
20	7.7393	9.9004	22.2536
21	7.8669	10.0524	22.6470
22	7.9732	10.1924	23.0589
23	8.0788	10.3317	23.5034
24	8.1837	10.4805	23.9918
25	8.3096	10.6610	24.5496
26	8.4669	10.8741	25.2098
27	8.6455	11.1192	25.9823
28	8.8560	11.3974	26.9018
29	9.0881	11.7079	28.0105
30	9.3410	12.0501	29.3319
31	9.6256	12.4556	30.9144
32	9.9617	12.9347	32.7842
33	10.3714	13.5204	34.9720
34	10.8759	14.2551	37.5066
35	11.5175	15.1623	40.4179
36	12.2968	16.2531	43.7201
37	13.2360	17.5405	47.4525
38	14.3367	19.0161	51.6427
39	15.5675	20.6580	56.3024
40	16.9287	22.4671	61.4724
41	18.4096	24.4426	67.1922
42	20.0206	26.6063	73.5185
43	21.7948	28.9930	80.5153
44	23.7546	31.6372	88.2579
45	25.9339	34.5747	96.8267
46	28.3563	37.8418	106.3041
47	31.0451	41.4641	116.7870
48	34.0250	45.4585	128.3907
49	37.2997	49.8516	141.2369
50	40.8942	54.6716	155.4578
51	44.8230	59.9470	171.2182
52	49.1121	65.7295	188.6856
53	53.8224	72.0975	208.0861
54	59.0046	79.1198	229.6614
55	64.7237	86.8704	253.7062
56	71.0365	95.4491	280.5720
57	78.0117	104.9255	310.6730
58	85.6994	115.3855	344.5024
59	94.1641	126.9316	382.6465
60	103.4972	139.6990	425.7038
61	113.7825	153.8301	474.2440
62	125.1590	169.5436	528.8339
63	137.7980	187.0887	590.0160
64	151.8966	206.7508	658.3167
65	167.6807	228.7547	734.5454

Table XIII (*Continued*)—Accumulated Cost of Insurance

$$1000 \ _nk_x = 1000 \ (M_x - M_{x+n})/D_{x+n}$$

x	n = 15	n = 20	n = 25
20	38.1414	60.0123	93.5166
21	39.0182	62.1811	98.1945
22	39.9926	64.6722	103.4665
23	41.1151	67.5374	109.4353
24	42.4427	70.8225	116.1978
25	44.0299	74.5948	123.8800
26	45.9273	78.9162	132.6035
27	48.1609	83.8436	142.4759
28	50.7638	89.4566	153.6246
29	53.7646	95.8310	166.1868
30	57.1936	103.0471	180.3113
31	61.1097	111.2216	196.1964
32	65.5690	120.4593	214.0587
33	70.6474	130.8815	234.1737
34	76.4193	142.6217	256.8322
35	82.9633	155.8241	282.3571
36	90.3404	170.6163	311.0968
37	98.6332	187.1829	343.4552
38	107.9021	205.7173	379.8902
39	118.2006	226.4026	420.8947
40	129.6215	249.4851	467.1189
41	142.2592	275.2553	519.3273
42	156.2575	304.0467	578.4997
43	171.8031	336.2844	645.8618
44	189.0927	372.4513	722.8757
45	208.3428	413.1246	811.1821
46	229.8105	458.9836	912.6203
47	253.7488	510.8468	1 029.2039
48	280.4662	569.7123	1 163.2452
49	310.3149	636.7701	1 317.3938
50	343.7192	713.3337	1 495.1845
51	381.1818	800.8522	1 701.2726
52	423.3340	900.9051	1 941.9438
53	470.9684	1 015.3116	2 225.6897
54	525.0045	1 146.0941	2 563.7784
55	586.4324	1 295.9888	2 970.5791
56	656.3185	1 468.6262	3 464.3392
57	735.7377	1 668.8581	4 068.5331
58	825.8459	1 903.1613	4 813.3780
59	927.9065	2 180.1523	5 738.5483
60	1 043.6945	2 510.6642	6 897.4979
61	1 175.5529	2 908.1113	8 363.1801
62	1 326.7658	3 389.6562	10 236.7397
63	1 501.7068	3 976.9290	12 660.2529
64	1 706.1491	4 697.7857	15 838.4347
65	1 947.1068	5 589.0310	20 074.7830

[176]

Table XIII (*Continued*)—Accumulated Cost of Insurance

$$1000 \; _nk_x = 1000 (M_x - M_{x+n})/D_{x+n}$$

x	n = 30	n = 60 − x	n = 65 − x
20	146.5332	379.5928	637.8701
21	155.7528	372.4760	628.5302
22	166.1169	365.4248	619.2763
23	177.7817	358.4793	610.1611
24	190.9113	351.6401	601.1855
25	205.7116	344.9427	592.3959
26	222.3897	338.3847	583.7893
27	241.1692	331.9312	575.3198
28	262.3374	325.5823	566.9877
29	285.1953	319.3071	558.7521
30	313.0771	313.0771	550.5760
31	343.4283	306.8960	542.4641
32	377.7036	300.7390	534.3837
33	416.4785	294.6109	526.3414
34	460.4048	288.4902	518.3086
35	510.2597	282.3571	510.2597
36	566.9195	276.1447	502.1066
37	631.5059	269.8166	493.8017
38	705.3506	263.3177	485.2726
39	790.0063	256.5540	476.3961
40	887.3039	249.4851	467.1189
41	999.3087	242.0549	457.3677
42	1 128.3869	234.2352	447.1052
43	1 277.3290	226.0226	436.3271
44	1 449.3651	217.3969	425.0070
45	1 648.7762	208.3428	413.1246
46	1 881.1785	198.8311	400.6416
47	2 154.0715	188.8219	387.5056
48	2 477.5178	178.2824	373.6738
49	2 864.9641	167.1718	359.0924
50	3 333.6990	155.4578	343.7192
51	3 905.8820	143.1024	327.5042
52	4 610.4676	130.0772	310.4101
53	5 485.3807	116.3773	292.4305
54	6 580.8709	101.9792	273.5348
55	7 965.3275	86.8704	253.7062
56	9 733.3919	71.0365	232.9261
57	12 017.1870	54.4513	211.1600
58	15 004.6026	37.0924	188.3784
59	18 969.6043	18.9422	164.5584
60	24 323.5113		139.6990
61	31 702.0680		113.7825
62	42 125.3370		86.8303
63	57 294.9066		58.8635
64	80 180.1648		29.9085
65	116 238.1908		

Answers to Exercises

CHAPTER 1

Page 5 (Section 1.4)

2. 1/4; 5/12; 2/3.
4. 1/36; 1/36; 1/18.

3. 1/55.
5. 0.72; 0.18; 0.1.

6. 1/221; 1/221; 4/663; 4/663; 8/663.
7. 1/5525; 2/5525; 16/5525.
8. (6): 1/169; 1/169; 1/169; 1/169; 2/169; (7): 1/2197; 1/2197; 6/2197.

9. 81/256.
11. 1/8; 3/8.
13. 1/6; 1/36; 1/18; 5/18.
15. 9/28.
17. 5/12.
19. 1/2.

10. 81/125.
12. 3/7; 1/840; 4/7; 839/840.
14. 26/49.
16. $1/2^n$; $n/2^n$.
18. 0.224.
20. 7/9.

Page 10 (Section 1.6)

2. 99,103; 297; 0.9970.

5. Age 96: 23; 0.793; 0.207; etc.
8. 0.05184; 0.11509; 0.22796.

7. 0.00925.
9. 0.2010.

Page 12 (Section 1.7)

1. 0.9363; 0.0051; 0.2247; 0.0685; 0.0317; 0.0297.

5. 0.5733.
9. 0.1262; 0.1379.

7. Age 85; 0.1611.
11. 0.1200; 0.1330; 0.2600; 0.3730.

Page 14 (Section 1.8)

6. 0.857; 1.214.

Page 16 (Section 1.9)

2. (0.99852)(0.99809)(0.99759)(0.99701).
3. (0.99886)(0.00133).
4. (0.99901)(0.99890)(0.99875)(0.99859)(0.99847)(0.99832)(0.99813)(0.99790).
5. 1 − (0.99908)(0.99890)(0.99867)(0.99839)(0.99805).
6. 0.00236; 1 − (0.99764)(0.99736)(0.99705)(0.99672)(0.99637).
7. (0.99908)(0.99890)(0.99859)(0.99847); 1 − (0.99908)(0.99890)(0.99867)
    (0.99859)(0.99847)(0.99832); (0.00092)(0.00141).
8. 1000 {(0.99864)(0.99826)(0.99780)(0.99728)(0.99668) − (0.99764)(0.99736)
    (0.99705)(0.99672)(0.99637)}.

Page 17 (Review Exercises)

1. Age 90: 400; 0.4706; 0.5294; 0.89; 1.39; etc.

3. 0.99716; 0.000939; 0.99824.
5. 0.855; 0.241.
8. 76 and 77; 0.0323.
10. 14/15; 32/35; 1/10.

4. 0.7 or 0.8.
6. 0.127; 0.638; 0.136.
9. 0.75.
11. (b): 0.6125; 1.1125.

CHAPTER 2

Page 22 (Section 2.2)

2. $1,138.16; $813.27.
3. (a): $3,612.22; $15,835.64; (b): $744.09; $52.03.
4. $12,136.31.
7. Between 23 and 24 years; between 37 and 38 years.

8. $612.91.
10. 12; $67.55.
12. $5,784.23.
14. $250.32.

9. $2,865.97.
11. $102.61.
13. $250.32.
15. $281.74.

Page 26 (Section 2.4)

2. $3,112.62.
8. $7,845.39.
10. 0.349475; 9.366331.

5. $1,911.22.
9. $358.45; $270.24.

Page 30 (Section 2.6)

1. $13,486.57; $14,086.57.   **2.** $859.50.
3. $4,826.38.   **4.** $1,173.88.
10. 96,064.0; 95,530.1.   **12.** $460.00.
13. $29,051.30.

Page 33 (Section 2.7)

5. $693.09; $658.44.   **6.** $1,484.26.
7. $1,292.62; $1,288.22.   **8.** $586.64.

9. $q_{90} = 0.167$; $p_{90} = 0.833$; $a_{90} = 1.972$; $e_{90} = 2.500$; $\overset{\circ}{e}_{90} = 3.000$; etc.

10. $2,012.32.   **11.** $481.92.
12. $647.91.   **13.** 3.80589.
14. $313.36.

Page 37 (Section 2.9)

4. $776.74.   **5.** $675.97.
6. $10,000\ D_{25}/(N_{18} - N_{22})$.   **7.** $26,790.89.
8. $50(N_{30} + N_{40})/D_{30}$.   **9.** $570.08.
10. $11,276.78.   **12.** $4,111.80.
13. $2,033.62.   **14.** $193.11; $237.80; $229.70.

Page 40 (Section 2.10)

4. $51.16.
5. $(10\ N_{24} + S_{25} - S_{40})/D_{24}$; $(100\ N_{30} - 5\ S_{31} + 5\ S_{51})/D_{30}$.
7. $8,461.37.
8. $100(S_{x+1} + 2\ S_{x+2} - 7\ S_{x+7} + 4\ S_{x+10})/D_x$.

9. $3,735.79.   **10.** $8,044.41.

Page 45 (Section 2.11)

1. $24,499.68; $23,999.68.   **2.** $1,844.37.
3. $8.65; $25.76.   **4.** $25.28.
9. $47.90.   **10.** $4,299.52.
11. $68.81.   **12.** $140.00.

184   The Mathematics of Life Insurance

Page 46 (Review Exercises)

3. $7,160.17.
4. $(N_{30}^{4\%} - N_{40}^{4\%} + D_{40}^{4\%} \cdot N_{40}^{5\%}/D_{40}^{5\%})/D_{30}^{4\%}.$
5. $2,697.31; $2,727.31; $2,742.31; $2,752.31.

7. 1.
11. $87.24.
13. $21,690.07.

10. $51.44; $50.11.
12. $25,203.26; $37,216.35.
14. $2,311.66.

CHAPTER 3

Page 51 (Section 3.2)

2. $988.08; $1,626.35; $3,484.66.   **3.** $4,919.02.
8. $1,959.05; $1,970.34.

Page 53 (Section 3.3)

6. 0.06.   **7.** $19.54.

Page 54 (Section 3.4)

1. $67.32; $36.34; $16.42.   **3.** $273.20; $81.98; $72.44.
6. $4,090.14.   **7.** $143.11.
8. 0.05.

Page 57 (Section 3.5)

3. $2.45; $6.06; $11.39.   **5.** $44.84; $48.72.
6. $18.80.   **7.** $113.90.
8. $118.10   **9.** $19,959.93.

Page 60 (Section 3.6)

2. $37.25; $39.62; $57.33.   **3.** $86.15; $52.04; $30.49.
4. $1,318.94.   **5.** $28.22.
8. $109.20.   **9.** $71.85.

Page 63 (Section 3.9)

2. $34.51.   **3.** $61.57.
4. $35.90.   **9.** $74.59.
10. 0.015.   **11.** $62.45.

Page 66 (Section 3.11)

4. $76.61; $16.43.   **6.** $46.00.

12. $M_x/(N_x - N_{x+20} - R_x + R_{x+20} + 20\, M_{x+20})$.

13. $M_x/(D_x - M_x)$; 0.55924.   **14.** $244.57.

Page 68 (Review Exercises)

1. $0.22.   **3.** $1000\, \ddot{a}_{\overline{10}|} M_x/D_x$.

5. $1000\, D_{x+n}/(D_x - M_x + M_{x+n})$.

8. $v - a_{x:\overline{20}|}/\ddot{a}_{x:\overline{20}|}$; $\ddot{a}_{x:\overline{21}|}/\ddot{a}_{x:\overline{20}|} - 1$.

10. $1,656.52.   **11.** 1.

13. $26(1 - .01\,x)$; $x/26(100 - x)$.

CHAPTER 4

Page 74 (Section 4.2)

1. 0.0167.

Page 76 (Section 4.3)

2. 0; A_{x+n}; 1.   **4.** $51.40; $91.53; $195.19; $0.63.

5. $110.32; $197.55; $422.82; $358.66.

6. $573.02; $866.35; $535.05.   **7.** $94.34; $282.00; $503.40; $503.40.

8. $427.02; $427.02.

Page 78 (Section 4.4)

2. $51.40; $91.53; $195.19; $0.64.   **3.** $(M_{x+25} - M_{x+30} + D_{x+30})/D_{x+25}$.

4. $327.77.

5. $176.80; $406.58; $863.63; $390.05.

8. $92.08.

Page 79 (Section 4.5)

8. $48.4128; $564.19; $564.19.   **9.** $610.45.

Page 84 (Section 4.7)

4. 10th terminal reserve: $91.86.   **6.** $208.73.

Page 88 (Section 4.10)

2. (a): $36.67; $74.49; $113.50; (b): $963.33; $925.51; $886.50;
(c): $1.86; $1.81; $1.76.

3. 0.18865.   **5.** $38.35.

7. $23.365; $46.17.

Page 93 (Section 4.11)

3. $31.56; $45.82.   **4.** $78.76; $103.92.

Page 95 (Section 4.12)

3. $55.96; 8 years, 228 days; $164.05; 21 years, 333 days.

4. $365.98; $1000 term insurance to 55 plus $304.59 pure endowment at 55.

5. $705.19; $1000 term insurance to 55 plus $689.07 pure endowment at 55.

Page 96 (Review Exercises)

2. $344.19.   **3.** $746.27.

6. 0.2761.

CHAPTER 5

Page 103 (Section 5.4)

3. $18.69; $10.78.   **4.** $16.8545; $56.8545; $597.44.

Page 106 (Section 5.6)

1. $61.30; $99.75.
3. $86.1535; $2.4369; $97.0619; $460.26; $409.18.
5. $0; $238.32; $484.25; $738.06; $1,000.00.
6. $4.1359; $79.6227; $325.89.

Page 109 (Section 5.8)

2. $8.0776; $35.5603; $112.75.   **3.** $1.7378; $15.7253; $146.38.

4. $3.4272; $21.6093; $75.79.
6. $2.0678; $20.2551; $313.02; $605.55.
7. 16th terminal reserves: $303.98; $308.26.

Page 111 (Section 5.9)

3. (a): $46.7895; $67.2343; (b): $18.2497; $38.6945; (c): $7.3857; $27.8305.
5. 5th terminal reserve: $451.12.
7. $5.1976; $23.0870; $379.13; $758.03.

Page 114 (Section 5.10)

1. $13.2126; $28.9124; $27.8703; $301.52; $887.92.
2. $4.3933; $30.7279; $276.69.
3. $5.4703; $23.3596; $384.47; $762.28.
5. $6.7866; $36.7128; $700.92.
6. 18th terminal reserves: $752.45; $756.27.

Page 116 (Section 5.11)

1. (a): 0.0134675; 0.0020679; 0.0139747; (b): 0.0211452; 0.0097456;
   0.0219622; (c): 0.0164248; 0.0050252; 0.0170494.
2. (a): 0.06212; 0.05095; 0.29048; 0.28203; (b): 0.10440; 0.09457; 0.51482;
   0.51482; (c): 0.07840; 0.06775; 0.37689; 0.37164.
5. $12.7647; $22.6778; $384.00; $759.92.

6. $12.6000; $27.4551; $270.46.   **7.** 18th terminal reserve: $751.51.

Page 121 (Review Exercises)

1. α^{Com}: $66.69; $56.98; $48.75; β^{Com}: $91.91; $82.20; $73.97;
   5th terminal reserves: $451.40; $398.44; $353.50.
2. α^I: $16.16; $7.28; $9.45; β^I: $43.82; $34.94; $37.11;
   5th terminal reserves: $414.96; $309.00; $334.94.
8. $353,489.49; $339,498.79; $3,651,192.03; $120,619.29.

9. 15 years.   **10.** $37.812.

11. $29.8434.

CHAPTER 6

Page 130 (Section 6.5)

1. $4.88.   **2.** $39.93.
3. $25.13.   **4.** $16.49.

Page 133 (Section 6.6)

1. −$3.39; $7.24; $19.67; $32.31; $45.11.
2. $20.39; $58.63; $98.14; $138.94; $181.05.
3. $3.72; $26.25; $49.43; $73.24; $97.66.

Page 134 (Section 6.7)

2. $32.2410; $38.78.   3. 0.001526; 0.08575.

Index

Numbers refer to pages